F

Simon and Schuster's

Guide to

INSECTS

By
Dr. Ross H. Arnett, Jr.,

and

Dr. Richard L. Jacques, Jr.

A Fireside Book

Published by Simon and Schuster

New York

Copyright © 1981 by Simon & Schuster, a Division of Gulf & Western Cor-
poration
All rights reserved
including the right of reproduction
in whole or in part in any form
A Fireside Book
Published by Simon and Schuster
A Division of Gulf & Western Corporation
Simon & Schuster Building
Rockefeller Center
1230 Avenue of the Americas
New York, New York 10020
FIRESIDE and colophon are trademarks of Simon & Schuster

Manufactured by Officine Grafiche di Arnoldo Mondadori Editore, Verona
Printed in Italy

10 9 8 7 6 5 4 3 2 1

Library of Congress Cataloging in Publication Data

Arnett, Ross H
      Simon and Schuster's guide to insects.
      (A Fireside Book)
      Includes index.
      1. Insects—North America—Identification.
I. Jacques, Richard L., joint author.
II. Title.
III. Title: Guide to insects.
QL473.A76   595.7097   80–29485

ISBN 0-671-25013-2
      0-671-25014-0 Pbk.

CONTENTS

NOTE
The symbols that accompany the individual entries are purely in-
dicative and approximate. In some cases, more than one symbol
in a particular category may be appropriate to the species, but
we have chosen to emphasize the most common or important activity, habitat, and ecological significance to humans.

EXPLANATION OF SYMBOLS

 PRIMARY ACTIVITY

Swimming

 Running

 Stinging

 Flying

 Jumping

 Bloodsucking

HABITAT

Forest or orchard

Aquatic

Grassland, flowers, grains, low vegetation

Desert or arid regions

ECOLOGICAL SIGNIFICANCE

S Stored-products insects in homes, warehouses, etc.

H Household pest

G Garden and ornamental pest

C Field crop pest

F Forest pest

O Orchard pest

L Livestock pest

D Human disease carrier or bloodsucker

B Beneficial insect (pollinator, predator, or parasite of insect pest)

W Wild species, not affecting humans

Insects live wherever a living organism can sustain itself with food and find a mate. This includes all wild habitats as well as the full range of human environments—homes, warehouses, cultivated ornamental plants, field crops, and sometimes even on or in our bodies and those of our domestic animals. Since we are unable to escape direct contact with a variety of insects, we are naturally curious about these small and often pesky forms of life.

This book will answer the following questions about our common North American insects:

1. What are they called?

About 90,000 species of insects live in the United States and Canada. Several hundred species have been selected for this book to illustrate their great diversity, and thus provide the means by which to identify the group name for any insect you discover. Take a few minutes to look at the insect and learn something about its anatomy. Small specimens may require that you use a hand lens to see some of the details necessary for a correct identification. You will find a shortcut guide to each of the twenty-nine insect orders on pages 65–73. Once you have determined the order name, turn to the corresponding description of the order (each numbered as in the guide table) for further information about the order. This will refer you to the entries for a discussion of the species included in that order. In this way you will find the name of the insect you are examining. You should be able to find an illustration that closely resembles your specimen and thus deduce that it is closely related to or possibly a species of the same genus or family, or the same species.

2. What do these insects do?

Most species of insects are wild and harmless to humans; many are beneficial because of their role in our ecosystems. Some are a part of the food chains of wild creatures; others, through predation and parasitism, hold in check many species populations. Once you know the group name of an insect, the descriptions of the orders and major families will tell you in general terms the life-style and behavior of these groups. The habits of each of the species illustrated are indicated by a marginal symbol which indicates its major activity and that of its close relatives.

3. Where do they live?

Many of the species of insects we find walking across our floors or flying against our windows do not normally inhabit our homes and buildings. They are usually harmless, although a few may sting. The question of their habitat is quickly answered by the appropriate marginal symbols next to each entry, with further details supplied in the text. For example, a large insect may be attracted to your porch lights at night. By finding a picture of the insect or one similar to it in the text, you can determine whether it is a forest, grassland, desert, or aquatic species.

4. Which insects are pests? Which are beneficial?

Marginal symbols combining letters and colors indicate the life activities of each of the entries. You will find that relatively few are pests; probably more are beneficial.

Note

The lives of insects are replete with endless details. Each life cycle, each courtship pattern offers new and interesting facts, most of which are yet to be recorded. Each species of insect now known to science, as well as each species of animal and plant, had to be formally described in the scientific literature before it could be named and otherwise referred to. Most of these descriptions are similar to the ones used here. That is, they give basic anatomical details and, if known, some information about how and where they live. Directions on how to record field observations will help you develop a scientifically valuable insect collection.

Many species of insects cannot be identified even as to genus unless one can see certain microscopic features found on the underside of the body or, sometimes, structures of the genitalia that are withdrawn into the body. A precise identification of a photograph is not always possible. Each of the illustrations has been checked by a professional entomologist, and the illustrated species is as accurately identified as possible without having the actual specimen at hand. Therefore, in a few cases the Latin name cited for the species in the entry may not be the one illustrated but a strikingly similar species.

THE SCIENCE OF ENTOMOLOGY

Entomology is the scientific study of insects and related arthropods. In America this branch of zoology came into being at the beginning of the nineteenth century. Thomas Say, a Philadelphia doctor, is considered the "father of American entomology." Along with a number of naturalists he founded the Academy of Natural Sciences of Philadelphia in 1812. Say published many articles and books on entomology and described a large number of insect species. His best known work is *American Entomology, or Descriptions of the Insects of North America.* Other prominent early entomologists include Thaddeus William Harris, the "father of American economic entomology" and author of reports on insects injurious to crops.

The works of Thomas Say and T. W. Harris stimulated interest in entomology and in 1853 the Federal Bureau of Agriculture was established, with a large section devoted to studies dealing with insect control. In 1878 it became the United States Department of Agriculture with a separate Bureau of Entomology. At about the same time, state entomologists were appointed in the major agricultural states, with the job of coordinating the research and application of insect control measures. Applied entomology in the United States received assistance from two pieces of legislation. The Morrill Act (1862) led to the establishment of "land grant" colleges which soon established departments of entomology: first at Cornell University, then at Purdue University, Michigan State University, the University of California, Ohio State University, Iowa State University, and Kansas State University. The Hatch Act of 1887 led to the formation of the state agricultural experiment stations, which are now the principal entomological research institutions in each state and are usually affiliated with the college of agriculture at the state university. Today more than 6,000 entomologists in the United States and Canada are working for the government, universities, research firms, private industry, and as businesspeople operating pest control services.

Entomology has become more complex since World War II, and the science now includes many subsciences that require special training. To become a professional entomologist it is usually necessary to specialize in one of the following branches of the field.

Disciplines within the science of entomology

Apiculture	Study of honey bees and honey production and marketing
Applied entomology	Study of various control methods for pest insects
Biological control	A spin-off of applied entomology using parasites, pathogens, and predators to control insects
Forest entomology	Study of forest pests and their control
Insect ecology	Habitat and life tables of insects including wild as well as pest insects
Insect physiology	Life systems of insects including the effect of pesticides on these systems
Medical entomology	Study of insects harmful to man and domestic animals
Industrial and home pest control	Application of pesticides and other means of control of insects, arachnids, rodents, and other pests of buildings and homes

General Features of the

Feature	Crustacea	Arachnida
Body Divisions	Cephalothorax and abdomen	Cephalothorax and abdomen
Legs	Numerous usually 5 pairs	4 pairs
Antennae	2 pairs	None
Habitat	Chiefly marine and freshwater, rarely terrestrial	Terrestrial

| Pest management | Use of ecological principles, pesticides, or a combination of these to control insect pest populations, particularly as this applies to the prevention of pollution |
| Systematics | Identification, description, classification, and evolution of insects |

The American Registry of Professional Entomologists (ARPE), 4603 Calvert Road, College Park, Maryland 20740, certifies qualified professionals in these various specialities. They have adopted a "code of ethics" for the practice of this profession. Certification is recognized by other professional fields.

CLASSIFICATION OF THE PHYLUM *ARTHROPODA*

The insects, as members of the phylum *Arthropoda,* share much of the evolutionary history of that phylum. In order to understand this evolution, it is necessary to examine arthropods in general. Fossil evidence indicates that the arthropods arose from an annelid (earthworm) type ancestor. The arthropod line further diverged into three major branches: the *chelicerates* (spiders, mites, ticks, scorpions, etc.); the *crustaceans* (crabs, lobsters, crayfish, etc.), and the *mandibulates* (the *Onychophora,* millipedes, centipedes, and insects). This last group is sometimes considered to be a separate phylum, the *Uniramia,* but it is certainly not very distinct from the rest of the arthropods. All of these groups display the same basic segmentation characteristic of the *Annelida.* The segments of arthropods are fused to form body sections or regions. These regions are termed the *head,* often fused to the next group of segments, the *thorax.* The hind group of segments form the *abdomen.* Each segment in the primitive state has simple, unspecialized appendages, but as the species evolved, these appendages became specialized to suit various specific functions such as eating, walking, jumping, and a great variety of other activities.

Five Major Classes of Arthropods

Class		
Diplopoda	Chilopoda	Insecta
Head and body	Head and body	Head, thorax, and abdomen
Many, usually 2 pairs per segment	Many, 1 pair per segment	Three pairs, 1 on each thoracic segment
1 pair	1 pair	1 pair
Terrestrial	Terrestrial	Terrestrial and freshwater, rarely marine

The number of species of the five major classes of the phylum Arthropoda.

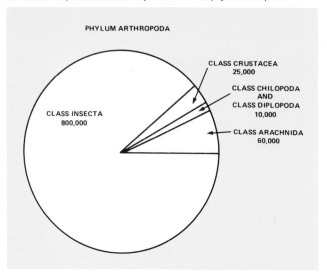

The tremendous diversity of the arthropods is apparently mainly due to two factors. First, their jointed appendages are susceptible to adaptive specialization. They may be modified, as previously indicated, for a wide variety of life activities. The word *arthropod* itself, meaning jointed foot, refers to these appendages composed of a number of segments, each capable of special movements according to the nature of their living habits. The second factor accounting for their diversity is that their exoskeleton gives not only protection, but a mechanical advantage in that the way the muscles are attached to the appendages and the body wall results in great strength in proportion to their size. Ants, for example, are well known for the great loads they are able to carry in their mandibles.

Of the ten classes of arthropods, five are considered major; the others are comparatively minor. The class *Arachnida*, spiders and relatives, is distinguished by bodies that are divided into two regions: the *cephalothorax*, composed of the fused head and thorax, and the abdomen. There are four pairs of legs attached to the cephalothorax in addition to the anterior appendages, which include the *chelicerae*, a mouthpart consisting of a stout base and a sharp terminal *fang*. The *pedipalps* are supplementary mouthparts consisting of an *apical* sensory feelerlike portion, and a *basal* stout mandibularlike part modified for crushing prey. This class of arthropods has more than 35,000 species, many of which are predaceous except for some mites who are plant juice suckers. A few of these mites are crop pests.

The class *Crustacea*, with over 30,000 species, gets its name from the hardened exoskeleton that is composed of calcium in addition to the basic chitin. This group includes lobsters, crayfish, crabs, shrimps, water fleas, wood lice, barnacles, sow bugs, and copepods. Although a few species are terrestrial, the majority live in marine or freshwater habitats. Crustaceans are distinguished from other arthropods by having five pairs of walking legs, two pairs of *antennae,* a pair of *mandibles,* and two pairs of *maxillae* for food manipulation.

The class *Chilopoda,* the centipedes, is a small class of active *predators* found under logs, stones, and debris. Each of the twenty or more *body segments* bears a pair of appendages, and those of the first segment have been modified into poison claws. The majority of species are harmless to man, but a few species in the tropics and in deserts can inflict a painful sting if handled.

The class *Diplopoda,* the millipedes, has cylindrical bodies with twenty-five to a hundred segments. Each of the four thoracic segments has one pair of legs and the abdominal segments have two each. Millipedes live in moist areas and are generally *herbivorous,* feeding on living plant material, or *saprophagous,* living on dead, decaying plants.

The class *Insecta* is readily distinguished from the other classes of arthropods by the following characteristics: a) body divided into three regions: head, thorax, and abdomen; b) three pairs of legs, rarely less, attached to the thorax, and generally two pairs of wings, sometimes only one pair, and sometimes none; c) one pair of antennae; and d) mouthparts composed of a pair of mandibles, the central pair of head appendages modified for chewing or cutting; a pair of maxillae, multisegmented head appendages located just behind the mandibles; a *hypopharynx,* a fleshy tonguelike structure located inside the head above the mandibles, and a *labium,* another modified pair of head appendages located behind the maxillae.

WHAT IS AN INSECT?

Many people confuse insects with other arthropods and related invertebrates. These small animals are often called fly, bug, maggot, grub, caterpillar, and beetle with no regard to their true scientific identity. Insects are invertebrate animals that belong to the phylum Arthropoda, the phylum that includes, as we have seen, crabs and lobsters. Insecta, as shown in the preceding chart, is only one class, albeit the largest, of this very numerous phylum. It is characterized in more detail below.

Characteristics of the Class *Insecta*

Body composed of three parts: head, thorax, and abdomen. One pair of antennae present (some wingless insects lack antennae).

Mouthparts composed of a pair of mandibles; a pair of maxillae with a pair of *palpi,* small, feelerlike sensory organs; a hypopharynx, the tonguelike organ, and a labium, the latter usually with palpi. Modifications of these basic parts account for the variety of mouthparts among insects.

The class Insecta comprises slightly over 50% of all living plants and animals.

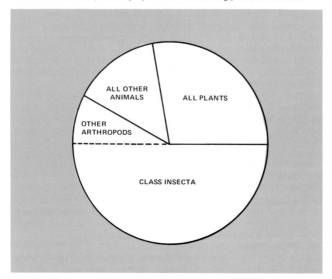

Three pairs of legs located on the thorax.

Usually two pairs of wings, or a pair of wings and a pair of *halteres,* small, modified club-shaped structures in place of the second pair of wings, or wingless in the immature stages and in certain primitive groups of insects. Most *ectoparasitic* insects lack wings.

The class Insecta contains more species than any other class of animals and far exceeds the total number of species in the entire plant kingdom and all of the rest of the animals combined. Approximately 800,000 species, about 80% of all the animal species now known, have been named and their external features described. One order of insects, the *Coleoptera,* or beetles and weevils, has as many species as all of the plant kingdom. Although estimates vary widely, there is little doubt that more than a million species and perhaps twice that number of insects exist. Whether or not we will ever discover the final number depends on how rapidly we destroy natural habitats.

You might ask why this group of animals is so successful, and why they are so abundant as species and individually. Some of the reasons have already been discussed; others are given below.

Features contributing to the success of insects

Exoskeleton to protect them against environmental trauma and predation.

Mobility: efficient muscle leverage; wings to disperse the species from area to area and to avoid predators; legs modified as tools for specialized feeding, digging, swimming, and related activities.

Small body size with physiological functions that maximize utilization of energy.

Reproductive fecundity and short length of life cycle permits rapid adaptive changes.

Complex metamorphosis under hormonal control permits two distinct life-styles in most species.

Protective coloration, mimicry, and defensive chemicals increase survival rate.

The arthropods, and in particular the insects, were the first organisms to overcome problems of terrestrial respiration, water conservation, and locomotion in a terrestrial environment. The hardened exoskeleton, adaptable legs, wings, and the ability to utilize atmospheric oxygen greatly enhanced their ability to survive in the changeable terrestrial environment.

NAMES OF INSECTS

With nearly one million species of insects and hundreds of thousands of other species of animals, a convenient system of naming is certainly a necessity. In 1758 Carl von Linné (Latin: Carlos Linnaeus) was the first person consistently to use the system now called *binomial nomenclature*. This system provides for two words that, when used conjointly, form the Latin or scientific name of each species of animal or plant: the generic name of the *genus* to which it is assigned, and the specific name for the particular *species*. Formalized in the early 1900s by a set of internationally accepted rules, this system is employed to name all known organisms. Two names, however, are not sufficient to organize the more than a million different species in a way that allows for convenient filing and retrieval. Therefore, several additional categories are used, and higher group names, or *taxa* (*taxon, sing.*) are given to a number of species. These taxa enable biologists to make generalizations, as we have done here, about arthropods and insects. That is, we can characterize these higher groups so that all of the species assigned to the group share certain features. The six major categories are shown in the following table, along with examples of each. Numerous minor categories are sometimes used as subcategories for each, but these refinements are of most concern only to the specialists. These categories provide an amazingly simple way to handle vast amounts of data in easily comprehensible blocks.

Assigning to them information about various kinds of organisms is the basis of all modern classifications of animals, as well as plants. Without such a system, the concise way in which we write about organisms would be impossible.

Categories and taxa of man, the house fly, and the honey bee

Category	Taxa		
	Man	*House fly*	*Honey bee*
Phylum	Chordata	Arthropoda	Arthropoda
Class	Mammalia	Insecta	Insecta
Order	Primates	Diptera	Hymenoptera

	Man	Taxa House fly	Honey bee
Family	Hominidae	Muscidae	Apidae
Genus	*Homo*	*Musca*	*Apis*
Species	*H. sapiens*	*M. domestica*	*A. mellifera*

Note that both the generic and the specific name must be used when referring to the species and that the specific name is not capitalized. Also note that both the generic and specific names are written in italic type to set them apart from the common names, as well as from the names used for higher taxa.

These scientific names are essential for accurate communication. Common names may vary from one part of the world, and even one part of the country, to another. For example, the insect called "bedbug" in some sections of the United States is known as "redcoat" in others, and in still other areas it is called a "bedlouse." *Cimex lectularis* is the accurate scientific name (uniformly accepted throughout the world) for this particular insect.

This book uses both common and scientific names and assigns them to the proper family and order. Given the number of species in each of the twenty-nine orders of insects (see following chart) and the details needed to describe them accurately, the task of covering even the most common American insects is enormous. However, since all members of the higher taxa have characteristics in common, it is possible for us to describe all of the twenty-nine orders of insects, the major families, and many of the species.

THE ORDERS OF INSECTS

All twenty-nine orders of insects found in the world are represented in North America. Some have many species assigned to them, others very few. The largest and most common orders are easily recognized. For example, butterflies and their close relatives, skippers and moths, are usually easy to spot identify on sight. They are members of the order *Lepidoptera.* Wasps, ants, and bees, similarly easy to recognize, belong to the order *Hymenoptera;* house flies and their relatives——gnats, mosquitoes, and horse flies——are all included in the order *Diptera,* the two-winged insects. The beetles and weevils, of the order *Coleoptera,* have hardened front wings without veins, and their hind wings fold beneath the front pair. The most numerous of all insect species, they abound everywhere. They are sometimes confused with cockroaches, earwigs, and certain bugs, making them somewhat less easy to identify on sight. Although nearly everyone senses that insect species can be grouped together in the manner we have here, more technical descriptions must be used to define each of the orders. To help you do this for yourself, a simple identification table is shown opposite.

INSECT ANATOMY
External anatomy

The exoskeleton, including the *integument,* or skin, of the insects, accounts for their size and shape. The integument consists of several parts, a basement membrane secreted by the

Number of species of each insect order

Order	Common Name	North American Species	World Species
Collembola	Springtails	660	6,000
Protura	Proturans	75	325
Thysanura	Silverfish and Bristle-tails	47	580
Diplura	Diplurans	51	660
Ephemeroptera	Mayflies	622	2,000
Odonata	Dragonflies and Dam-selflies	450	4,950
Plecoptera	Stoneflies	485	1,550
Grylloblattodea	Rock crawlers	10	20
Orthoptera	Grasshoppers, Katy-dids, etc.	1,018	12,500
Phasmida	Walkingsticks	27	2,000
Dictyoptera	Cockroaches and Mantids	79	5,500
Isoptera	Termites	41	1,900
Dermaptera	Earwigs	18	1,100
Embiidina	Webspinners	10	149
Zoraptera	Zorapterans	2	22
Psocoptera	Book lice and Bark lice	143	1,100
Mallophaga	Chewing lice	318	2,675
Anoplura	Sucking lice	62	250
Thysanoptera	Thrips	606	4,000
Hemiptera	True bugs	4,500	23,000
Homoptera	Aphids, Leafhoppers, etc.	6,500	32,000
Neuroptera	Dobsonflies, Lace-wings, etc.	338	4,600
Coleoptera	Beetles and Weevils	28,600	290,000
Mecoptera	Scorpionflies and Allies	66	350
Trichoptera	Caddisflies	975	4,500
Lepidoptera	Moths, Butterflies, and Skippers	13,700	180,000
Hymenoptera	Wasps, Ants, and Bees	17,429	103,000
Diptera	Flies	16,130	85,000
Siphonaptera	Fleas	238	1,370

cells, epidermal cells responsible also for secreting the upper, nonliving exoskeleton, and the cuticle, the complex noncellular layer that is the bulk of the outer covering. The latter is a nitrogenous polysaccharide, basically tan but may be pigmented, and a protein, *sclerotin*. As the exoskeleton develops during molting of the larval or nymphal skin, or during pupal transformation to the adult, sclerotin mixes with the other cuticular chemicals to form a relatively impervious, flexible struc-

Details of the anatomy of the integument (exoskeleton) of an insect. The epidermis is the only living portion of this structure. The remaining parts are chemical secretions of specialized epidermal (skin) cells.

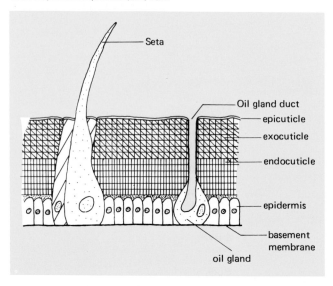

- Seta
- Oil gland duct
- epicuticle
- exocuticle
- endocuticle
- epidermis
- basement membrane

oil gland

ture. The process of hardening after mixing is termed *sclerotization*. The functions of the integument are: a) to prevent water loss; b) to protect from predators, pathogens, and parasites; and c) to provide a site for muscle attachment.

The head, the fused anterior series of body segments, is heavily sclerotized. Its appendages are: a pair of antennae, the two compound eyes, often one to three simple eyes or *ocelli,* and the mouthparts. The antennae vary greatly among the species of each insect order and are one of the morphological characteristics that are used for identifying the order, family, and sometimes even species of insects. They function as sensory organs to detect chemicals, including food, and *pheromones,* chemicals secreted into the air by the opposite sex. The compound eye is composed of numerous facets, each with a lens, united to form a single functional eye. Besides these two eyes there are often ocelli, or simple eyes. The insect's compound eyes can detect color, especially those of the bees and other pollinators, movement and, to some extent, distance. The ocelli apparently record daily changes in light intensity useful to insects strongly diurnal or nocturnal.

The structure of the insect's mouthparts determines its range of life habits. (It is also a useful means of identification since the structure varies from group to group.) Some insects can bite and chew plant material, others provide tools for predation, and still others suck plant juices or blood. They are responsible for causing a great deal of damage and injury to plants and animals.

The chewing type of mouthparts consists of, from front to back, an upper lip, or *labrum,* which connects to the front of the

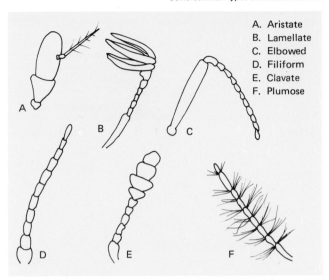

A. Aristate
B. Lamellate
C. Elbowed
D. Filiform
E. Clavate
F. Plumose

head; a pair of jawlike mandibles; and a pair of maxillae, which are less massive than the mandibles but also act as jaws. Each maxilla has, in addition, a small antennalike palpus connected to its base. The lower lip, or labium, completes the externally visible mouthparts, and is also equipped with a pair of palpi. Inside the mouth, lying on the labium, is the tonguelike hypopharynx. The chewing type of mouthparts is found in many insect orders, particularly beetles, grasshoppers, cockroaches, termites, and most of the wingless primitive insects. This basic structure is modified in other orders, usually into a thin, elongated, piercing shape from which certain parts, particularly the labial palpi and major portions of the maxillae, have been removed. Thus piercing-sucking, sponging, chewing-lapping, lacerating-sucking, and siphoning mouthparts are formed.

Mouthpart Types

Mouthparts	*Adult Insects*
Chewing	Collembola, Thysanura, Diplura, Odonata, Orthoptera, Isoptera, Plecoptera, Dermaptera, Embiidina, Zoraptera, Psocoptera, Mallophaga, Coleoptera, Neuroptera, Mecoptera, Trichoptera
Piercing-sucking	Protura, Anoplura, Diptera (part), Thysanoptera, Hemiptera, Homoptera, Siphonaptera
Lacerating-sucking	Diptera (part)
Chewing-lapping	Hymenoptera (part)
Sponging	Diptera (part)
Siphoning	Lepidoptera

The head and mouthparts of a grasshopper showing the arrangement of these basic structures on the head.

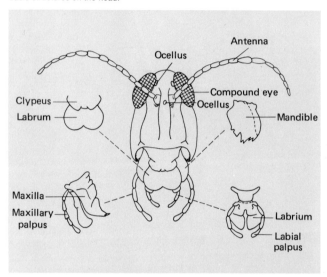

The three segments of the insect's thorax, moving from anterior to posterior, are termed the pro-, meso-, and metathorax. Each of the segments usually bears a pair of legs. As discussed previously, these are rarely absent but variously modified, and in some insects the front pair of legs is greatly reduced and may even function as sense organs only.

The wings, borne only on the meso- and meta-thorax, are present in most insects. They are absent (or apterous) in all of the *apterygote* orders (the primitive wingless orders) and in most ectoparasites such as bedbugs, keds (particular flies), lice, fleas, and certain species of most of the other orders. The true flies (order Diptera) have one pair of wings, located on the mesothorax, and a pair of halteres, or balancing organs, on the metathorax. These sensory structures, stubby appendages with a terminal knob, have apparently replaced the true wings. The forewings of beetles and earwigs are hardened, modified veinless wing covers, or *elytra,* that protect the flying wings which fold beneath them when the insect is at rest. The front wings of Orthoptera are more leathery than those of beetles, but are used in part at least for flying. The true bugs, Hemiptera, have wings that are hardened at the basal half, but the outer or apical portion is membranous as is their second pair of wings. Moths, butterflies, and skippers have scales that form various color patterns on the surface of the otherwise transparent wings.

Wing shape and the arrangement of the veins of the wings are used for identification purposes, especially in the Diptera, Hymenoptera, and Lepidoptera. A unique system has been devel-

Hind leg of a grasshopper showing the arrangement of the basic parts.

A hypothetical insect wing showing the arrangement and names of the veins and cross veins using standard terminology for wing venation. C = costa; Sc = sub-costa; R = radius; M = media; Cu = cubitus; A = anal veins; r = radial cross vein; m = medial cross vein; r–m = radial–medial cross vein; m–cu = medial–cubital cross vein; a = anal cross vein.

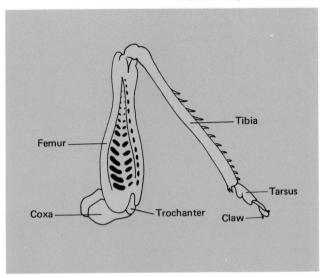

oped to name the wing veins. It has been shown that the position and number of veins have changed from the primitive orders to the more advanced orders and within each order. This, along with the fossil remains of the wings of ancient insects, has made possible a classification of the insects which probably closely parallels the actual evolution of the class.

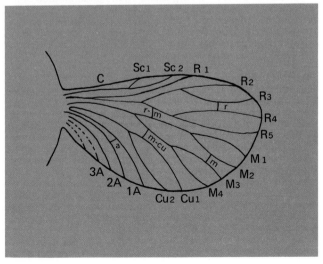

Structure of the abdomen showing the cercus, ovipositor, and the claspers which, in this case, are modified for digging.

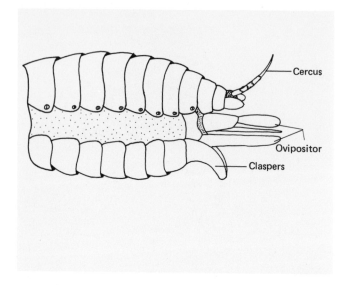

The abdomen has no appendages except for the female's egg-laying apparatus, the *ovipositor,* and the copulatory structure of males and, in some groups, *cerci,* antennaelike organs projecting from the last abdominal segment. Some cerci have been modified into forcepslike structures that are used for grasping. In rare instances, nonfunctional, short styletlike paired projections are found on the undersurface of the abdomen of such primitive insects as the Thysanura, and, for no apparent reason, on a few beetles. These structures may be remnants of legs. The abdomen is usually rather soft compared to the rest of the body, so that it can expand as food is consumed or as eggs develop.

Internal anatomy
The internal organs have a number of interesting adaptations which are responsible for the group's successful endurance and abundance. The *respiratory system* is perhaps most responsible for the insect's mastery of terrestrial life. Air is taken in through a series of openings, *spiracles,* on the sides of the insect's body. Inside the body are air tubes, *tracheae,* and air sacs through which air can flow to the organs and tissues. Waste gases also travel through the tracheal system and are expelled through the spiracles. However, anterior spiracles are generally used for air intake and posterior ones for carbon dioxide exhalation. Note that the respiratory system is completely independent of the *circulatory system.* The latter consists of a series of open blood sinuses through which the blood flows freely and eliminates the need for a complex network of veins and arteries as found in the vertebrates. Since the circu-

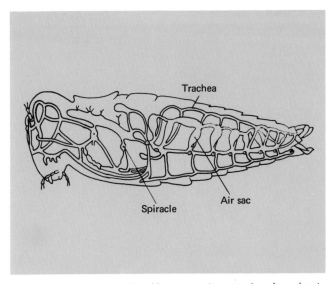

latory system is not involved in oxygen transport, only a simple heart, consisting of a *dorsal tube* open at both ends, is necessary. Blood is sucked into the posterior end by the relaxation of the alary muscles, which flatten the tube upon contraction and force the blood along the tube toward the anterior. A series of valves prevent the backward flow of blood by closing under pressure. The posterior portion of this dorsal aorta also has a series of lateral openings, or *ostia,* through which blood can enter. Oddly enough, and for obscure physical and chemical reasons, the heart may pump in the reverse direction, perhaps because of an ion imbalance or simply to protect the brain from damage by poisonous materials in the blood. Normally the brain receives the blood first. Remember, however, that the blood contains only food material and metabolic waste products, not oxygen. It is thus unnecessary for insects to have a circulation as efficient and high pressure as that found in mammals and birds who depend upon their blood for oxygen.

The insect digestive system is usually complete; that is, the tube extends from the mouth through the body to the anal opening. The many modifications to the system directly relate to the type of food the insect ingests. Thus, plant juice and blood-feeding insects have filtering mechanisms that remove water from the fluid and enable them to handle large volumes of liquid. Aphids, for example, do not have a complete digestive tract. Water is eliminated instead through a filtering device, and most, if not all, of the sugar which is totally digestible is retained. Some sugar is passed out when water is excreted, as anyone who has parked a car under trees in the summer may have noted. Fluid drops expelled by the aphids drip onto

Digestive system of a hypothetical insect. Note that the three main regions are labeled. In actual species each of these regions is modified according to the type of food consumed.

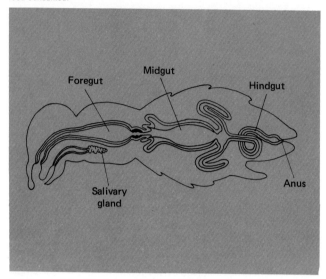

the car and the heat evaporates the water, resulting in a sticky, dust-trapping mess. Conversely, caterpillars busily feeding on the leaves of those same trees will excrete dry pellets. Their massive consumption of leaf tissue is proportionally far greater than the daily volume of food consumed by elephants, whose daily dung piles weigh only a few hundred pounds, a fraction of their body weight. In comparison, the nocturnal dung production of caterpillars, who eat more than their own weight each day, would be measured in tons were they elephants.

The *central nervous system* located ventrally along the body wall, as opposed to the dorsal location in the spine of vertebrates, consists of the brain, which is little more than a large *ganglion* (nerve center), and the *nerve cord*. The latter extends the entire length of the body, but in the more advanced forms, such as flies and bees, it is located only in the thorax. The thoracic ganglia have long nerves that pass into the abdomen. You may have noted that the abdomen of a bee, even when completely detached from the rest of the body, will continue to contract and the stinger will continue to function. This is because of a somewhat independent network of nerve connections that send impulses to the stinger muscles so it continues to pump venom.

Most insects are bisexual, with as many males as females. Some bees, beetles, and aphids are *parthenogenic* in some stages; that is, females reproduce without males. Female insects may lay eggs after fertilization or, in a few specialized species, the eggs and sometimes even part of the larval stage remain inside the female, and the young are born alive. In some flies, such as the disease-carrying tsetse fly, not only are

the egg and *larva* retained inside the female to develop, but a *prepupa* is formed that is close to the adult stage when it passes out of the female's body. The courtship habits and oviposition processes of insects are remarkably varied and worthy of careful observation.

Metamorphosis, the change that occurs in most insects during the various stages of their life histories, differs from group to group. The apterygote insects are *ametabolous;* they have no evident metamorphosis. Many orders have incomplete, or *hemimetabolous,* metamorphosis. These insects develop gradually after hatching from the egg, by a series of skin sheddings, or *molts,* into the adult stage. In addition to the egg stage, they have a nymphal stage that resembles the adult in external appearance but is otherwise different. The nymphs lack wings but gradually develop wing pads, and then, as adults, usually develop wings. During the final molt, the reproductive system matures and becomes functional after the molt is completed. Aquatic nymphs who are often very different in shape and structure from their adult stage are frequently referred to as naiads to distinguish them from other nymphs and to indicate that they are aquatic.

The most advanced form of insect metamorphosis is termed *holometabolous.* In a number of species, most insects have complete metamorphosis consisting of the four stages: egg, larva, pupa, and adult. The larval, or feeding, stage during which all growth takes place is entirely different from the adult, and larvae always have chewing or rasping mouthparts. Upon reaching maximum size, the larva enters the pupal, or transformation, stage during which most of the internal anatomy is

Adult, larva, and chrysalis of the monarch butterfly, an example of complete meta-morphosis.

broken down and rearranged to form the structure from which the adult emerges. Metamorphosis is controlled by a balance of three internal hormones secreted by glands located in the head or thorax. One of these, *ecdysone,* is responsible for the final transformation of the larva to the pupa, and the pupa to the adult. As might be suspected, these immature stages differ from species to species. Therefore, different names have been applied to these stages in the various orders. Those referred to throughout this book are defined in the glossary.

ADAPTIVE COLORATION
More than any other group of animals, insects exhibit color patterns, sometimes combined with mimic shapes, that have been selected through evolutionary processes to protect them. We might expect protective colors of necessity to be dull or mottled, so that insects blend into their background. Yet, scanning the pages of this book, we see that most insects display beautiful, bright, strong colors. How then are insects protected from their predators? These bright red, orange, or yellow hues, combined with black or dark blue, are warning, or *aposematic,* colors. They delight the eye but warn would-be predators that chemical poisons lurk within the body tissues of an otherwise tasty morsel of food; in the case of many species, they lack the chemicals which provide that protection. These striking colors, however, fool predators, and the insects usually escape harm. For example, one family of beetles, the Lycidae (entry no. 132), has many brightly marked species which are all very poisonous. Predators, either instinctively or through learning, avoid them and all similarly marked species.

Thus, other species, such as certain moths (entry no. 260) and many other beetles, benefit by mimicking the color and shape of lycid beetles. In fact, this color pattern is repeated so often among insects that it becomes almost monotonous.

Another example of this phenomenon is the poisonous larvae of the monarch butterfly (entry no. 239, lower). Birds carefully avoid these green and black creatures whose colors serve as a warning when fully exposed. The monarch caterpillar feeds on the leaf surface, but when necessary it crawls to the base of a leaf or clings to the stem of the milkweed food plant, its disruptive color pattern protecting it from view. The adults (entry no. 239, upper) have used the "standard" red and black pattern for their protection. Occasionally a young bird will attempt to eat these insects, but the internal fluids, a poison extracted from the milkweed plant, will cause the bird to vomit. Even though the caterpillar and, occasionally, the adult butterfly have been killed by these experimental forays on the part of the younger birds, the remainder of the population escapes unharmed. However, nature is not static and the evolutionary process continues. Adept birds have learned that the poison in the adult butterfly is stored in the surface tissue of the body and will scoop out the inner tissues which are not poisonous. Entomologists do not yet know whether the monarch is heading for extinction because of this new development in bird behavior.

Other kinds of bright color patterns provide protective coloration. Certain moths, for example, have brightly colored hind wings that are exposed when the moth is in flight. As soon as it alights, however, the duller front wings cover the hind ones, and the moth effectively "disappears." The predator flies on, overshooting its mark, and goes hungry.

Large "eyespots" on the wings or bodies offer still another form of protection by creating the illusion of a much larger animal that ought not to be attacked. In the case of many butterflies (entry no. 215, lower) the predator will be confused by the eyespots and make them the target of attack. The butterfly will no longer be as attractive a specimen without these pretty markings, but it will live. Beetles (entry no. 122) and even larvae (entry no. 207, lower) are apparently also protected by these patterns.

A seemingly endless parade of mimics and their protective resemblances have been described by naturalists. Some proven examples are shown in this book. Not all of those that have been reported to be examples of *mimicry* actually are. Insects that look alike side by side in collections may, in fact, inhabit areas hundreds of miles apart, so it seems unlikely that one is mimicking the other and is actually protected in this way. More careful study and experimentation is needed before it is possible to know the extent of functional protective resemblance, coloration, and mimicry.

INSECT BEHAVIOR

The great differences between insect and human behavior may not always be obvious. For example, the bee's sting is not an

Anthophora Stanfordiana, a bee mimic of the bumble bee.

aggressive act in the human sense but, rather, the result of a series of triggering stimuli causing a fixed pattern of response. It is thus possible to apply what we know about insect behavior so that it may appear that we have trained them. The beekeeper is well aware of these principles and is thus able to avoid painful stings.

Innate behavior (sometimes referred to as *instinct*) is defined as a fixed response or series of responses to a particular stimulus or series of stimuli. The stance and movement patterns of all insect species are characteristic of the species. We recognize the flight pattern of the house fly, as distinguished from that of the honey bee or wasp, and our reactions vary accordingly. Some true flies look almost exactly like bees and mimic their behavior. Although they are completely without stingers, the human response is the same toward the harmless fly as it is toward the honey bee.

Much more complicated behavioral patterns occur among ants, bees, certain wasps, and to a lesser extent in other insect groups. Fixed action patterns, a more descriptive term than instinct, are unlearned reactions to life situations. The insect's nervous system is programmed genetically to react in a particular way to a releaser stimulus or series of releaser stimuli.

The famous nineteenth-century French naturalist, Jean Henri Fabre, recorded his observations of and experiments with the complex behavior patterns among insects. A few of the species he worked with are illustrated here. Fabre experimented with sexton beetles (entry no. 91), whose normal activity is to bury dead mice, frogs, or other small cadavers for food for their larvae by digging below the carcass until it is lowered into the ground, and then covering it with soil. The beetles must dig quickly in order to prevent flies from getting to the food source

31

A sexton beetle, *Nicrophorus* species, will gnaw the strings that prevent this dead shrew from burial. To the sexton beetle, the strings are merely grass rootlets, an ordinary problem frequently encountered in this instinctive process. Note the hordes of other insects that are attracted to this carrion. The sexton beetles must work rapidly to bury this animal if they are to save their food from consumption by these other necrophilous insects.

first. Fabre tied a dead shrew to sticks in a way that prevented its being buried, but this stopped the beetles only temporarily. They scurried around, found the string holding the shrew, and quickly chewed it in two. An act of reasoning? Not at all. The beetles often encounter small roots as they dig. To them the string was only a form of root, another in a series of releaser stimuli.

Similar experiments have been performed with the potter wasp (entry no. 283), who constructs a small clay pot on a branch or on the side of a building. As soon as the pot has been completed, the wasp stocks it with paralyzed caterpillars to which she attaches her eggs. Having filled the pot, the wasp caps it with a mud cover and flies away, never to return. What happens when a hole is broken through the bottom of the pot so that the paralyzed caterpillars fall through and the pot is never filled? Fabre and others found that the reaction to this depended upon the species of potter wasp and the stage in the construction of the pot. In some cases, if the pot had not been completed, the female would simply repair the damage caused by the experimenter. Obviously pots are damaged during construction by birds or other hazards and need to be repaired. Once the pot has been completed, however, the damage is ignored, and a new response is initiated. The pot must now be filled with caterpillars and it can no longer be repaired. One experimenter observed a remarkable phenomenon: Some wasps appeared to be able to count! A fixed number of caterpillars were placed in the pot, although they fell through the bottom and none remained inside. As soon as the pot was "full"—a specific number of caterpillars had been dropped in—the pot was capped and away flew the female wasp, blissfully unaware of the futility of her efforts. Other species that could not "count" went on trying to fill the pot until they died of exhaustion, ran out of eggs, or lost interest because the initial stimulus wore off.

These are only brief examples of fascinating observations that can be made by anyone who takes the time to look at what is going on in a woods, field, stream, or even on the back porch. Behavior also involves the acts that lead to mate location, courtship, and mating processes. Some insects (entry no. 235, note) stake out territories, others brood their young, and a few (some ants, bees, etc.) feed their young or tend the young of other insects (entry no. 224). Escape and defense tactics also utilize behavioral patterns. The list is almost endless, and the behavior of only a few insects is known, leaving a vast frontier of study open to any curious person.

AQUATIC INSECTS

Approximately 5% of insects spend all or part of their life cycle in water. The majority of these *aquatic* insects are found in fresh water, but a few species live in the open ocean, many in intertidal zones, and a considerable number in brackish water. All species of four orders of insects have aquatic nymphs, naiads, or larvae. They are the mayflies (Ephemeroptera), the dragonflies and damselflies (Odonata), the stoneflies (Plecoptera), and the caddisflies (Trichoptera). A number of families in the larger orders, particularly the beetles (Coleoptera), true bugs (Hemiptera), and flies (Diptera), have aquatic stages.

In adapting to the aquatic environment, these insects underwent various anatomical changes, for example, developing abdominal *gills*, terminal breathing tubes (*siphons*), and in some, internal gills in order to use the oxygen dissolved in the water. Siphons allow some to remain in the water and still use the atmospheric oxygen at the surface. The bodies of aquatic insects are usually streamlined to cut down resistance, and their legs are often modified to form swimming paddles. Many such insects feed on organic debris on the bottom of the body of water. A large number are predators and relatively few feed on living plants.

Aquatic insects are beneficial to man in that they provide food for fish and other aquatic or semiaquatic vertebrates desirable to man. A few species are indicators of environmental pollution: They are so sensitive to changes in environmental conditions that biologists can detect small variations in water quality by noting shifts in the populations of these species. Some aquatic larvae, such as mosquitoes and blackflies, are of great concern because their adults transmit human disease organisms from person to person. One way to stop the spread of these diseases is by killing the larvae of the *vectors,* but this may also disrupt many aquatic ecosystems since beneficial species are killed along with the disease transmitters.

SOCIAL INSECTS

The majority of insect species are solitary, living out their lives alone, only intermittently in contact with a mate. They compete with one another for food and, occasionally, for shelter and mates. Two orders of insects, however, the termites (Isoptera) and certain ants, wasps, and bees (Hymenoptera) have complex societies whose members carry on sustained interaction. These *eusocial,* or true social, insects are characterized by cooperation among family members, caring for the immature, and usually dividing the labor according to their caste. The generations overlap, enabling the offspring to aid the parents in the colony's work. Termites, ants, honeybees, yellowjackets, hornets, and some wasps are eusocial.

Social behavior is classified in a way that perhaps represents stages in the development of advanced social life, as follows:

Subsocial: Adult insects display maternal care for or protection of their offspring (some earwigs, crickets, beetles, cockroaches, and true bugs).

Communal: Adults of the same generation share the nest or hive but do not cooperate in the care of the offspring (some bees and wasps).

Quasisocial: Adults use the same nests and cooperate in the care of the offspring (some bees and wasps).

Semisocial: A worker caste of the same generation as the reproductive caste cares for the young (some bees).

Eusocial: As discussed earlier, and in contrast to the previous four, they have overlapping generations. Their offspring include worker and reproductive castes which cooperate in the care of the young, division of labor, and assistance to the parents.

Further details about eusocial life among insects is given in the following examples and in some of the entries.

1. Termites
All species of termites are eusocial. It is likely that termites evolved from the subsocial cockroaches. The *caste* system of termites includes: *primary reproductives, secondary reproductives, workers, soldiers,* and sometimes *naustes.* The latter are members of a special caste of soldiers that secrete chemicals for defense. Their heads are funnel shaped and they are thus able to squirt the defensive chemicals which they secrete. The primary reproductives are the queen and the males. The secondary reproductives are nymphlike workers who can develop into primary reproductives should something happen to the queen or the males. Soldiers are nonreproductives modified by large jaws on enlarged heads and capable of defending the nest. Termites are best known for their damage to wood and wood products. They usually make their nest in soil, but use chewed wood as food for themselves and their young. They cannot actually digest wood, but their digestive tracts contain bacteria or protozoa that secrete wood-digesting enzymes. The product of this digestion is the food of both the termites and bacteria or protozoa.

2. Ants
Ants, family *Formicidae,* are good examples of eusocial Hymenoptera. The caste system of ants includes males, queens, and several types of workers. The workers care for the larvae and pupae. Many ants are predaceous on other arthropods; others are plant feeders or scavengers. Ants are often confused with termites, especially when the adult reproductives swarm. Because homeowners often confuse these two very distinct insects, the following table explains how they differ.

Comparison of termites and ants

Termites	Ants
Antennae straight	Antennae elbowed or angled
Two pairs of wings of equal length	Two pairs of wings of unequal length
Wing veins simple, more or less straight, without closed cells	Wing veins curved, united to form many cells
Eyes usually absent	Eyes usually large
Waist thick, no constriction between thorax and abdomen	Waist with constriction between thorax and abdomen, with a little scalelike bump in the middle of the abdominal stem
Wings milky white, opaque, or black	Wings transparent or dusky brown

The great variety of ant colonies have attracted the attention of naturalists and philosophers alike. Some colonies of ants "farm" fungus gardens; some make slaves of other ants; and some, aptly called "army" ants, go on bivouacs, massive raiding parties involving all the members of the colony, including even the larvae and pupae.

3. Honey bees

Many species of wasps, hornets, and bees show some degree of eusocial life, but few are organized to the extent of the honey bee hive. The castes of bees are: *drones* (sexually active males), a single queen (the egg-laying female), and workers (sexless females). The queen and workers are capable of stinging, the stinger being a modified ovipositor. Metamorphosis, as in all Hymenoptera, is complete, and the larval and pupal stages depend upon the workers for their feeding and care. The bee mouthparts are greatly modified into a combination of chewing and lapping, effective for feeding on plant nectar and pollen and for making the hive out of plant material and wax. Some social Hymenoptera feed upon other insects and provision their nests with caterpillars, spiders, and other arthropods, but although honey bees may kill other insects, they never feed on them. The queen, with a small staff of workers, spends the winter in the hive and starts a new colony in the spring. Depending upon the supply of the food store, there may be considerable activity in the hive during the winter, and workers will leave the hive on warm days on the chance they may find early blooming flowers. Drones are most numerous during the summer, but as food becomes scarce the workers kill the drones and remove them from the hive. New colonies are formed when young queens are permitted to live and fly from the old hive with some of the workers and a few drones. This swarming process usually takes place when an established colony becomes too large. Many of the social Hymenoptera are beneficial as pollinators and sometimes as predators upon insect pests. This is discussed in several of the entries of Hymenoptera.

PLANT PESTS

No species of flowering plant escapes injury from *phytophagous* insects who attack all parts of the plant, including foliage, stems, roots, flowers, fruits, and seeds. Some also transmit plant *pathogens* (bacteria, viruses, fungi, etc.) that cause plant diseases. These pests of crops or ornamental plants cause damage amounting to millions of dollars annually. Some species are responsible for the destruction of conifers and hardwood trees in our already depleted forests at the cost of billions of dollars in lost lumber in the United States and Canada. The type of damage inflicted depends upon the insect pest's mouthparts. Although chewing is the most visible form of destruction and, with piercing-sucking, accounts for most of the harm done to plants by insects, egg-laying scars, nest-building, and insect secretions also take their toll. The order Homoptera is exclusively phytophagous; all species are therefore potential pests of cultivated plants.

Insects that Damage Plants

Order	Common names	Damage
Orthoptera	Grasshoppers, crickets, katydids	Nymphs and adults feed on leaves
Hemiptera	Plant bugs, seed bugs	Nymphs and adults damage stems, leaves, flowers, and seeds
Homoptera	Aphids, cicadas, scale insects, whiteflies, treehoppers, and leafhoppers	Piercing-sucking mouthparts damage all parts of the plant; vectors of plant diseases
Thysanoptera	Thrips	Mechanical damage to leaves and flowers; plant disease vectors
Coleoptera	Beetles and weevils	Grubs cause root damage; adults and larvae attack all parts of the plant; seed infestation by many
Diptera	Flies	Leaf miners; gall formation
Hymenoptera	Sawflies, gall makers, webspinners	Larvae of some are leaf feeders; webspinners cause leaf damage
Lepidoptera	Moth and butterfly larvae	Caterpillar damage to all parts of the plant, including flowers and seeds

Some plants are attacked by only a few pest species; others, such as corn and rice, have over 100 insect pests feeding on their various parts. The damage includes defoliation, leaf-mining (the larvae feed on the tissues between the upper and lower epidermis), skeletonization of leaf tissue so that only the leaf veins remain intact, and gall formation (galls are a type of cancerous growth of plant tissue). Stem and leaf galls provide a haven for many different insect species who feed on the excessive tissue growth. Stems are attacked by boring insects such as the billbugs (weevils) and long-horned beetles. A heavy infestation of insects feeding on plants with piercing-sucking mouthparts causes serious loss of plant juices which stunts the growth of the plants.

Root damage inflicted by insects weakens the plant, often to the extent that the plant wilts or is easily knocked down by wind or rain. Many beetle grubs and moth caterpillars cause extensive harm to root systems of cultivated plants. Fruits and seeds may be damaged by insects with either chewing mouthparts or piercing-sucking mouthparts. The slightest damage by these feeding actions to fruits such as apples, peaches, pears, plums, and citrus greatly reduces their commercial value and often makes them unmarketable. Discoloration by scale insects and the presence of froghopper spittle also reduces the commercial value of the fruit even though the fruit itself is not harmed.

Bacteria, fungi, and viruses are transmitted mechanically by species of Hemiptera, Homoptera, and Thysanura through direct contact. Rarely, they are transmitted indirectly, with some development of the pathogen taking place in the insect's digestive system before it is transmitted. The infamous Dutch elm disease of the American elm, for example, is transmitted by the elm bark beetle which has special pockets that carry the spores of the disease-causing fungi.

Control of plant pests is a major concern of many entomologists. Most ecologists believe that the use of chemicals is detrimental to the environment because the residues enter various ecosystems; chemical buildup has killed many non-pest species, both vertebrate and invertebrate, particularly aquatic food chains, and entomologists are therefore experimenting to find alternate means of control.

INSECTS HARMFUL TO MAN AND ANIMALS.

Medical and veterinary entomology, the branch of the science that deals with insects in relation to the health of humans and domestic animals, involves many other branches of biology, including epidemiology, microbiology, parasitology, virology, and public health administration. The insects of medical or veterinary concern are those that cause injury to humans and animals either directly, through bites and stings, or indirectly, by transmission. They range from the nuisance of cockroaches who persist in living in homes, restaurants, and warehouses, to the world's deadliest killer, the anopheline mosquitoes that transmit malaria. The major orders of insects whose species are involved in disease transmission are listed in the following table.

Insects that transmit disease to humans and animals

Order	Pest or Vector	Injury or Disease
Dictyoptera	Cockroaches	Sometimes mechanical transport of pathogens
Hemiptera	Bed bugs	Loss of blood through bites
	Kissing bugs	Painful bites around mouth; vector of Chagas disease in New World tropics

Order	Pest or Vector	Injury or Disease
Mallophaga	Chewing lice	Ectoparasites of birds and mammals; heavy infestations may cause death through secondary infection
Anoplura	Sucking lice	Ectoparasites of man and mammals; vectors of diseases; may cause serious dermatosis
Diptera	Mosquitoes	Irritating bites; vectors of many diseases including malaria and yellow fever
	Black flies	Irritating bites; vectors of diseases
	Deer flies	Vectors of serious eye disease
	Tsetse flies	Vectors of African sleeping sickness
	Sand flies	Vectors of several tropical diseases
	House fly	Vectors of amoebic dysentery; typhoid; cholera
	Horse flies	Vectors of anthrax
	Blow flies	Vectors of typhoid and cholera
Siphonaptera	Fleas	Vectors of epidemic typhus and plague
Hymenoptera	Bees, ants, and wasps	Some species inflict painful stings

Some evidence shows that cockroaches are capable of carrying certain pathogens on their legs and mouthparts, but they are usually not disease carriers. Bed bugs inflict painless bites, but they too are not disease vectors. Kissing bugs, found throughout North, Central, and South America, are painful nocturnal bloodsuckers whose salivary glands secrete an anesthetic that temporarily suppresses the pain until some hours later when painful swelling occurs. Some species are vectors of the New World sleeping sickness, Chagas disease, which is prevalent in parts of tropical America.

The two orders of lice, Mallophaga and Anoplura, are ectoparasites who infest birds, mammals, and humans. Under conditions of stress such as war, famine, or poverty, human body lice transmit epidemic typhus. All lice are, at the very least, an irritant and may also cause both loss of blood and lowered resistance to disease that can lead to death of the host.

Flies are, at the present time, by far the most serious disease transmitters of all insects, just as fleas and lice were vectors of the infamous bubonic plague during the Middle Ages. Their types of mouthparts include piercing-sucking, lacerating-sucking, and sponging-lapping. Only a few species of this very large order actually attack vertebrates, but a great number are parasitic as larvae on other insects.

Mosquitoes, house flies, flesh flies, and black flies are among the species that transmit disease, and no part of the world is completely free of them. Buzzing around humans and animals, tracking fecal material across food, and often biting, in order to draw the animal "nectar," blood, they are nuisances even if not disease transmitters.

Mosquitoes (but only the females) not only use animal blood for food, but they carry a long list of human and animal diseases. Malaria remains the number one killer of humans throughout the world. Only recently have heart disease and cancer approached the mortality rate of this disease. Yellow fever, once a disease that through its debilitation delayed the building of the Panama Canal and other development of tropical regions, is now nearly under control. Taking its place, however, is another mosquito-borne disease, encephalitis.

The aquatic larvae of mosquitoes are called *wigglers* and the aquatic pupae *tumblers* by nonentomologists in areas where it is necessary for human survival to know whether or not disease-transmitting mosquitoes are present. These people learn to recognize not only these stages but the major kinds of mosquitoes. They know that the mosquito that "stands on its head" will cause a malaria outbreak and the one with the "lyre on its back" will bring the dreaded yellow fever. They also know that the mouthparts of the adult female mosquito are for piercing the skin and sucking blood. Male mosquitoes are plant juice or nectar feeders. Not all female mosquitoes take a blood meal, and those that do, do so only prior to egg formation and laying. Most mosquito species feed on nonhuman animals including both warm-blooded and cold-blooded animals. The elephant mosquitoes do not suck blood at all. Their larvae are carnivorous and often beneficial because they eat other mosquito larvae.

Black fly bites are itchy and in most parts of the world black flies are merely pests, but in western tropical Africa they are the vectors of the dreaded "river blindness," or onchoceriasis, caused by a worm parasite transmitted through the bites of the female black fly. The disease causes almost complete loss of sight in children and adults alike.

The house fly with its sponging-lapping mouthparts is not a true disease vector because no pathogen develops within the fly's body. Nevertheless, it is capable of mechanically transmitting typhoid, cholera, and probably other diseases contained in human and animal waste.

Adult horse and deer flies have lacerating-sponging mouthparts, and many domestic and wild animals suffer from their severe bites and resulting blood loss. They also transmit diseases to these animals and occasionally to humans.

Blow flies and other house flylike flies, whose larvae may infest animal wounds, are abundant around barnyards and houses. The screwworm, for example, is a serious cattle pest. To bring it under control, a unique method has been devised by U.S. Department of Agriculture entomologists. Mass reared male flies are separated and irradiated by low doses of radioactive materials that will sterilize but not kill them. These neutered flies are then released in great numbers in the screwworm areas. Because the wild female mates only once in her lifetime, and because of the greater number of these sterilized males as compared to the wild ones, most of the eggs laid by the females are incapable of developing. Eventually the populations are reduced to zero. However, new infestations of wild flies may occur by invasion from other areas, making it necessary to repeat the procedure. Still other flies are known to cause myiasis, or fly larval infestation. The larvae usually feed on dead or dying tissue so their excrement harbors infectious bacteria. A secondary infection may spread to other parts of the animal's body.

Fleas are well-known ectoparasites of mammals and some birds. Most dogs and cats who spend time outdoors harbor these wingless, bloodsucking ectoparasites. Flea larvae are scavengers who live in animal nests, including dog and cat beds and surrounding areas. Once matured into the adult stage, however, they require a blood meal for egg development. Ordinarily they are relatively harmless, but fleas of ground squirrels may transmit sylvatic plague, and occasional outbreaks still occur in the western United States. Rat fleas, particularly those of the Orient, are often involved in the transmission of endemic typhus, now a worldwide disease.

Even though most bees and wasps are harmless, those with stingers have a universal reputation because of the pain they cause, and most of us avoid all of these flying insects. Some of their wingless relatives, such as the fire ants of the southern states, are known to sting and may be dangerous. However, the claim that they cause the death of domestic animals and humans is exaggerated. Nevertheless, anyone who has been stung by them will agree that the pain is not something that warrants repetition. The female Hymenoptera use their modified ovipositors to sting, although this modification does not occur in all species. For some, a sting from a bee or a wasp can be very serious. The venom injected may be not only painful but can cause anaphylaxis, a hypersensitive allergic reaction which can lead to death through respiratory difficulties, heart disturbances, and other physiological problems. A victim who shows symptoms of weakness, confusion, and heart rate change requires prompt medical attention and treatment.

BENEFICIAL INSECTS

We would be unable to enjoy many fruits and flowers were it not for the insects who pollinate them, and make possible billions of dollars worth of crops each year. Honey bees top the list of pollinating insects, but other bees and a few species of flies also provide this service. Certain beetles gather pollen, but only rarely are they actually responsible for pollination.

Some crops that require insect pollination

Alfalfa	Cranberries	Cantaloupe	Radishes
Apples	Cucumbers	Peaches	Raspberries
Blackberries	Currants	Pears	Turnips
Blueberries	Eggplant	Plums	Onions
Cherries	Muskmelons	Pumpkins	Watermelons

Honey bees, in addition to their beneficial role as pollinators, produce valuable honey and beeswax. Beekeeping is a multi-million-dollar industry, and the United States alone produces an estimated 200 million pounds of honey a year.

Commercial silk is produced by a number of species of silk-worms, but most of it comes from the cocoons of *Bombyx mori,* a completely domesticated species, no longer living in the wild. Several dyes are produced by scale insects, and shellac is the product secreted by the related lac insect.

Entomophagous insects, those that feed upon other insects, are increasingly important for biological control and are particularly useful to home gardeners. The ladybird beetle larvae and their adults help control scale insects and aphids in gardens and orchards. Lacewing larvae and adults are used to control aphids and other crop insect pests. Praying mantids, vigorously predaceous insects, are used by many gardeners to control insects. Unfortunately, all predaceous insects do not distinguish between those pests causing damage and insects that are beneficial pollinators or beneficial predators themselves. Some of the most beneficial of the parasitic insects are the tiny wasps of the hymenopterous family *Braconidae* which are used to control a number of caterpillars such as the tomato and tobacco hornworms that cause extensive damage to crops.

A considerable number of insect species are scavengers, important to the recycling phase of all ecosystems. Dung beetles, carrion beetles, dung flies, carpenter ants, termites, and wood-boring beetles hasten the conversion of dung, carrion, decaying wood, and plant and animal debris into humus which adds to the fertility of the soil. Without detritus converters the recycling time for animal dung and carrion, in particular, would be much longer and enable numerous generations of pestiferous flies to develop on that material.

One acre of soil is estimated to have more than one million individual arthropods living in it. Insects and other arthropods, as well as earthworms, assist in the aeration of the soil which improves the plant-growing quality of the soil.

Some insects are used to destroy plants accidentally introduced by commerce from one country to another. Prickly pear cacti in Australia, alligatorweed, and Klamath weed in the United States are foreign plants now controlled by species of moths or beetles. Entomologists travel to the country of origin of the weed to determine its natural pests. After long experimentation in carefully protected test chambers, it is possible to select an insect that can be safely introduced into the area of the plant pest to bring it under control without danger of its becoming a pest.

Insects are the major food source of many species of birds, fish, amphibians, and mammals. Freshwater fish feed upon caddisflies, mayflies, stoneflies, dragonflies, damselflies, mosquito larvae, and beetle larvae. The woodpecker's well-known beak is used to dig out wood-boring beetles. Frogs and lizards are adept at catching flies. Skunks, opossums, and raccoons are among the animals who search out tasty, fat, nutty-flavored beetle larvae in rotting logs. All of these insects are high in protein and are an excellent food source.

To primitive peoples of Australia, Papua-New Guinea, and certain other regions, insects are prized delicacies. Grubs and grasshoppers (the locusts of the Bible) are often eaten in some countries, although this is uncommon in the United States. Caterpillars are customarily eaten in parts of Latin America (the fritos of Mexico, for example). As food, particularly beef, becomes more expensive and scarcer, more attention will be given to the high-protein insects.

Biological research with insects started at the turn of the twentieth century when Nobel Prizewinner Thomas Hunt Morgan used fruit flies to demonstrate the basic principles of genetics. Mendel was able to describe the mathematical principles of heredity; Morgan saw the units of inheritance, the chromosomes and genes, by studying the tiny abundant two-winged fly, *Drosophila melanogaster*. It is likely that most modern biologists learned the rudiments of critical experimentation through their classroom studies of this interesting insect. Much more has been learned since Morgan's time, not only about genetics, but about basic physiological principles through experiments with these six-legged guinea pigs. Carol Williams of Harvard and Sir Vincent B. Wigglesworth of Cambridge are among those who have used insects in their tests and have contributed greatly to biology.

CONTROL MEASURES

Less than 5% of all the insect species in the United States and Canada are pests, but since our economy is so dependent on agriculture, domestic animals, and our own health, the reproduction of these species must be checked. Several means of applied controls, those that involve human intervention as opposed to natural population restrictions, have been developed.

Major types of applied insect control

Physical methods	Mechanical methods	Chemical poisons
Cultural control	Biological control	Plant breeding

The laws that regulate applied entomology specify the proper use of chemicals, provide for plant and animal quarantines, and for the inspection of goods at air- and seaports. Physical control measures involve use of temperature (high and low), light, and sound. Light traps, the most widely used physical control, attract and kill moths and beetles. Mechanical controls include fly swatters, window screen barriers, sticky "tangle foot," and trap barriers such as mosquito netting. Cultural control results from the practice of crop rotation, waste removal for fly control, and planting and harvesting when the insect pest is dormant. Chemical insect control is the only satisfactory type used in the United States today, even though the persistent use of insecticides is of great concern because of the serious contamination of the environment. The disadvantage of the contact poisons, fumigants, attractants, repellents, growth regulators, and sterilants is that they kill both pests and harmless or beneficial insects. For this reason and because of the residual contamination, entomologists are exploring more efficient biological control methods.

Chemical insecticides are also known to bring about rather rapid changes in the genetic makeup of an insect population. In a fly population of 1,000, suppose there is a genetically controlled range of resistance to the effects of a certain insecticide. If that population is sprayed with the insecticide, perhaps fifty of the flies will be so resistant that they will not be killed by it. Within two or three weeks they will be the parents of a new generation of flies with an inherited resistance greater than that of the original population was, and within the span of several generations, the insecticide is no longer effective at any practical dosage.

Insects are biologically controlled by parasites, pathogens, and predators, whose selection depends on the particular kind of insect pest. If they infect or feed on only one kind of insect then beneficial insects remain unharmed. Ladybird beetles control scale insects in orchards, and lacewing larvae and adults keep aphids in check. The breeding of insect-resistant varieties of plants has reduced the amount of chemicals needed for pest control. The manipulation of a pest population can induce sterility, alter an insect's ability to survive certain environmental conditions, or reduce its immunity to certain parasites. Much of this type of control is still in the experimental stage.

COLLECTING INSECTS

Some insects can be collected during any season of the year and at any time of the day. When the weather is too severe for collecting, there is always a large backlog of specimens to mount, identify, and arrange in boxes.

The collector uses a number of special techniques to gather representatives of each species of any particular region. The best time to collect most species is during the warm weather when more insects are active, but your collection will have gaps in it if you add to it only during these seasons. Insects are usually either day flying or night flying, rarely both. Certain species fly only at certain times of the day or night. The serious collector must be aware of and take into consideration the various aspects of the species' habits as well as its habitats.

WHERE INSECTS ARE FOUND

A species' habitat is usually rather limited. Meadows, swampy areas, fence rows, along railroad tracks, at the margins of woodlands, mixed forest stands, deserts, grasslands, coniferous forests, and so on have their particular insect faunas. Fields of cultivated crops will yield a variety of pests, predators, and incidentals, depending upon the effectiveness and time of application of control measures. If you are looking for a particular pest species, you must keep track of this, and usually you can find a small pocket of infestation that has survived.

Certain generalizations about insect distribution will help you to locate good collection areas. Some species are very widely distributed; a few are even cosmopolitan, but this is exceptional. Most insect species have very restricted distribution. Most of the so-called common species are common only in certain areas. Even crop pest species are often confined to a part of a field. Obviously, knowledge of an insect's habits and its preferred habitat is very helpful for finding a particular species. Unfortunately, entomologists are aware of the habitats of only a very small percentage of the species. It is very important, therefore, that collectors record details about where an insect is discovered, in order to add to our knowledge of entomology.

Many insects are closely associated with plants, either directly as plant feeders or indirectly as predators or parasites of plant pests. Their distribution is determined by the distribution of the plants, and therefore tied into weather conditions. Therefore, we can see distribution patterns emerge that parallel the distribution of plant types.

The major plant communities or *biomes* are shown on the following map.

The area of the far north and above the treeline is the *tundra*, a region typified by a variety of short quick-growing plants and insects with short life cycles.

Farther south are vast stands of closely growing coniferous trees, the *coniferous forests* or *taiga*, rarely with open areas of grass or shrubbery. The insect fauna of this region and the tundra are limited in number of species, but the populations of the few species represented, as with the plant species, are usually very abundant. Great swarms of mosquitoes and black flies are present during the brief spring and summer. Both regions extend into the mountains of the United States and typical arctic insects may be found there.

Much of eastern United States is mixed *deciduous forest,* an area that harbors a great variety of insect species. The insects of this biome are the best known because they have been intensively studied. The great variety of plant life makes possible an equally varied insect fauna, and almost all known families of insects are represented there.

45

Map showing the vegetation regions, the major biomes, of North America.

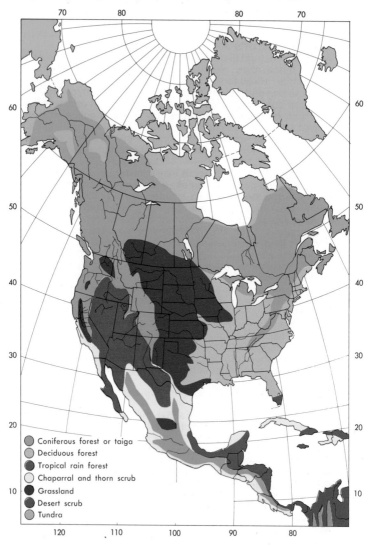

Coniferous forest or taiga
Deciduous forest
Tropical rain forest
Chaparral and thorn scrub
Grassland
Desert scrub
Tundra

The central portion of North America is *grassland* covered with natural stands of many species of grasses except where grain crops are now grown, a natural substitute for the native grasses. Grasshoppers, true bugs, and many kinds of moths are abundant there. Trees do not grow naturally in these grasslands or in the few remaining areas of *prairie* because of unsuitable soil conditions. The western portion does not receive enough rainfall to support cultivated grains, but it is used as grazing land instead. Although the insect species are limited, those represented are abundant.

As you travel west through the central plains, rainfall decreases until very sparse grassland turns into *desert*. Oddly enough, the variety of insect life does not dwindle; if anything, the number of species is greater in the desert. Desert habitats support a specialized and interesting insect fauna that disappears during the long dry periods, but emerges in a great variety of colorful and strange species as soon as the brief rainy period begins.

Still farther west, in coastal southern California and northern Baja California, Mexico, are the *chaparral* and *thorn scrub* regions. This specialized, dry area supports a peculiar flora characterized by short, spiny, shrubby plants, grasses, and a variety of oaks, and many insect species live only in this region.

Finally, the lowland *tropical rain forests* of the United States in southern Florida, and in parts of Mexico and the West Indies, are characterized by high rainfall, a very great number of large-leaved plants, and tall trees. These regions boast by far the greatest number of insect species with their bright colors and weird shapes.

WHAT IS NEEDED FOR COLLECTING

Equipment for capturing, killing, and storing specimens are basic items for any collecting trip, and may be conveniently carried in a small canvas bag similar to the Army musette bag sold in surplus stores. Some collectors prefer to pack their equipment in a hunter's jacket or vest. Two important factors must be considered: safety and convenience. Safely store poisons you will use to kill insects, and beware of glass breakage. Arrange your gear as conveniently as possible; the more efficiently you use it, the fewer the insects that will escape. You may find nets bulky and hard to manage, especially on public transportation, but some neatly folding nets are commercially available.

Killing jars are glass jars of convenient size containing one of several poisons. They are easy to make at home or they may be purchased from one of the biological supply houses. The difficulty is in obtaining a suitable killing agent. The three most commonly used are *potassium cyanide, ethyl acetate,* and *carbon tetrachloride,* listed here in descending order of preference. If you are connected with a university or similar institution, you will probably be able to obtain all three. Ethyl acetate may be purchased from a biological supply company and car-

Cyanide killing jar.

Ethyl acetate or carbona killing jar.

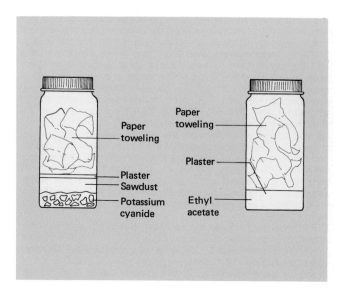

Paper toweling

Paper toweling

Plaster

Paper toweling

Plaster
Sawdust

Potassium cyanide

Ethyl acetate

bon tetrachloride (Carbona) can usually be bought in drug-stores.

Select jars of various sizes, with at least one very large jar marked specifically for Lepidoptera, which tend to lose some of their wing scales. This usually does not seriously damage the specimen, but if very small insects are placed in the same jar, they will pick up Lepidoptera scales, thereby obscuring identifying or diagnostic features. A general rule to follow is: a large jar for large insects, medium jar for medium insects, and a selection of smaller jars for small insects. Isolate scaly insects to prevent loose scales from spreading onto scaleless insects; do not put insects with dense pile (for example, bumble bees) into liquid preservatives. Ethyl or isopropyl alcohol can be used both to kill and store many insects. Label all jars *poison*. Wrapping tape around the bottom and near the top of the jar will prevent the glass from shattering if dropped. Leave an open space so you can look in and see what is happening. Be sure that the lid can be tightly closed. This requires a metal top (plastic tops tend to work loose) and threaded, rather than crimped, rims. A killing jar with a loose top is a danger to you and those around you.

Prepare the jar in a well-ventilated room. If you are using potassium cyanide, place about an inch in the bottom of the jar. Press it down tightly with the end of a piece of dowling, then add and tap down a layer of sawdust to absorb excess moisture and to control the rate of gas generation. Place ½- to ¾-inch layer of wet plaster of Paris on top of the sawdust to hold sawdust and cyanide in place. Mix the plaster with enough

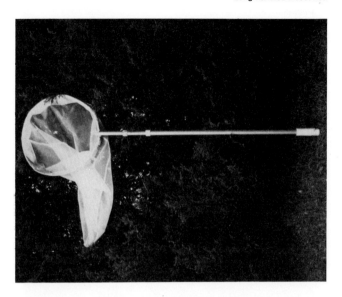

water so it will just pour off the end of a spoon. If it is too wet, the cyanide will expend itself too soon; if too dry, the surface will be rough and unsatisfactory. Tap the jar lightly on the table to eliminate any bubbles in the plaster and to smooth the top. Leave the cover off for several hours to let the plaster dry, away from direct sunlight. Cover the jar as soon as the moisture from the plaster reaches the cyanide, and deadly cyanide gas begins to generate from the potassium cyanide and water mixture. AVOID BREATHING: IT IS DEADLY!

If you use ethyl acetate, follow the same directions but in place of the cyanide, add more sawdust. If you wish, you may place a cork in the center, over the sawdust. Add the plaster around the cork. When the plaster is dry, remove the cork and pour in some ethyl acetate. Replace the cork tightly so sawdust cannot work out or small insects work in.

Carbon tetrachloride jars are made in the same way as the ethyl acetate jar. REMEMBER: Both of these substances are POISONOUS. AVOID BREATHING THEM. Check and recharge this type of jar before each collecting trip.

You can buy professionally constructed nets. However, you can make a good net of fine mesh for capturing flying insects. Sew a double thickness of muslin around the edge of the netting to protect it and to form a channel through which the ring, made of heavy steel wire, is threaded. The ring is attached to the handle in such a way that it can be removed and opened to replace the netting as it wears out. The net pole should be of hard wood or aluminum. A heavier net of similar construction, with a bag of light canvas or heavy muslin, is useful for beating

49

Details for the home construction of an insect net.

A beating sheet.

An aspirator.

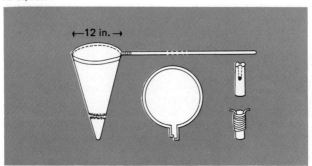

←12 in.→

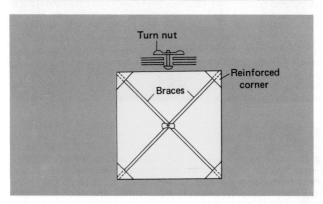

Turn nut

Braces

Reinforced corner

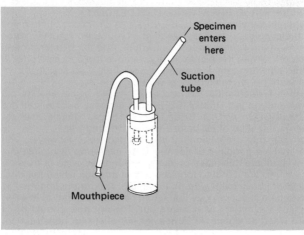

Specimen enters here

Suction tube

Mouthpiece

and sweeping vegetation, such as brambles, where the air net's netting would be quickly torn and useless.

A white beating umbrella with a small pole (or a net handle) is also useful for beating vegetation. A square of heavy cloth can be attached to two crossed poles to form the "umbrella" if a white umbrella is unavailable. Beat vegetation with the pole to loosen insects that cling to branches of woody plants. They will drop into the umbrella below, and you can pick them out and place them into your killing jar or alcohol vial.

Specimens are sometimes too small or fragile to be handled. An *aspirator* is a device you can use to suck small insects into a vial without any danger of swallowing them, and is useful for collecting active insects from the beating net or any other surface. Another method of picking up tiny specimens is to wet a finger and touch it to the insect, or use a small watercolor brush in the same way.

Light traps, which are commercially obtainable, are used to collect night-flying insects, especially moths and beetles. Set in place, a trap will attract the insect, which hits the upright baffle in the trap and drops into a jar or pail of alcohol where it quickly dies. One drawback to this method of collecting is that the moths enter the trap in large numbers, and their loose scales will contaminate the alcohol and cling to the nonscaly specimens. If this is a problem, instead of using a light trap,

simply hang a blacklight trap near a white wall or a bed sheet tied between tree branches. This will attract the same insects and you may select whatever you want from the attracted assembly of species.

A *Malaise trap* is primarily an automatic daytime collecting device, made of green or brown netting with netting baffles that lead trapped day-flying insects into a killing jar at the top. Insects tend to fly upward when they hit a barrier and thus will fly directly into a jar of alcohol. Place this trap, which will cost less from a commercial supplier than homemade, across woodland flyways. A little experimentation will soon tell you the best place to erect it.

You can make a pitfall trap by digging a small hole in the ground and putting in it a coffee can fitted with a funnel at the open end. Cover it with a rain baffle and pour alcohol or antifreeze into the can. Many insects walk into this kind of trap as they search for food on the ground. You can also put bait——dead animals, dung, or artificial bait——in the bottom of the can, and place a fine screen over the bait so that the insect cannot get to it. Of course this kind of trap must be examined frequently and specimens removed before they leave or kill each other in their scramble to get to the food.

A *Berlese funnel,* which may be homemade from sheets of alu-

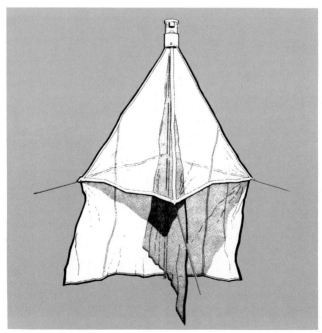

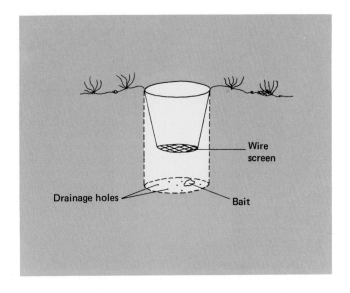

Wire screen

Drainage holes

Bait

minum, is another type of *insect separator*. This consists of a metal funnel placed over a jar of alcohol. Put debris, gathered at the base of forest trees, stream banks, and from decaying vegetation, in the funnel after placing a coarse screen baffle inside near the top of the funnel, to prevent the debris from dropping into the alcohol. A light bulb suspended over the top of the funnel is the heat source that forces small insects, mites, and other invertebrates hiding in this material to crawl away from the heat. Eventually they drop through the screen and into the alcohol. The Berlese funnel may be used year round and many uncommon specimens are obtained in this way.

Small jars or vials of 80% ethyl or isopropyl alcohol can serve both as killing jars and storage vials. Fragile specimens should be stored in alcohol rather than mounted. Because of their flexibility, "wet" specimens are often easier to identify than dry and brittle ones mounted on pins or points. When there are large numbers of specimens in a vial, the alcohol must be changed after a few days; fresh specimens contain a lot of water which will dilute the alcohol enough to prevent its effectiveness as a preserving agent. Vials stored for long periods of time must be checked to be sure the alcohol hasn't evaporated because of a loose top. One precaution to follow is to add a very small amount of glycerine to the alcohol. If all the alcohol should evaporate, the glycerine, which does not evaporate, will keep the specimens pliable until more alcohol is added. Aquatic collecting can be challenging as well as fun. Aquatic nets with flat edges are used to collect naiads of mayflies, stoneflies, dragonflies, and damselflies, and nymphs, larvae,

A Berlese funnel.

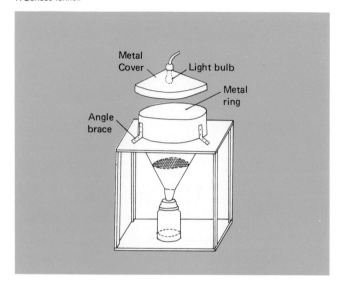

and adults of other aquatic insects from streams, ponds, and swamps. Some aquatic scoop nets have mesh covers that keep out aquatic plants but allow insects to filter through. An open net will collect aquatic vegetation and debris as well, making it necessary to sort the material for insects by emptying the collection into a flat white enamel pan. Using your fingers and forceps (a few aquatic bugs bite), you can drop specimens into vials of alcohol or into aquaria for rearing. Aquatic nets may be obtained from various supply houses.

Ectoparasites may be collected from live animals, or from freshly killed birds or mammals, in which case special techniques must be used to kill the ectoparasites. Put the dead animal and a chloroform-saturated cotton ball into a plastic bag and seal. Then shake the parasites out of the bag or from the animal itself onto a black cloth. Do this almost as soon as the animal is killed before the parasites have removed themselves from the animal, or you probably won't be able to find them. You may have to comb off specimens killed while still clinging to the host, and forceps may be necessary to remove some. A camel's hair brush moistened in alcohol is helpful to pick up small specimens. Store the ectoparasites in 80% alcohol until you are ready to mount them on slides. Be sure you put the proper collecting data plus the name of the host animal into the vial with the specimen. *Note:* It is best to wear gloves when handling dead animals since the animal may have diseases that can be transmitted to humans.

Once you have collected and killed your specimens they must be mounted, stored, and arranged in your collection. Speci-

An aquatic scoop net.

Pillbox storage of insects.

A relaxing box.

mens collected dry in killing jars must either be mounted the same day or dried stored on layers of cotton in small boxes with tightly fitting covers. Dried specimens remain in perfect condition indefinitely if protected from dermestid beetles that will eat them or from mold that will grow on them if any mois-

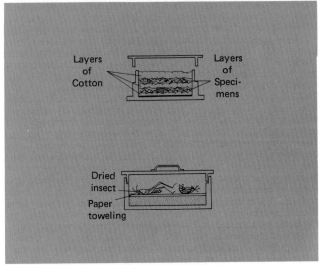

Layers of Cotton

Layers of Specimens

Dried insect

Paper toweling

How to mount small insects.

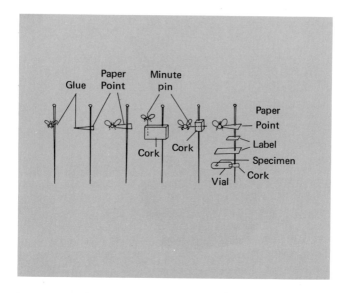

ture remains. Dried specimens, which are very fragile, may be prepared for mounting by placing them in a relaxing chamber. This permits water to be reintroduced into the specimens and they again become flexible and will not break. The chamber may be made from a wide-mouthed gallon jar with an airtight cover, or better, a metal box with a tightly fitting cover. Place some wet sand or wet paper in the bottom of the jar and add a little carbolic acid to prevent mold and mildew from growing. Put your specimens in a small open box or in uncovered Petri dishes in the chamber, keeping them from actual contact with the water in the sand or paper. Allow them to remain there for a day to two, depending on the size of the insects, until they are flexible. They may now be pinned without breaking.

Pinning insects is the most common way of preserving dead specimens. They will dry and remain in perfect condition on the pins without any further treatment, retaining the shape and color indefinitely. Of course it is only the exoskeleton that remains, the inner soft tissue dry and decayed, and in this dried condition, they are very fragile and must be handled with care. Use only standard length insect pins which can be purchased from an entomological supply company. They are available in a range of sizes from very fine to stout (sizes 000–8), but most collectors find that numbers 2–4 are best. Smaller specimens should be mounted on points. Pin the insects vertically through the body with the aid of a pinning block to position both the insects and the labels. For uniformity, most insects are pinned through the thorax slightly to the right of the midline. This also prevents the insect pin from obscuring identification features.

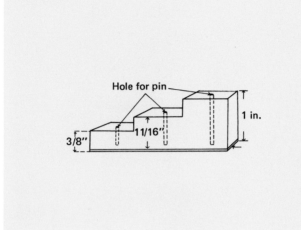

You should position the legs and antennae so they do not droop. If necessary you can support the abdomen with pins crossed beneath it to form a platform to prevent the abdomen from sagging while drying. Be sure to put a temporary label on each specimen so you know where and when you collected it. Permanent labels, which are discussed later, can be added when the specimens are dry.

Spread the wings of Lepidoptera and other large-winged insects such as caddisflies (unless kept in alcohol), dragonflies and damselflies (unless kept in cellophane envelopes), and the wings on the left side of grasshoppers (those of the right side are kept folded back to take less space in the insect box). This requires a bit more time and patience than routine pinning. Insert an insect pin through the body of the insect to be spread, and then push the pin through the cork in the groove in the specially made spreading board so that its body rests in the center groove. Using an insect pin, move the wings into place on each side of the board and hold them there by pushing another pin, placed near the base of each wing just behind the large first vein, into the wood. The front wings are lined up first, and the hind wings are brought into place slightly under the hind portion of the front wings to form at this junction a straight line at right angles to the insect's body. After the wings are in position, pin paper or cellophane over them, taking care not to put the pins through the wings. Fold the paper lengthwise to form a narrow double strip, and place the fold near the base of the wing (thus preventing the raw cut edge of the paper from cutting into the wing or forming a pressed line on the wing).

Various kinds of insects are pinned as indicated by the pinhole shown as a black dot on the top surface of the insects.

Detailed plan of a spreading board showing construction and how to set butterflies and moths.

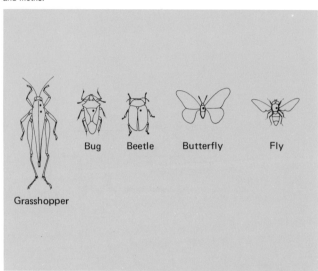

Bug   Beetle   Butterfly   Fly

Grasshopper

Remove the initial base pins. When the specimens have dried on the boards for several days, remove the pins and papers, add a permanent label to the specimens, and place in insect boxes or trays. In humid areas it will be necessary to place the spreading boards in a cabinet heated by an electric light bulb

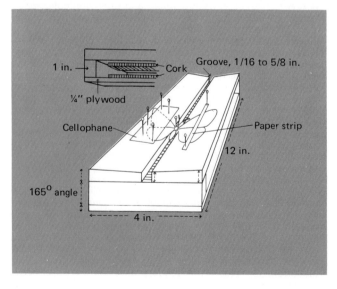

1 in.   Cork   Groove, 1/16 to 5/8 in.

¼″ plywood

Cellophane   Paper strip

12 in.

165° angle

4 in.

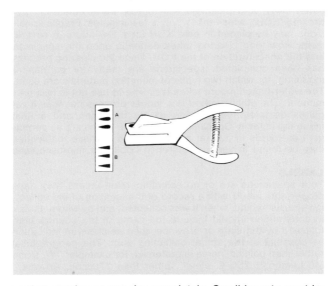

so that specimens can dry completely. Small insects must be mounted on paper points if they are too small for an insect pin. A point punch may be purchased from a supply company for this purpose, or you can cut points out of file cards or heavy drawing paper. Place a point on a step block so that the base is over the top hole of the block. Push a number 3 insect pin through the base of the point and insert the pin into the top hole of the step block as far as it will go. This will adjust the height of each point uniformly on the pin. Bend down the very tip of the point to form a small surface on which to glue the specimen. Apply a drop of adhesive by touching the point to the glue, and then to the thorax of the insect you are mounting. Attach the insect on the right side so that all specimens face the same direction. A water-soluble milk-base glue is usually used. It should be thick enough so that it dries rapidly or the specimen can fall off or change its position. Pins may be placed in a propped-up insect box so that specimens hang in position while the glue dries. Use as little glue as possible— too much glue may cover parts that need to be examined for identification purposes.

Mounting ectoparasites from mammals and birds requires special skills. These specimens are first preserved in alcohol, but then must be mounted on microscope slides so they can be examined under high-magnification lenses. Certain other small insects, such as thrips, midges, gnats, fruit flies, mosquitoes, mites, and ticks, and the larvae of many small insects, may also be mounted this way. Before some heavily pigmented, hard-bodied specimens can be mounted on a permanent slide, they must be cleared, i.e., the specimen softened, its muscle eaten away, and bleached with hot or warm potassium hydroxide (KOH), which takes only a few minutes. Fragile specimens may be placed in cold KOH for a few hours to several days. How long clearing takes depends upon the specimen and the concentration of the KOH. Once the clearing process has been completed, specimens are ready for permanent mounting, for which two types of mounting materials are used. The water-based mount takes less time to use but is less permanent. The other method is a longer process because it requires complete dehydration of the specimen and a final mounting in resin. Specimens mounted in resins are as permanent as fossils in natural amber. Details of these techniques may be found in various reference books for microscopists.

LABELS

Your specimens are of no scientific value unless they have proper data labels with a record of the location of the collecting site, its habitat, when it was collected, and by whom. Locality information should include the name of the country first, followed by the state or province, then as close an indication as possible of the actual collecting spot. The geographical rather than political name is preferred, for example, "W. slope Mt. Lemon, 6,250 ft. elev." rather than "Tucson, Arizona." The county and nearest post office names may be given, but indicate direction and distance, e.g., "15 mi. N.E. Tucson." Dates should be specific. Use Roman numbers or abbreviations for the month: "X-5-1979" or "5 Oct. 1979" instead of "10-5-79" which can be confused for "5-10-79." Note that the century is included in the year date. No end of ecological data can be added to the label. Sometimes a separate habitat data label is used. Examples of brief statements for the label are: at light; in leaf litter; under bark; in fresh water. The collector's name is included as a reference for possible further information, field notes, or other records. All available information can be useful to specialists, especially if the species happens to be rare or previously unknown.

Labels may be obtained from a commercial printer, or hand printed with India ink. The printing should be as small as possible and, of course, legible.

Labels are placed at a uniform position on the pin beneath the insect. They should run lengthwise to the specimen with the top line to the right. Adjust their height on the pin by using a pinning or step block, a tool consisting of three pieces of wood nailed or glued together to form a step, each piece 8 mm. (0.3 in.) thick and 25 mm. (1 in.) wide. The thickness of the wood is exactly one quarter the length of a standard insect pin. The top piece of wood is 25 mm. (1 in.) long, the middle piece 50 mm. (2 in.) long, and the bottom piece 75 mm. (3 in.) long. Drill a vertical hole slightly larger than an insect pin through the center of each step. To use, place the insect at the height of the top step. Then place the locality label over the hole at the middle step, and push the pin through. Repeat for the remaining label at the lower step.

Locality data labels. These are easily cut out after inking in with India ink the dates of collecting.

U.S.A., Florida	Ross H. Arnett, Jr.	Ross H. Arnett, Jr.	Ross H. Arnett, Jr.
Leon County	Collector	Collector	Collector
Tall Timbers	June , 19	July , 19	August , 19
Research Station			

U.S.A., Florida	Ross H. Arnett, Jr.	Ross H. Arnett, Jr.	Ross H. Arnett, Jr.
Leon County	Collector	Collector	Collector
Tall Timbers	June , 19	July , 19	August , 19
Research Station			

U.S.A., Florida	Ross H. Arnett, Jr.	Ross H. Arnett, Jr.	Ross H. Arnett, Jr.
Leon County	Collector	Collector	Collector
Tall Timbers	June , 19	July , 19	August , 19
Research Station			

U.S.A., Florida	Ross H. Arnett, Jr.	Ross H. Arnett, Jr.	Ross H. Arnett, Jr.
Leon County	Collector	Collector	Collector
Tall Timbers	June , 19	July , 19	August , 19
Research Station			

U.S.A., Florida	Ross H. Arnett, Jr.	Ross H. Arnett, Jr.	Ross H. Arnett, Jr.
Leon County	Collector	Collector	Collector
Tall Timbers	June , 19	July , 19	August , 19
Research Station			

U.S.A., Florida	Ross H. Arnett, Jr.	Ross H. Arnett, Jr.	Ross H. Arnett, Jr.
Leon County	Collector	Collector	Collector
Tall Timbers	June , 19	July , 19	August , 19
Research Station			

U.S.A., Florida	Ross H. Arnett, Jr.	Ross H. Arnett, Jr.	Ross H. Arnett, Jr.
Leon County	Collector	Collector	Collector
Tall Timbers	June , 19	July , 19	August , 19
Research Station			

U.S.A., Florida	Ross H. Arnett, Jr.	Ross H. Arnett, Jr.	Ross H. Arnett, Jr.
Leon County	Collector	Collector	Collector
Tall Timbers	June , 19	July , 19	August , 19
Research Station			

U.S.A., Florida	Ross H. Arnett, Jr.	Ross H. Arnett, Jr.	Ross H. Arnett, Jr.
Leon County	Collector	Collector	Collector
Tall Timbers	June , 19	July , 19	August , 19
Research Station			

Ecology data labels.

Collected	Collected in	Collected	Collected	Collected
by beating	decaying veg.	on carrion	in dung	on:
Collected	Collected in	Collected	Collected	Collected
by beating	decaying veg.	on carrion	in dung	on:
Collected	Collected in	Collected	Collected	Collected
by beating	decaying veg.	on carrion	in dung	on:
Collected	Collected in	Collected	Collected	Collected
by beating	decaying veg.	on carrion	in dung	on:
Collected	Collected in	Collected	Collected	Collected
by beating	decaying veg.	on carrion	in dung	on:
Collected	Collected in	Collected	Collected	Collected
by beating	decaying veg.	on carrion	in dung	on:
Collected	Collected in	Collected	Collected	Collected
by beating	decaying veg.	on carrion	in dung	on:
Collected	Collected in	Collected	Collected	Collected
by beating	decaying veg.	on carrion	in dung	or.
Collected	Collected in	Collected	Collected	Collected
by beating	decaying veg.	on carrion	in dung	on:
Collected	Collected in	Collected	Collected	Collected
by beating	decaying veg.	on carrion	in dung	on:
Collected	Collected in	Collected	Collected	Collected
by beating	decaying veg.	on carrion	in dung	on:
Collected	Collected in	Collected	Collected	Collected
by beating	decaying veg.	on carrion	in dung	on:
Collected	Collected in	Collected	Collected	Collected
by beating	decaying veg.	on carrion	in dung	on:
Collected	Collected in	Collected	Collected	Collected
by beating	decaying veg.	on carrion	in dung	on:
Collected	Collected in	Collected	Collected	Collected
by beating	decaying veg.	on carrion	in dung	on:
Collected	Collected in	Collected	Collected	Collected
by beating	decaying veg.	on carrion	in dung	on:

Determination (identification) labels indicating the specific name of the species are the last to be added. Each specimen should be labeled. Put the label for the first specimen of a series to the left side of the pin so that it can be read without removing the specimen from the insect box or tray.

STORAGE OF THE COLLECTION

Once the specimens have been mounted, labeled, and identified, they should be arranged for study and display. Beginners

A sturdy wooden insect box.

often use cigar boxes or cardboard boxes for this purpose. Line the bottom of the box with a double layer of corrugated cardboard or preferably 8 mm. (5/16 in.) thick sheets of polyethylene foam. A variety of insect boxes and drawers are also available commercially. Although relatively expensive compared to cigar boxes or cardboard boxes, they have tightly fitting covers that help protect the collection. Serious collectors often use glass-topped drawers containing variously sized trays, each of which contains representatives of a single species. The size of the tray depends upon how many specimens of a particular species you are storing. Another advantage of the trays is that you can move them to make room for additional species without having to repin all of the specimens.

Specimens are arranged in the boxes phylogenetically (according to their evolutionary sequence), in the same manner in which the orders are listed in this book. Families, genera, and species are arranged within the orders either in phylogenetic sequence or alphabetically. Catalogs of the species of various orders are often available. Collections are arranged according to these listings much the same as stamps are arranged in stamp albums according to country, date of issue, and variations.

It is very important that specimens be protected by fumigation from the several species of insects that invade collections and eat the dried specimens. Paradichlorobenzene crystals, a killing agent sold in drugstores, are generally used. Put a small

A Cornell-type drawer for insect collections.

Trays used for pinning insects and storing in Cornell drawers.

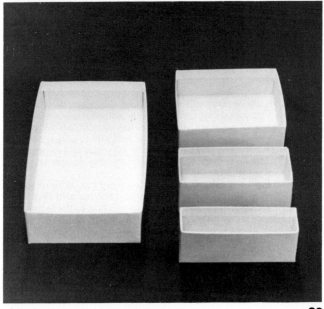

container of the crystals in a small tray or a cheesecloth bag in one corner of the box. They will remain effective for about a year in a tight box. Naphthalene crystals (moth crystals or mothballs) are a good repellent, but they do not kill the pests (or clothes moths). They are carcinogenic, so do not inhale them. Collections should be examined frequently for signs of infestation. If live pests are present, carbon tetrachloride may be used to kill them. Place the infected box in a large airtight container with a small dish of the fumigant and leave for several hours. Re-inspect several weeks after the box has been returned to the collection to make sure that eggs which might have been present haven't hatched out and started a new generation of pests.

HOW TO IDENTIFY AN INSECT TO SPECIES

First, read the section "What is an insect?" p. 15, to be certain the specimen you have is an insect. Most noninsect invertebrates have more than six legs, or lack legs entirely. A few are illustrated in the third part of the following identification table. It will also be helpful if you have read the section of the introduction that defines insects and explains the parts that are used in these tables as identification characteristics.

Once you have determined that your specimen is an insect, you must assign it to its proper order. Compare the specimen with the figures illustrating each of the orders listed in the tables. Each order has been assigned a number. After you have selected one of the orders as the most likely one to which your specimen is assigned, turn to the description of that order, which follows the table and bears the same number as that in the table. This will give you further information about the order and will also tell you what entry numbers describe and illustrate the species of this order.

You will find, as you use the table of orders, that you will soon learn the major characteristics of each order. Note the three major sections: The first separates the most common insects; the second, those less often seen; and the third, organisms commonly confused with insects but actually belonging to other classes of animals. Compare the illustration of each order with your specimen. Remember that this is only a single example, or at most a few examples, of very diversified groups and only rarely will they exactly resemble the specimen you have.

Finally, after you have accurately determined the order of your specimen, you will be able to turn to the entries and find the species or a closely related species. In addition to the account of the anatomical features of the species, you will find many other details about the life of the insect and about related insects.

TABLE OF INSECT ORDERS

Table I: Common Insect Orders

Main Features	Further Details	Order
1. WITHOUT WINGS AT ALL STAGES		
A. FREE-LIVING, not attached to another animal for feeding		
	a. ABDOMEN with three tails; body size moderate, 3–30 mm. (0.1–1.2 in.); antennae long; abdomen without jumping mechanism	3. THYSANURA, thysanurans
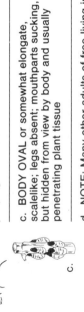	b. ABDOMEN without tails; body size usually less than 5 mm. (0.2 in.); antennae moderate to long; abdomen often with a jumping mechanism	1. COLLEMBOLA, springtails and relatives
	c. BODY OVAL or somewhat elongate, scalelike; legs absent; mouthparts sucking, but hidden from view by body and usually penetrating plant tissue	21. HOMOPTERA, scale insects
	d. NOTE: Many other adults of free-living insects lack wings, but these all resemble the winged adults of the same order and generally are not confused with these forms. For example, ants usually are wingless, although there are winged stages, but they would never be confused with any of the above. Therefore, if the specimen does not agree with the above, continue reading this table.	

Table I: Common Insect Orders (Cont.)

Main Features   Further Details   Order

1. WITHOUT WINGS AT ALL STAGES (Cont.)

B. ECTOPARASITES, attached to another animal for feeding, or in nests; not free-living

a.

b.

c.

d.

a. BODY FLATTENED: long, visible antennae; body color dark red or brown — 20. HEMIPTERA, bed bugs

b. BODY FLATTENED; whitish; sucking mouthparts; live on mammals and man; antennae very short — 18. ANOPLURA, lice

c. BODY FLATTENED; whitish; chewing mouthparts; antennae very short; found on mammals and birds and in their nests — 17. MALLOPHAGA, chewing lice

d. BODY COMPRESSED: brownish or red; with jumping hind legs; on mammals and birds, in their nests, rarely on man — 29. SIPHONAPTERA, fleas

2. WITHOUT WINGS AT CERTAIN STAGES

a. NYMPHS, NAIADS, LARVAE, PUPAE, and, of course, EGGS do not have wings, but are the immature stages of winged adults of the orders that follow; some resemble the adults; others (caterpillars, grubs, maggots, and pupae) are very different from the adult stage

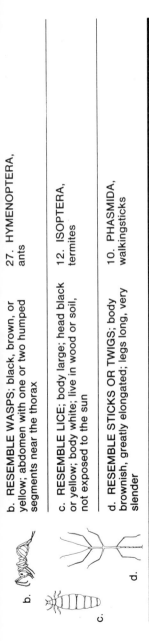

b. RESEMBLE WASPS; black, brown, or yellow; abdomen with one or two humped segments near the thorax — 27. HYMENOPTERA, ants

c. RESEMBLE LICE; body large; head black or yellow; body white; live in wood or soil, not exposed to the sun — 12. ISOPTERA, termites

d. RESEMBLE STICKS OR TWIGS; body brownish, greatly elongated; legs long, very slender — 10. PHASMIDA, walkingsticks

3. ALWAYS WITH WINGS AS ADULTS

A. WITH ONE PAIR OF WINGS ONLY

a. HIND PAIR OF WINGS reduced to small clublike organs — 28. DIPTERA, flies

B. FRONT WINGS UNIFORMLY THICKER THAN HIND WINGS; chewing mouthparts

a. HIND WINGS FOLD BENEATH SHORT FRONT WINGS to form covers; abdomen with terminal forcepslike pinchers — 13. DERMAPTERA, earwigs

b. HIND WINGS FOLD BENEATH FRONT WING COVERS that usually extend to the end of the abdomen which lacks terminal forcepslike pinchers — 23. COLEOPTERA, beetles and weevils

Table I: Common Insect Orders (Cont.)

Main Features   **Further Details**   **Order**

3. ALWAYS WITH WINGS AS ADULTS (Cont.)

Main Features	Further Details	Order
 c.	c. HIND WINGS FOLD LENGTHWISE under leathery front wings; hind legs enlarged, used for jumping	9. ORTHOPTERA, grasshoppers, crickets, and katydids.
d.	d. HIND WINGS FOLD LENGTHWISE under leathery front wings; hind legs slender, not used for jumping; front legs enlarged, used to grasp prey	11. DICTYOPTERA, praying mantids
e.	e. HIND WINGS FOLD LENGTHWISE under leathery front wings; both front and hind legs slender; body broad, flattened	11. DICTYOPTERA, cockroaches
f.	f. HIND WINGS FOLD LENGTHWISE under leathery front wings; both front and hind legs slender; body greatly elongate, cylindrical.	10. PHASMIDA, walkingsticks
g.	g. HIND WINGS NOT FOLDED; both pairs of wings held tentlike over abdomen; long sucking mouthparts projecting backward between front legs	21. HOMOPTERA, cicadas, leafhoppers, aphids, and allies

C. FRONT WINGS WITH BASAL PORTION THICK, APICAL PORTION THIN, membranous, transparent

a. MOUTHPARTS SUCKING; body broad, or narrow and elongate; wings cross apically when held in repose; usually with a large triangular portion between base of front wings

20. HEMIPTERA, bugs

D. BOTH PAIRS OF WINGS MEMBRANOUS, USUALLY TRANSPARENT UNLESS PIGMENTED, with many cross veins

a. ABDOMEN WITH TWO OR THREE LONG apical tails

5. EPHEMEROPTERA, mayflies

b. ABDOMEN WITH VERY SHORT TAILS or tails absent; body broad, more or less flattened; legs widely separate at base; body brown to black

7. PLECOPTERA, stoneflies

c. ABDOMEN ALWAYS WITHOUT TAILS, but may have exposed genital structures; antennae moderate or long; wings held roof-like over and close to abdomen

22. NEUROPTERA, neuropterans

d. ABDOMEN WITHOUT TAILS, but with exposed small pincherlike genital structures; body and sometimes wings brightly colored; antennae very short; wings held out at sides or closed well above abdomen

6. ODONATA, damselflies and dragonflies

Table I: Common Insect Orders (Cont.)

Main Features	Further Details	Order

3. ALWAYS WITH WINGS AS ADULTS (Cont.)

Main Features	Further Details	Order
e.	e. ABDOMEN WITHOUT APICAL APPENDAGES, except some with small peglike subapical projections; body broadly cylindrical; wings held tentlike over abdomen; long sucking mouthparts projecting backward between front legs	21. HOMOPTERA, cicadas, leafhoppers, aphids, and allies

E. WINGS COVERED WITH FINE HAIRS

Main Features	Further Details	Order
a.	a. RESEMBLE MOTHS; wing held tentlike over abdomen; antennae very long and slender; usually near bodies of water	25. TRICHOPTERA, caddisflies

F. WINGS COVERED WITH SCALES, rarely with transparent areas

Main Features	Further Details	Order
a.	a. Wings held close together above body, or more or less tentlike over abdomen; body covered with scales	26. LEPIDOPTERA, butterflies, skippers, and moths

G. WINGS WITHOUT SCALES OR NOTICEABLE HAIRS, with few cross veins

Main Features	Further Details	Order
a.	a. WINGS WITH LONG FRINGES OF HAIRLIKE SETAE on each side; very small insects	19. THYSANOPTERA, thrips

b.

WINGS WITHOUT FRINGES OF SETAE; often with stingers; abdomen usually narrowly attached to thorax

27. HYMENOPTERA, wasps, ants, and bees

Table II: Less Common Insect Orders

Main Features		Further Details	Order
1. WINGLESS			
A. WITH TWO TAILS OR A PAIR OF FORCEPS AT THE END ON THE ABDOMEN			
	b.	a. TAILS LONG OR FORCEPS PRESENT; legs short; antennae stout	4. DIPLURA, diplurans
		b. TAILS SHORT; legs long; head large; antennae long and slender	8. GRYLLOBLATTO-DEA, rockcrawlers
a.	c.	c. TAILS VERY SHORT, 1-segmented; body compact	15. ZORAPTERA, zorapterans
B. WITHOUT ABDOMINAL TAILS OR FORCEPS			
		a. RESEMBLE BED BUGS; body flattened; ectoparasites of sheep; some with or without a single pair of short wings, found on bats	28. DIPTERA, sheep keds and bat bugs
a.	b.	b. THREE PAIRS OF LEGS, BUT FIRST PAIR USED AS ANTENNAE; true antennae absent; very small	2. PROTURA, proturans

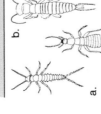

Table II: Less Common Insect Orders (Cont.)

Main Features	Further Details	Order
1. WINGLESS (Cont.)		
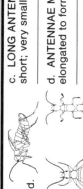 d.	c. LONG ANTENNAE PRESENT; head short; very small	16. PSOCOPTERA, barklice and booklice
	d. ANTENNAE MODERATELY LONG; head elongated to form a snout; larger insects	24. MECOPTERA, scorpionflies and allies
e.	e. FRONT TARSI ENLARGED; live in silk galleries	14. EMBIIDINA, webspinners
2. WITH TWO PAIRS OF WINGS		
a.	a. WINGS (PRESENT IN MALES ONLY) long, narrow, capable of flexing forward; front legs with enlarged first tarsal segment; live in silk galleries	14. EMBIIDINA, webspinners
b.	b. WINGS SHORTER, NOT FLEXIBLE; front tarsi not enlarged	15. ZORAPTERA, zorapterans
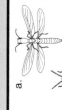 c.	c. WING VEINS NUMEROUS; head elongate forming a snout; abdomen of some males with enlarged scorpionlike apex	24. MECOPTERA, scorpionflies and allies

Table III: Not Insects, have more than six legs

Main Feature	Further Details	Class and Order
1. WITH FOUR PAIRS OF LEGS		
	a. WITH ABDOMINAL STINGER CURVED OVER BACK; front pair of legs with pinchers	Class ARACHNIDA, order SCORPIONES (not included)
	b. WITH LONG WHIPLIKE TAIL, without stinger; front pair of legs with small pinchers	Class ARACHNIDA, order UROPYGI, whip-scorpions (not included)
	c. ABDOMEN WITHOUT TAIL, but with silk spinning glands; front pair of legs without pinchers	Class ARACHNIDA, order ARANEAE, spiders (not included)
	d. NOTE: Small to minute organisms with four pairs of legs belong to other orders of the Arachnida, and larger forms such as daddy-longlegs and others are not included in this book.	
2. WITH MORE THAN FOUR PAIRS OF LEGS: Various Arthropods not included in this book		

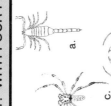

1. COLLEMBOLA, the Springtails and allies (See entry no. 1)
These wingless insects are small, rarely longer than 0.25-5.0 mm. The body is elongate, slender, or reduced to a short, compact, somewhat humpbacked shape. Most species are white or gray, but some are purple, yellow, or green.

The species are distinguished primarily by their abdominal *furcula,* or jumping apparatus, which is unique among insects. The insect can flex the furcula, held by a catch on the underside of the abdomen, thus catapulting itself several centimeters into the air. It is this feature that gives these insects their common name, but not all species have it. They do not undergo metamorphosis.

Collembola are very abundant in the soil and in leaf mold. They may be found in most aquatic habitats, including along the shore of the ocean where they are very common in marine vegetation. Sometimes they are found in large numbers on snow and are often called snow fleas.

Collembola are worldwide in distribution with approximately 6,000 species, of which about 660 species occur in North America, north of Mexico. They are extremely abundant but seldom seen except occasionally when they become pests in greenhouses and in mushroom caves.

2. PROTURA, the Proturans (See entry no. 2)
Proturans lack antennae. The front pair of legs are elevated and projected forward and apparently serve as sensory organs similar to antennae. Their small white or pale amber bodies (0.6–2.5 mm) are elongate, very similar to that of some springtails. The mouthparts are considered to be primitive, for sucking, with long, thin mandibles. All species are wingless, eyeless, and without cerci on the abdomen, but there is a median short tail termed the *telson.* The basal three abdominal segments have paired ventral appendages. Metamorphosis in these insects is very slight, and the early stages closely resemble the adults.

These insects are seldom seen by collectors because they live in moist soil around roots, in humus, moss, and under bark of rotting logs. Most of the species are not well known. At the present time all 325 species found throughout the world are assigned to only four families. About seventy-five species are now known to inhabit the United States and Canada.

3.THYSANURA, the Thysanurans (See entry no. 3)
These are also all wingless; some are rather large, their size ranging from 3–30 mm. The body is flattened or convex, rounded in front, tapered behind, and sometimes covered with scales. Most species are brown or earth colored, but some are white or gray. The antennae are nearly as long as the many-segmented body. Some species have compound eyes and ocelli. The abdomen has a median and two lateral many-segmented apical filaments; the several abdominal segments have short, ventral paired appendages of no apparent function.

Their metamorphosis is very slight, all nymphal stages resembling the adults.

Thysanurans are usually found in humid places among rocks, along shores, wet soil, in caves, in ant and termite nests, and in homes and buildings.

Four families occur in the United States and Canada. The Lepismatidae, or silverfish, are those most often seen. The firebrat (*Thermobia domestica*) is one of the common species in homes. A few additional species have been found in homes and buildings in the United States and Canada, but otherwise, the species, forty-seven in all in our area, are seldom seen. About 580 species have been recorded in the world.

4. DIPLURA, the Diplurans (See entry no. 4)

These insects resemble the larvae of other insects more than they do the adults. They range in size from 2–50 mm. Their bodies are elongate, slender, slightly flattened, pale tan, with the abdominal apex in some species darker. The antennae are longer than the head; eyes absent; mouthparts biting; wingless; legs are short and slender; the abdomen has a pair of apical segmented cerci, or unsegmented forceps, segments 2–7 with ventral paired appendages. As with the previous three orders, the metamorphosis is slight.

These insects are found in decaying vegetation, soil, under stones or logs, or in caves. Some species are predatory, others feed on plant material.

5. EPHEMEROPTERA, the Mayflies (See entry no. 5)

Mayflies are the most primitive of the winged insects. Their bodies are cylindrical and elongate; the thorax is enlarged to accommodate the wing muscles. They range in size from 1–30 mm. The body is rather soft, usually pale brown or tan but sometimes with reddish, olive-brown, or yellowish markings. The abdomen has two or three hairlike filaments extending from the apex. The forewings are large and triangular with many veins; the hindwings are small and rounded or, in a few species, absent. Most species have transparent wings, but some are marked with white or brown.

Immature mayflies, called naiads, are aquatic with gills along the sides of the abdomen and with two or three hairlike apical abdominal filaments.

Adult mayflies live a very short time, sometimes only a day. They fly near lakes, streams, and rivers, sometimes in very large swarms. Mating takes place during these flights. Their greatly reduced mouthparts prevent them from feeding. Eggs are laid within a few hours of mating and the adults die. Aquatic naiads develop in various freshwater habitats depending upon the species. It takes a year or more for them to develop to maturity. The naiads are sensitive to industrial pollutants because they feed on organic debris and small aquatic organisms. This concentrates chemicals in the food chain because at each feeding step pollutants are added, finally causing the extermination of many populations of these insects.

6. ODONATA, the Dragonflies and the Damselflies (See entry nos. 6–12)

The Odonata and the Ephemeroptera are the only two surviving representatives of the ancient flying insects. The fossil record shows some remains of giant dragonflies with wingspans of over a foot. Most species of this order have a wingspan ranging from 50–100 mm; some of the very small specimens have only about a 20 mm wingspan, while some of the tropical species measure at least 190 mm. Their bodies are brightly marked with brown, blue, green, red, yellow, and shades of these on a black background. The abdomen is elongate, cylindrical; the head spherical or broad, with very short setaelike antennae, shorter than the width of the head; eyes are very large, with three ocelli present; mouthparts are large and well developed for chewing. The thorax is very large in order to accommodate the powerful wing muscles. The wings are narrow, many times longer than broad, with the hind wings the same or very similar to the front wings. They may be transparent, or marked with white, yellow, brown, and black. The legs are long and slender, fitted with long spines and modified for capturing prey. The long abdomen is terminated by short cerci.

The immature stages are aquatic naiads that take from one to several years to mature. They are predaceous, feeding on small crustaceans and insects. The adults also are predaceous. The dragonflies, which represent a separate suborder, are strong fliers capable of capturing many kinds of flying insects. To do this they form a basket with their legs and scoop up their prey in flight. Damselflies, members of the second suborder, are weaker fliers and depend upon capturing less active prey. Both types of Odonata are common around most aquatic locations. A few dragonflies are known to fly great distances and have been seen flying across desert areas far from any permanent collection of water. Reports of them, alighting on ships far out at sea are not uncommon, although no species breed in salt water.

More than 4,950 species occur throughout the world, with about 450 species in the United States and Canada. There are no pest species. Because of their predatory habits, they are an important part of many aquatic ecosystems, both as naiads and as adults. Some attempts have been made to utilize them in the biological control of mosquitoes but with little success.

7. PLECOPTERA, the Stoneflies (See entry no. 13)

Stonefly adults are soft-bodied, elongate, flattened insects with long and threadlike antennae; mouthparts of the chewing type, but usually weak and nonfunctional. Their wings are nearly equal in length, many-veined, and held flat over the abdomen when not in use. The body is usually a dull brown to black, but some species are yellow or green.

The immature stages are aquatic. These naiads develop very slowly in freshwater streams. The adults are rather poor fliers and are more likely to be found on aquatic vegetation or shrubbery near streams than flying. They are often seen resting on bridges.

8. GRYLLOBLATTODEA, the Rockcrawlers (See entry no. 14)
Rockcrawlers are extremely rare insects found only in very specialized habitats. They are elongate, slender, ranging in length from 14–30 mm, pale brown or gray. They lack wings. The antennae are about half as long as the body and filamentous; the abdomen has long projecting cerci; ovipositor is long and sword-shaped.
The nymphs are terrestrial and resemble the adults. The long life cycle sometimes takes up to eight years to complete. Both the adults and the nymphs prefer cool, mountainous areas, usually at high altitudes. They are scavengers, living under stones, logs, often near the end of a glacier, or in caves.

9. ORTHOPTERA, the Grasshoppers, Crickets, and Katydids (See entries nos. 15–30)
The enlarged hind femora of the species of this order provides an easy recognition feature. They vary in length from 5–150 mm, but usually they are between 10–50 mm. The body is elongate, cylindrical, usually brown or green, but some species are brightly colored, marked with red, blue, yellow, and black. Most species are winged; the head has large eyes; usually 3 ocelli; antennae are moderate to very long, sometimes much longer than the body; mouthparts are for chewing; the membranous hind wings fold fanlike under the front wings which are usually smaller and thicker than the hind wings, to form a protective cover when the insect is not flying; front and middle legs are slender, and sometimes front legs are fitted for digging; hind legs usually have an enlarged femur for jumping; abdomen is usually short and stout, with a prominent ovipositor present in the female.
Nymphs resemble adults but have wing pads instead of wings. Nymphs and adults are usually phytophagous, a few are carnivorous, and some are scavengers; some rather rare species are aquatic.
More than 12,500 species occur throughout the world, with about 11,018 species in the United States and Canada.
Grasshoppers are very destructive, accounting for millions of dollars of crop loss each year. The infamous locust plagues described in the Bible continue today in some parts of the world. The migratory locusts that are responsible cause widespread famine.

10. PHASMIDA, the Walkingsticks (See entry nos. 31–32)
These insects are masters of camouflage; they resemble sticks, twigs, and sometimes, among the tropical species, they resemble leaves. Our species range in length from 10–70 mm, but some of the tropical species are as long as 30 cm. They are green or brown, blending into the background surface of

their habitat. The head is small, with small eyes and very long antennae. The legs are long and very slender. Our North American species are usually wingless, but most of the tropical species can fly, although rather feebly. They have incomplete metamorphosis, and the nymphs resemble the adults except for their lack of wings.

Walkingsticks are phytophagous and are usually found in trees and shrubs. Eggs are deposited on twigs in overlapping rows, or sometimes dropped from the tree to the forest floor where they may overwinter. The nymphs hatch and feed on vegetation. Walkingsticks can emit protective chemicals from special glands located on the thorax. Sprayed into the eyes of birds or onto other predators, it is usually an effective defense mechanism. Unlike most adult insects, walkingsticks are capable of regenerating lost limbs.

11. DICTYOPTERA, the Mantids and Cockroaches (See entry nos. 34–37)

This order is divided into two closely related but distinctive suborders, Mantodea, the praying mantids, and Blattaria, the cockroaches. Each suborder is discussed separately here.

Suborder Mantodea: The praying mantids in many ways resemble the walkingsticks, but at the same time have features in common with cockroaches. Their body is elongate, cylindrical, slightly flattened, green or brown, rarely pink (resembling a flower), and ranging from 10–165 mm in length. The head is large, triangular, with large eyes; the thorax is elongate. The front legs, the most distinctive feature of these insects, are enlarged and modified for grasping prey. The second and third pairs of legs are slender. The wings are similar to those of the grasshoppers. The abdomen has short cerci.

Eggs are laid in masses in a distinctive egg case which is attached to vegetation. This is one of their similarities to cockroaches. The nymphs hatch out and are immediately predaceous, often feeding on each other before they disperse. They resemble the adults but lack wings. Nymphs and adults frequent vegetation in search of aphids, and flowers for larger insects, including flies, bees, and even butterflies, all of which they carefully stalk, finally grasping them with deadly accuracy.

Suborder Blattaria: The cockroaches are generally despised, in contrast to their cousins, the praying mantids. Some of the tropical species of cockroaches are 15 cm in length, but most species range between 10–50 mm. Their bodies are oval, flattened, and usually brown or black, but some of the tropical species are marked with white and yellow spots. The head is usually partly covered by the pronotum of the thorax; their eyes are large and the antennae long, filiform. Cockroaches have chewing mouthparts. Most species have two pairs of wings similar to those of grasshoppers, but others are wingless. The abdomen has short apical cerci. Their eggs are laid in an ootheca, or egg case, similar to that of the mantids. The nymphs resemble the adults but are wingless.

Most cockroaches are wild, living in tropical forests and feeding on organic debris. The domestic species are well known to most people and have attained a considerable reputation as pests. They are quite common in most public buildings and often in homes. Their flattened shape and nocturnal habits enable them easily to inhabit dwellings, restaurants, and warehouses. Cockroaches feed on most organic matter. They hide their egg cases throughout the building (a few species carry the ootheca attached to their abdomen until the nymphs are ready to hatch). These ootheca may contain up to sixteen developing nymphs. The domestic species can invade most parts of a home but prefer warm, moist areas where food is available. They are especially fond of the greasy trash spilled in restaurant kitchens. They are rapid runners and hard to step on, as anyone knows who has surprised them late at night by turning on lights. Cockroaches are active throughout the year. A few species are known to migrate from building to building which adds to the difficulty of controlling them.

Four domestic species are of economic importance because they are pests in homes and in public buildings. The German cockroach (*Blattella germanica*) is the most common of the four (see entry no. 37 for more details). The Oriental cockroach (*Blatta orientalis*) is common in warm areas of buildings, near steampipes and sinks, especially in heating plants, bakeries, and restaurants. They are about 18–30 mm long and black; the females are wingless. The American cockroach (*Periplaneta americana*) is larger (28–45 mm) and is light brown to cherry. It is common in basements, sewers, alleyways, and steam tunnels. In the southern part of the United States this roach lives outdoors, especially in large outdoor dumps and landfills. The most recent intruder among cockroaches is the brown-banded cockroach (*Supella supellectilium*) which is about 10–14 mm in length. It has two transverse bands at the base of the wings, but is otherwise similar to the German cockroach with which it may be confused. It has become common in homes, often in all of the rooms, and seems to be most common around electrical appliances.

Cockroaches in restaurants and warehouses where food is available are difficult to control. Professional services are available for these situations. Controlling cockroaches in homes varies from a simple cleanup around the kitchen, to an intensive control program involving insecticides. In the North, cockroaches are less likely to migrate; therefore, once an infestation has been eliminated it is unlikely that it will return. In warmer climates it is a different matter. Cockroach ootheca are brought in with food packages, and migrating adults are often present. Apartment dwellers find it nearly impossible to control these pests unless the entire building complex is sprayed by a professional extermination service.

12. ISOPTERA, the Termites (See entry nos. 39–40)
Termites are elongate, cylindrical insects, 3–10 mm, with

queens up to 80 mm in length. Their white or light tan bodies serve to distinguish them from ants with which they are often confused. The head of the soldier is greatly enlarged and dark brown to black. Termites are soft-bodied; the head has chewing mouthparts; antennae are short and filiform (shaped like a filament); thorax is without wings except during the migratory stage, when both pairs of wings are equally long; veins have very few cells and wings are deciduous at the base. All species are social with a caste system. Usually there is only one pair of reproductives, a queen, greatly enlarged with eggs, and the male or king. Their offspring are nymphs which resemble their parents, but never reach sexual maturity unless the royal pair die. Some nymphs are workers and others soldiers. Workers are smaller than the reproductives, lack eyes, and never develop wings. They feed the queen and soldiers and take care of eggs and newly hatched nymphs. Soldiers have well-developed, enlarged mandibles. Their heads are usually much larger than those of the other castes because of the massive jaw muscles. Some species have an additional caste, the nasute, a specially adapted soldier with a drawn-out head able to squirt out a defensive fluid at colony invaders. Their metamorphosis is incomplete, and nymphs develop into various castes. Termites build nests in the soil, in wood, or, some tropical species, in trees. The workers of all species chew wood, making it necessary for them to be in contact with wood either in the soil, fallen logs, or in buildings. They do not infest living wood. Some species build their nest inside the wood itself. Others build closed runways to the wood. They do not expose themselves to light, and therefore may go unrecognized in buildings until great damage has been done. Although termites destroy wood by chewing it, they are actually unable to digest it for food without the aid of symbiotic bacteria or protozoa. These organisms inhabit their intestinal tract where they supply the necessary enzymes to convert complex cellulose molecules into simpler carbohydrates.

Termites are serious structural pests, often causing extensive damage to homes and other wooden buildings. All new construction is rendered termite-proof by chemically treating the wood and by metal barriers. Older buildings should be inspected frequently for signs of damage. This requires the aid of a professional entomologist.

13. DERMAPTERA, the Earwigs (See entry no. 33)
Earwigs range in length from 5–15 mm. Their body is elongate, somewhat flattened, brownish to black, hard or leathery. The head is large, bearing simple, filiform antennae, small eyes, chewing mouthparts. The thorax is large, with prothorax dorsally forming a hood, or pronotum, over this segment; winged, with front wings modified as wing covers (elytra), and hind wings which when not in use fold fanlike under the wing covers; abdomen with a pair of stout terminal forceps that are sexually dimorphic. Their metamorphosis is incomplete;

nymphs resemble the adults except for the lack of wings, and they have weak forceps.

Earwigs build small nests in the ground. The female guards her eggs and the young nymphs. They feed on a variety of materials and sometimes infest flowers. They crawl into crevices, under bark, stones, and logs. Campers are sometimes invaded by these creatures looking for a hiding place. Although they can crawl into a camper's ear (the source of their common name, earwig) there are no reports of this actually having happened. Rarely they are garden pests damaging flowers.

14. EMBIIDINA, the Webspinners (See entry no. 38)

These rare, rather odd, insects are 4–7 mm in length. One reaches nearly an inch in length (22 mm). They are elongate, cylindrical, pale tan to black. The antennae are slender. The mouthparts of the nymphs and adult females are well developed and used for chewing, but the male mouthparts are used only to grasp females during mating. Only the males are winged, with long and narrow wings, veins long with few cross-veins. Front legs of all stages have enlarged first segment of the tarsi containing silk glands; these spinning tarsi distinguish all species of the order from any other insect. Abdomen with short, two-segmented cerci. Metamorphosis is incomplete; nymphs resemble the adults.

These insects live gregariously in a community of silken tunnels. These are usually in forests at the base of trees. They feed on dried leaves and bark.

15. ZORAPTERA, the Zorapterans (See entry no. 41)

This is another rare order of insects. They are elongate, cylindrical, 2–2.5 mm in length, very pale tan to brownish. The antennae are short, simple; mouthparts are for biting; wings are present on some individuals, absent on others of both sexes and have few veins; abdomen with short, unsegmented cerci. They have incomplete metamorphosis. The nymphs are of two types, with or without wing pads according to the type of adult into which they will develop.

Zorapterans live under bark, in decaying wood, frequently in old sawdust piles, and sometimes in termite nests.

16. PSOCOPTERA, the Booklice and Barklice (See entry no. 42)

The adults of these insects resemble lice, but they are not ectoparasites. They range in size from 1.5–5 mm in length, rarely reaching 10 mm (0.4 in.). The body is pale tan to dusky brown. Antennae are long and slender, 12-to-50-segmented in contrast to the very short antennae of true lice. Their mouthparts are fitted for chewing. Some species are wingless, some with wings that have few veins and a few closed cells. The legs are slender. The abdomen lacks cerci. The nymphs are often gregarious and may be found along with the adults congregated in large numbers.

Psocoptera live on foliage, bark, under bark, on fungi, and in nests of birds and mammals. They are often found in buildings as scavengers.

Some species infest houses where they feed on bookbindings, wallpaper paste, and similar starchy materials. They are sometimes pests of certain stored products such as spices.

17. MALLOPHAGA, the Chewing Lice (See entry no. 43)

Lice are ectoparasites ranging in length from 0.5–6 mm, rarely as long as 10 mm, or even larger. The body is oval to elongate, somewhat flattened. They are pale tan, rarely with yellow or black markings. The head is large, about the same size as the thorax, with small antennae with three to five segments. These lice have chewing mouthparts. Their eyes are very small, and there are no ocelli. All lice are wingless; their legs are small and modified for clinging to feathers and hair. The abdomen is without cerci.

Chewing lice predominantly infest birds, but some species occur on mammals, particularly marsupials, rodents, some hoofed mammals, and a few on primates. The nymphs and adults live together on their hosts.

The order is divided into eleven families. Most species are host specific, that is, restricted to a single host. Their classification, therefore, to a great extent parallels the classification of the birds and mammals upon whom they live; they evolved along with their hosts. So far 2,675 species of chewing lice have been described, but probably many more are yet to be found. North America has 318 species.

Some species are severe pests of poultry, weakening them and subjecting them to disease and attack by other members of the flock. Other domestic animals have lice pests. They are not, however, involved in the transmission of disease as are the members of the order Anoplura.

18. ANOPLURA, the Sucking Lice (See entry no. 44)

Sucking lice feed upon the blood of their host and are serious pests. As a group they are somewhat smaller than the chewing lice, ranging in length from 0.4–5 mm. The body is similar to the preceding group, oval to elongate oval, somewhat flattened, very pale tan to gray or brownish. The head is small, with very small eyes or completely without eyes or ocelli. The antennae are 3–5-segmented. Mouthparts are modified for piercing the skin and sucking blood. They are wingless, but with legs modified for grasping hair. Abdominal cerci are absent.

All species, both as nymphs and as adults, are blood-sucking ectoparasites of mammals. The 250 species are assigned to six distinct families. Only sixty-two species are known to occur in the United States and Canada, with three of these species exclusively ectoparasites of humans.

In addition to being annoyances as bloodsuckers, they transmit serious and often fatal diseases to humans and other animals.

19. THYSANOPTERA, the Thrips (See entry no. 45)

Thrips are generally very small, but they range in length from 0.4–14 mm. Most flower species are only 2–3 mm. They are elongate, cylindrical, black, brown, or yellowish, sometimes with white, red, or black markings. The head is small, with eyes small to moderate; antennae short and stout; mouthparts fitted for piercing and sucking plants or sometimes animals. Some species are wingless. Others have very narrow wings, almost without veins except for one large main vein, but with a fringe of long anterior and posterior setae on each wing, a very distinctive feature of the order. The legs are rather small. The abdomen lacks cerci.

An advanced form of incomplete metamorphosis occurs in this order. The nymphal stage resembles the adults, but this is followed by a prepupal and pupal stage before transformation to the adult stage.

Most species of thrips are plant-juice suckers and live on flowers and vegetation. Some are predators on other insects such as whiteflies.

Although most species pass unnoticed, and some are even beneficial because they prey upon certain plant pests, a number of species are serious pests of crops, particularly ornamental flowers, coffee, and tobacco. They also transmit plant fungus diseases.

20. HEMIPTERA, the Bugs (See entry nos. 46-64)

Bugs, or "true" bugs as they are often called, are a large order of insects, one of the so-called major orders. They range in size from 0.5–55 mm. The body is oval to triangular, somewhat to very flat, or elongate and cylindrical. They are usually brown or green, often black, and many species, especially those of tropical regions, are brightly marked with primary colors, especially red, yellow, and blue.

The head is closely attached to the thorax; antennae are moderate to long, sometimes short in aquatic forms; eyes are usually large, one to three ocelli usually present; mouthparts are for piercing-sucking, deflected downward between front legs; the thorax has a large scutellum; front wings with basal half-thickened, apically half-membranous; hind wings are membranous and held crossed over the abdomen beneath the front wings; wings cover the short, broad abdomen; abdomen without cerci. The nymphs resemble adults, older nymphs with wing pads.

Several families are aquatic or subaquatic; terrestrial species are usually phytophagous, but some are predators, and a few are bloodsuckers and live as ectoparasites.

The so-called true bugs, because of the great variety of feeding habits, vary widely in importance. Although the term *bug* is applied to many kinds of insects, and even to other kinds of small invertebrates and bacteria, technically it is properly applied only to this group of insects. The plant bugs are pests of all kinds of herbaceous plants. If present in large numbers, the damage they do by penetrating the surface of the plant with their beaks causes the plant to die. These wounds also form an entrance for plant-disease fungus and bacteria. Trees and other perennial plants are not immune to the attacks of bugs of many different kinds. On the other hand, many species are predaceous and probably rank as beneficial insects. At the very least, they play a role in balanced ecosystems. A large number of species are hematophagous, attacking people as well as domestic animals. The bed bug is the best known of this group.

21. HOMOPTERA, the Cicadas, Leafhoppers, Aphids, Scale Insects, and Allies (See entry nos. 65–77)
Members of this order are very similar in many respects to the previous order and are often called bugs. They range in length from 1–55 mm, rarely as long as 90 mm. Generally they are triangular in shape in the winged species, oval in the sedentary scale insects. Aphids have a characteristic shape that some-what resembles lice with long legs; hence, they are often called plant lice. Most species of Homoptera are green or brown; many are marked with red, yellow, or black, or other primary color combinations. The antennae are usually short and bristlelike, but in some, longer and filamentous; mouth-parts are for piercing and sucking, held at rest directed back-ward between the legs; eyes and ocelli present or absent, de-pending upon the group; both winged and wingless species occur, and sometimes different stages, as aphids, are winged or wingless; both pairs of wings membranous and of the same texture throughout; wing veins are simple with relatively few closed cells; wings are held rooflike over the abdomen; abdo-men may have apical cornicles (in aphids), but usually they lack appendages or cerci. The nymphs resemble the adults; a primitive pupa is present in some forms.
All species are phytophagous, feeding on plants of all kinds. The order is separated into several distinctive superfamilies, each with a number of families. The family classification is based upon highly technical characteristics.
More than 6,500 species occur in the United States and Can-ada, with a total of 32,000 species in the world.
Many species are serious pests of cultivated crops, ornamen-tals, fruit trees, forest trees, and greenhouse plants. Damage is done by the piercing-sucking mouthparts. The loss of plant fluids stunts the plant, causes distortion and discoloration of leaves, flowers, and fruits, and often induces the spread of var-ious plant diseases.
Many species are very small and soft-bodied. Only the ci-cadas, treehoppers, and leafhoppers have hardened exoskel-etons so that they can be pinned. Others are stored in 80% al-cohol or mounted on microscope slides. Those that can be pinned are collected in the usual way on their host plants. The others are removed by the use of a fine brush moistened in al-cohol. Scale insects are usually left intact on the plant where

they are firmly attached. A sample of the infestation is taken and mounted on herbarium sheets as botanical specimens.

22. NEUROPTERA, the Neuropterans (See entry nos. 78–80)
These insects show a great diversity of size and shape. Their length varies from 5–160 mm. All are elongate, cylindrical, and most species are brown or black, some green, and some with wings marked with brown or black; otherwise the wings are transparent. The head is small; eyes are moderate to large; ocelli are usually present; antennae are usually long and fili-form, but they may be short and clubbed. The mouthparts are of the chewing type, or a combined chewing and sucking; the mandibles, when hollow, are used for sucking. The thorax may be elongate; wings with many veins and cross-veins, front and hind wings usually about the same size, held rooflike over the body; legs are short to moderate, with the front pair sometimes modified for grasping prey and similar to those of praying mantids; abdomen is elongate, without apical cerci. Their met-amorphosis is complete; larvae resemble the adults and are very active; pupae are in cocoons or in pupal cases in soil.
The larvae of many species are aquatic and predaceous. Some live in freshwater sponges; some are actively preda-ceous in various freshwater habitats. The larvae of others are terrestrial and also actively predaceous, often attacking plant pests such as aphids on the host plant. Adults are rather fee-ble flyers. They are often attracted to lights at night. Some adults are predaceous.
None are of economic importance, except the aquatic forms which may be important fish food; they are often used as fish bait.

23. COLEOPTERA, the Beetles, Weevils, and Stylopids (See entry nos. 81–193)
Beetles are the most abundant in number of species of any group of organisms. Beetles and the entire plant kingdom have approximately the same number of species. Not only abundant in species, they are, without doubt, the most diverse of all in-sect orders. They are also the easiest to collect and preserve. Their length varies from 0.025 to 150 mm, usually 2 to 20 mm. The smallest beetle is also the smallest insect; the largest bee-tle competes with the largest moth for size, but the beetle far outweighs the moth.
The body ranges from elongate and cylindrical to flat, round, and hemispherical. The shape of beetles is often characteristic of the species, but it is extremely diverse within the order and frequently within a particular family. Many beetles are black or brown, but several families have species that are very colorful, ranging from red and orange to green, blue, spotted, and striped with many colors including gold and silver. The hind or flying wings, when not in use, are folded and covered by the front pair of wings, termed the elytra. These are hard and form a hull-like cover. When closed they meet in a straight line

along the back. This feature alone distinguishes beetles from all other insects except for the earwigs (Dermaptera). Earwigs, unlike the beetles, have a pair of terminal abdominal forceps (see entry 33). Beetles have chewing mouthparts (or, rarely, as in some Meloidae, a long sucking tube as well). The antennae of beetles are almost always 11-segmented but vary greatly in length and shape from group to group. Often the type of antennae (as for example, those of the Scarabaeidae) will distinguish a particular family. The compound eyes are usually large and well developed, occasionally divided and appearing as four eyes (see Gyrinidae). Ocelli are almost never present. The legs of beetles are modified in various ways, and used for running, grasping, swimming, digging, and sometimes for jumping. There are usually five tarsal segments, but the number may be reduced in various combinations. The number of segments of each leg is expressed as a tarsal formula. Thus, the tarsal formula showing the number of segments on the fore, middle, and hind tarsi respectively is written as: 5-5-5, 5-5-4, 4-4-4, and so on, according to the count for one side. This formula is usually uniform for a family or a group of families and is used in characterizing some groups. The prothorax is enlarged dorsally and is called the *pronotum,* which includes all of the thorax, except for a small triangular part, the *scutellum,* which can be seen dorsally. The remaining two thoracic segments are hidden in the closed elytra. The abdomen is soft above where it is covered by the wings and elytra. In a few groups, the elytra are short (see Staphylinidae), exposing several segments of the abdomen. In such cases, the abdominal tergites are hardened. The ventral surface of the abdomen is hard. From five to eight ventral segments are exposed. The remaining segments are withdrawn into the abdomen and are modified to form the copulatory and egg-laying apparatus. Metamorphosis is complete. Very little is known about beetle eggs. The larvae are of various shapes, usually have legs, and are active. They are variously adapted according to their habitat. Many live under bark or bore into stems, wood, seeds, and roots. Some are predators, living in leaf litter, leaf mold, soil, or in gravel. Others feed on carrion, decaying vegetation, or fungi, and many are leaf feeders. Several families have aquatic larvae. The larvae transform into pupae in the soil, wood, or under bark, or other habitats. Very few make a cocoon. Some of the pupae overwinter so that the adults emerge in the spring. Others emerge a few days after pupation and repeat their life cycle. Most beetle life cycles are completed within a year, but wood boring larvae may take several years to mature. Obviously this abundant and diverse order of insects occupies a wide range of habitats. Almost every location harbors species of beetles. Adults are attracted to light at night, and they are abundant on flowers, foliage, and branches during the day. Only a very few are parasitic, the least exploited habitat for beetles. Although they are seldom dominant in aquatic habitats, they are abundant there.

Although many species of beetles can be identified by their distinctive shape and color patterns, most species must be identified with keys and compared with the technical descriptions and illustrations before they can be correctly named. Obviously the vast number of species makes this difficult without a great expenditure of time and effort. Most beetle collectors, therefore, specialize in certain groups and learn as much as they can about these. Although they may collect all kinds of beetles, they usually enlist the help of other specialists for identification of much of their material.

Many of the leaf-feeding beetles are restricted in their distribution by the range of the host plants. Others are more widely distributed, apparently adaptable to a wide range of conditions. Most species are restricted to very limited habitats, which no doubt accounts for the evolution of such a great number of species. Not much is known about the life requirements and ecology of most beetle species.

It is difficult to know which group of insects causes the most crop damage. Certainly the cotton-boll weevil, a member of the largest of all insect families, the Curculionidae, has caused great economic loss. Many other weevils are serious crop pests, along with the leaf beetles (family Chrysomelidae) and the various wood borers (for example, the families Buprestidae and Cerambycidae). Dozens of species are pests in stored grain and similar stored foods. Several species of the family Dermestidae are household pests, feeding on rugs, clothing, and other fabrics. Fortunately, unlike the flies, no species are involved in the transmission of human disease, although a few are implicated in livestock diseases. No beetles sting, and even the largest with powerful mandibles, unless handled carelessly, are not known to bite people. Some of the carrion-infesting beetles are active in the processing of this decaying material. Probably the most important role played by beetles in their part of an ecosystem is in the mixing of leaf mold, leaf litter, and soil, to increase the amount of humus. But, again, this has been poorly studied.

24. MECOPTERA, the Scorpionflies and their Allies (See entry no. 194)

Mecoptera are retiring insects, usually found in sunny areas of forests or in fields nearby. Most people confuse them with large flies unless they look closely. They range in length from 3–30 mm, usually about 10–12 mm. The body is elongate, cylindrical; wings are long and narrow, usually rounded apically. Most species are reddish brown to dark. The wings are transparent, sometimes marked with black, or entirely dark. The head is extended into a beak with chewing mouthparts at the end. Antennae are filiform (threadlike); the eyes large. The thorax has two pairs of wings of similar shape and color. The legs are long and slender, sometimes very long. The abdomen of the male of some species has genital claspers and may be upturned over the abdomen, giving the appearance of a scorpion, hence one of the common names. (Another common name is hangingfly, because some species have the habit of hanging by their long legs on the underside of leaves.) Their metamorphosis is complete. Scorpionflies usually deposit their eggs on the ground. The larval stage is caterpillarlike.

Adults are found most often in areas of dense vegetation. They are predaceous and omnivorous.

Note: Male scorpionflies do not bite or sting. However, the males of some species may bring a captured insect as a present to the females they are courting. In one case, at least, males are known to mimic females in order to get a free meal from an unsuspecting suitor.

25. TRICHOPTERA, the Caddisflies (See entry no. 196)

Caddisflies look like moths that have lost their scales. They are closely related to the Lepidoptera, but may be distinguished by the presence of short, fine hairs on their wings instead of scales. Length varies from 1.5–40 mm, usually 8–20 mm. The body is elongate, cylindrical; wings are triangular, front wings usually larger than the hind wings. These insects are brown or yellowish brown; wings are sometimes marked with black, or are otherwise either transparent or the same color as the body. The head is small, eyes are large; the antennae are filiform and usually very long, sometimes extending well beyond the length of the abdomen. The mouthparts are of the chewing type, but usually reduced and used only for drinking water and perhaps nectar. Wings similar to each other, held tentlike over the abdomen when not in use. The legs are slender, often with stout spines. The abdomen is simple, without terminal filaments or cerci. Their metamorphosis is complete. The larval stage is aquatic. Eggs are deposited in water, and the newly hatched larva constructs a case, often characteristic of the species, made out of bits of stone, wood, leaves, sand, or plant debris. These particles are held together with silk. Some species construct a netlike case of silk. As the larvae grow, the case is enlarged. The larvae feed on algae and organic debris; rarely they are predaceous; a few are herbivores. Pupation takes place in the water. The pupa is active and swims to shore where the adult emerges.

The adults are shortlived, nocturnal, and are often attracted to light near bodies of water. They do not feed and die shortly after mating.

Over 975 species occur in United States and Canada. These species are assigned to eighteen families. They are not easy to identify because of the need to use obscure anatomical features. Cooler waters seem to be preferred by most of the 4,500 species in the world; therefore, they are more abundant in temperate regions than tropical. They are important fish food in many regions and therefore contribute substantially to the aquatic (freshwater) food chains.

26. LEPIDOPTERA, the Moths, Butterflies, and Skippers (See entry nos. 197–263)

Lepidoptera are considered to be among the most beautiful of creatures. Butterflies, especially, have always been prized by collectors. Some of the large tropical species are very valuable and sell for thousands of dollars.

In length they vary from 2–150 mm, usually at least 5 mm and less than 80 mm (3 in.). The body is uniformly elongate. There are always two pairs of scale-covered wings, which are usually broad, but may be variously shaped; a few species have their wings cleft so there appears to be more than two pairs of wings, but this is unusual (Alucitidae and Pterophoridae), and often the very small species have lanceolate wings, and some have scaleless, transparent areas. A few species have wingless females. Many species of moths and most species of butterflies are brightly colored with every imaginable shade and combination of color patterns. Usually these bright colors are warnings to would-be predators that the insect's body contains a poison (see, for example, the monarch butterfly). The head is small; mouthparts consist of a long coiled sucking tube in many species or, rarely, some of the very primitive moths have biting mouthparts; others have the mouthparts greatly reduced or absent. Many species have large maxillary palpi which project forward. The antennae are usually only about half the length of the body and consist of many segments. They vary from slender to plumose (featherlike). Those of the butterflies are clubbed at the tip. The thorax is enlarged because of the large wing muscles. The legs are slender, usually three pairs of equal size, but in some of the butterflies (family Nymphalidae), and a few others, the front pair is greatly reduced in size. They are covered with scales and hairlike setae. The abdomen is round, elongate, and lacks any external cerci. The male copulatory organs and the female ovipositor are retracted into the abdomen.

The adults lay eggs which hatch into larvae. Lepidoptera larvae are of various shapes. Some are without scales or setae; others are thickly clothed with long hairlike setae. These caterpillars, as they are termed, have chewing mouthparts, three pairs of small thoracic legs, and abdominal prolegs which are not true legs because they are unsegmented. They have circles of hooklets at the foot end. Lepidoptera larvae can only be confused with the larvae of some of the primitive Hymenoptera, the sawflies. However, the latter have six to eight pairs of abdominal prolegs, whereas true caterpillars have at most only five pairs, and often less.

The caterpillar stage is the feeding stage of the moth or butterfly. After reaching full size, these creatures, which are so different from their parents, transform into pupae. The larvae often spin cocoons of silk to protect them during this transformation stage. Others make a cell in the soil for protection. Butterfly larvae spin a small button of silk, attach it to a twig or leaf, and suspend themselves from this. As they transform, they secrete a shiny cover that protects them from drying out. It takes several days to weeks for the pupae to change into moths or butterflies. When they first emerge, their wings are folded and crumpled, and they cannot fly until fluid has been pumped through the wing veins and the wings unfold. Finally the wings harden and the adult flies away to mate, thus completing the cycle.

The larval habitat is much different from that of the adult. Most caterpillars are leaf feeders and often host specific, restricted to a single kind of plant. Others will feed on a wide variety of leaves. One of the best ways to gather beautiful specimens, as well as to learn the details of the life cycles of moths, is to raise them from eggs. Moths will often lay their eggs on a twig or leaf in a jar. When the eggs hatch, the young larvae will feed in captivity, eventually pupate, and later perfect specimens will emerge. Other larvae infest plant stems; some are root feeders, wood borers, or leaf miners, and still others infest seeds. A wide variety of species live in various kinds of stored products, especially grain and grain products. A very few species have aquatic larvae.

The adults are nectar feeders. Some of the primitive species are pollen feeders, but this is rare. Many adults do not feed, but only fly about in search of a mate. After mating and egg laying the adults of most species die. Some of the tropical and subtropical species, and very occasionally, other species, may have more than one brood a year, and some may live for more than one year. A considerable number of adults overwinter, hibernating under leaves, or behind loose bark through the long northern winters. The adults of moths are usually night flyers and are attracted to lights. Butterflies and skippers are day flyers and are usually found around flowers or at mud puddles drinking water.

Classification: The species of Lepidoptera are assigned to seventy-five families distributed among five suborders. However, all but nine primitive families belong in one suborder, Ditrysia. This comprises most of the moths and all of the butterflies and skippers. There are approximately 180,000 described species in the world and about 13,700 species in the United States and Canada.

Many moths are difficult to identify to family without the use of technical identification tables and descriptions, usually involving details of the arrangement of the wing veins and similar features. This is particularly true of the large number of families referred to as the *microlepidoptera* because they are usually very small. Many species are drab browns and obscurely marked. A few of the brighter colored species are illustrated in this book. However, many species of micros are of economic importance and should not be ignored. The *macrolepidoptera* are usually larger species, but not always. There are about nine families of macros. Another nine families comprise the butterflies, and one family, the skippers. A great many of these species can be recognized by their color patterns and wing shape alone, the ''spot'' identification method used by most beginners. Many species of these Lepidoptera are illustrated in this book.

Most species of Lepidoptera are restricted in their distribution by the range of the larval food plant. Thus there are eastern species with closely related western species on a different food plant, or northern species with very similar species in the south, and so on. Some species of butterflies are very widely distributed and at least one common species, the painted lady (*Vanessa cardui*), is worldwide in distribution. Several species, most notably the monarch, migrate as adults.

A great many species cause extensive crop damage if left unchecked. One familiar to many of us is the corn earworm, or corn borer. Although harmless to humans, the larvae of this moth make corn ears unsightly and therefore unsuitable for market. More serious is the cotton bollworm that may destroy a large portion of the cotton crop in some areas. Many other species of moth larvae and a few butterfly larvae attack our crops. In fact, it is safe to say that no flowering plant is immune to the attack of the larvae of Lepidoptera—and so they become an important part of the checks and balances we know function in all ecosystems, the balance of nature.

27. HYMENOPTERA, the Wasps, Ants, and Bees (See entry nos. 264–308)

Wasps, ants, and bees are well known for their stings and nest building. Except for the mimics, it is fairly easy to recognize the members of this order. They are as much fun to watch as they are to collect and identify.

They range in length from 0.2–115 mm. The body is cylindrical with a distinct, movable head, a more or less humpbacked thorax, and distinct abdomen, usually narrowly connected to the thorax. They are generally brown to black, or yellow with black-and-white markings, or metallic blue or green, rarely marked with other primary colors. The head is usually big, with large eyes and, generally, three ocelli; antennae are usually 11- or 12-segmented, filiform, moderate in length, sometimes very long; mouthparts are usually for chewing or of a modified chewing and lapping structure; the thorax is compact, legs moderate to long, sometimes modified for digging or carrying pollen or grasping prey; wings, usually present in some males, are elongate-oval, the hind wings shorter than the front, with veins curved, usually with several closed cells; the abdomen may be broadly attached to the thorax, or more generally, it is attached by a narrow petiole; abdominal appendages are absent; the female ovipositor is often modified to form a stinger. The larvae may be caterpillarlike or a legless grub; pupae transform in a pupal case, cocoon, or in a pupal cell in a nest.

Members of this large order occupy a great many habitats; many are phytophagous; a large number are parasitic as larvae inside other insects; many are social and build nests.

The order is divided into more than eighty families placed in three distinct groups. The classification is based on wing venation, structure of the thorax, and to some extent their habits. More than 103,000 species have been described, but many more remain undescribed, especially those that are parasitic as larvae. The latest catalog of the species of United States and Canada lists 17,429 species.

A few species are plant pests in the larval stage. These resemble caterpillars of moths and feed on leaves, especially on conifers. The majority of species are beneficial as parasites of other insects and as flower pollinators.

28. DIPTERA, the Flies (See entry nos. 309–400)

Flies belong to the fourth largest order of insects. Although there are many species, most of them seem, at first sight, rather drab. Look at a few under a microscope, however, and you will admire their remarkable body construction and delicate beauty.

Flies range in length from 0.5–50 mm, rarely up to 75 mm. Their body is compact; the head is usually large; thorax is compact, more or less humpbacked; the abdomen is short, oval, usually widely attached to the thorax. They are usually brown or black, sometimes metallic blue, green, or copper, rarely brightly colored. The head usually has large eyes, and ocelli are often present; antennae of *various* shapes, sometimes long and filiform, but except for the more primitive species, the antennae are short and composed of a few segments; mouthparts are usually of a modified biting type, but may be elongated for bloodsucking, or greatly modified for sponging (see a house fly). The thorax has only one pair of wings; the second pair of wings are modified into short balancing sensory organs; wing venation is distinctive for each family and often for the genus and even the species. Head, thorax, and abdomen are clothed with setae, spines, and scales. Their placement on the body is genetically determined. The arrangement of these structures varies from species to species but is constant within the species; therefore, they are extensively used for identification characters. Some flies are wingless, ectoparasitic insects similar to ticks, but unlike ticks, they have three pairs of legs instead of four.

The larval stages of many species are called maggots. They are legless, but are active and able to crawl throughout their food material, including boring in plant tissue. Aquatic larvae are usually good swimmers. The pupal stage takes place in a cuticlelike covering termed the puparium. Aquatic pupae are also active swimmers.

Flies of one kind or another are found almost everywhere. Many of the more primitive species are aquatic in the larval stage, while their adults, such as mosquitoes, tend to be bloodsuckers. Other species infest carrion, dung, and decaying vegetable materials and are an important part of the detritus cycle. Others, including leaf miners and gall makers, are pests of plants. Some are important parasites of other insects and are extremely beneficial in controlling natural populations. Flies as disease transmitters are discussed on p. 40. As pointed out, a large number of species are annoying pests, and many others are beneficial. Relatively few are involved in plant crop loss, but well over fifty species are known to be plant pests in our area, and some, such as the Mediterranean fruit fly that sometimes invades this country, cost us millions of dollars to keep them out of our groves of fruit trees.

Some flies are attracted to lights at night; many others are found around decaying organic matter of all types; still others visit flowers (often the most attractive species), and many fly into Malaise traps. (Incidentally, various commercially available fly traps are sold as a means of controlling flies. These usually attract many wild species and, if anything, increase the fly problem rather than decrease it. However, the abundance of specimens in these traps will delight any fly collector.)

29. SIPHONAPTERA, the Fleas (See entry no. 195)

Fleas are ectoparasites but do not spend their entire lives on their hosts. They are all small, ranging in length from 1–5 mm. They are strongly compressed laterally, with the head fused to the small thorax. Although the abdomen is short, it is the largest part of the brown to black body. All are hard-bodied with numerous depressed spines and setae which are uniformly placed on the individuals of each species, but because the location varies from species to species, this feature is used for identification and classification. The antennae are very short and held in grooves at the side of the head; mouthparts are of the modified piercing-sucking type. Fleas never have wings. The hind legs are modified for jumping. The abdomen has small claspers and other copulatory structures at the apical end.

Unlike most other ectoparasites, fleas have a complete metamorphosis. Their larvae live in mammal nests, on the ground in mammal runs, or in homes in areas frequented by pets. They feed on organic debris. The adults feed on the blood of mammals and birds, but they leave their host to lay eggs. Most fleas are very host specific, but they will take blood from other than their normal host if they cannot find the right host.

The order is divided into seventeen families based mostly on the arrangement of spines and teeth on the body and legs. Only 238 species, out of the 1,370 known species in the world, have been recorded in the United States and Canada. They have, of course, the same distribution as their animal hosts.

Fleas are pests of all mammals and many birds. Heavy infestation may cause weakness of the host which, in turn, may bring about death through infection or attack from other animals. These insects are vectors of serious diseases, including the dreaded bubonic plague or "black death," of domestic animals and humans.

1 ORCHESELLA AINSLIEI
Slender Sphagnum Springtail

Family Entomobryidae
Order Collembola
Length ±1.8 mm.
Recognition marks Pale yellow to blackish purple; antennae are 6-segmented. This group is very distinctive because of the large fourth abdominal segment, at least twice the length of the third segment as seen from dorsal view.
Habitat Found on sphagnum moss growing in woodland pools.
Distribution This species belongs to a family of 138 species in northeastern United States and Canada.
Note Springtails are among the most abundant of insects, yet they are very seldom seen by nonprofessional collectors. Nearly any moist soil sample will yield hundreds of individuals. If you watch the activity going on in a bowl containing wood's moss, you will see these creatures plying their way through the vegetation. Springtails undoubtedly are a main food source for many small beetle larvae and for centipedes. Very few details are known about their lives. It is known that the males place spermatophores in strategic positions on the soil so that the females will encounter them. She engulfs these gelatinous masses into her reproductive tract where the sperm are released and fertilize her eggs.

2 ACERELLA BARBERI
Soil Proturan

Family Acerentomidae
Order Protura
Length ±1.8 mm.
Recognition marks Body white; front pair of legs projected forward and used as sense organs rather than for locomotion.
Habitat Soil; these insects are seldom seen.
Distribution Poorly known, probably throughout eastern North America.
Note These primitive insects need further study. Some authorities do not consider them to be insects but a separate group by themselves. They show some relationship to the springtails. Spiracles and Malpighian tubules (excretory organs), both characteristic of insects, are absent in this and similar species of the order. In addition, unlike "true" insects, they add abdominal segments during each molt. Other insects have a complete complement of segments upon hatching.

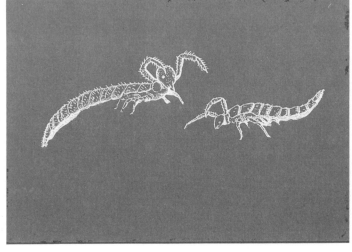

3 LEPISMA SACCHARINA
Silverfish

Family Lepismatidae
Order Thysanura
Length ±12 mm.
Recognition marks Uniformly slate gray; body is covered with scales; eyes are small with separate elements.
Habitat Warm, humid places, including home, but also in the wild in southern Florida and in other tropical regions.
Distribution Cosmopolitan.
Note This species is often a pest in homes and libraries. It feeds on starchy materials, such as glue, but requires high humidity. It can be reared in glass jars where it will feed on oatmeal and other starchy foods. Potatoes will provide the necessary water. Do not let it mold or let the jar get too dry. Other species of this poorly known order can be captured in the wild. They are found in leaf litter and among rocks and in debris along the shore. These insects are considered to be very primitive, perhaps the most primitive of living forms. The appendages on the ventral surface of the abdomen are one indication of this even though these are not functional locomotive appendages. Silverfish might well be considered living fossils; they are much older than the dinosaurs.

---

4 JAPYX DIVERSIUNGUS
Slender Dipluran

Family Japygidae
Order Diplura
Length 8–10 mm.
Recognition marks Elongate; pale tan, with central portion of each abdominal segment darker, apical segment dark brown, with a pair of stout forceps.
Habitat Soil-inhabiting species.
Distribution Widespread, but local, spotty distribution.
Note Although all of these primitive wingless insects are rather small and devoid of attractive colors, they are worthy of study if for nothing more than the fact that so little is known about them. The wingless primitive insect pictured at the introduction to this section is a wild thysanuran. They are fast runners. They must be closely examined to distinguish them from the nymphs of some other order. Perhaps this is why they have been overlooked for so long.

PRIMITIVE
WINGED INSECTS

5   HEXAGENIA BILINEATA
Burrowing Mayfly

Family   Ephemeridae
Order   Ephemeroptera
Length   14–18 mm.
Recognition marks   Yellow with brown prothorax and abdominal stripes; wings are opaque, veins marked with brown.
Habitat   Naiads are found in large rivers; they feed on plant debris.
Distribution   Common; southeastern United States. Mayflies such as these are becoming very rare because of the pollution of the rivers and streams throughout the United States and Canada.
Note   The burrowing mayfly family contains some of the largest species of the order. Their common name refers to the naiads' habit of burrowing into the sand and silt in streams and lakes. This affords them protection from predatory fish. Flies for fishing are made to mimic species of this family.

6   OCTOGOMPHUS SPECULARIS
Clubtail

Family   Gomphidae
Order   Odonata
Wingspan   58–65 mm.
Description   Dark brown to black with pale yellow markings; easily recognized by the inverted urn marking on the front of the thorax.
Habitat   Naiads are found in bottom mud of streams or in leaf trash at the edge of mountain streams. Adults are found near streams, and seldom fly. They rest, well camouflaged, on vegetation.
Distribution   Throughout western mountain areas.
Note   These and other large dragonflies are often called "devil's darning needles" and similar names, implying that they can inflict some sort of an injury, but this is not so. No species of Odonata stings. It is possible that they could bite if a finger were placed near their large mandibles, but there are no records of this ever having happened.

7 CORDULEGASTER DORSALIS
Biddie

Family Cordulegastridae
Order Odonata
Wingspan 85–100 mm.
Recognition marks Chocolate brown to black with bright yellow markings on the abdomen. Females have a long ovipositor. Eyes are large but do not meet dorsally.
Habitat Naiads are found in small woodland streams. Adults are found along the shores of streams.
Distribution West Coast from Alaska to California and east to Utah. This is one of several closely similar species. Biddies are common throughout North America.
Note Naiads of Gomphidae may be taken from mud and silt. Adults are difficult to net as are most dragonflies.

---

8 PLATHEMIS LYDIA
White-tailed Skimmer

Family Libellulidae
Order Odonata
Wingspan 65–75 mm.
Recognition marks Crossband of males' wings are uniformly dark brown; female has brown wing tips; front of head is yellowish to olive green; thorax is brown to blackish marked with two longitudinal white or yellow stripes; front stripe may be broken into a line of spots; abdomen of male is white apically; female abdomen has yellow spots.
Habitat Flies along the margin of ponds, hovering over the water, and perches on shore vegetation; usually flies a regular route, often with species of *Libellula*. Naiads are found in ponds and swampy areas. Adults are usually found near the habitat of the naiads, but they are also often seen flying around puddles in blacktop parking areas.
Distribution Common throughout North America from southern Canada to Florida and California.
Note The Libellulidae is probably the most common family of dragonflies in North America. Many species have patches or bands of color on wings. They are large insects with wingspans from 40–160 mm.

9 · LIBELLULA FORENSIS
Western Widow

Family Libellulidae
Order Odonata
Wingspan 80–85 mm.
Recognition marks Wing tips lack color; central and basal bands are irregular, dark brown or black; subapical and subbasal spots are pale brown; front of head is yellow, densely covered with black hairlike setae; thorax is brown, sides have two yellow streaks; abdomen is brown to black. This species is similar to *Libellula pulchella* except that the latter species has black wing tips. These two species often fly with *Plathemis lydia*.
Habitat Naiads are hairy, living in stagnant ponds in the bottom ooze.
Distribution Western Canada and the United States.
Note The southwestern big red is illustrated on the opening pages of this section. It is also a member of the genus *Libellula*, *L. saturata*. It is the only entirely red species in the United States. Adults are not strong fliers and are easily collected. It occurs in southwestern United States, occasionally straying north to Idaho and Montana. The western widow is found throughout western Canada and the United States; species of *Libellula* occur throughout North America.

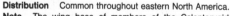

10 HETAERINA AMERICANA
American Ruby Spot

Family Calopterygidae
Order Odonata
Wingspan 56–60 mm.
Recognition marks The body is reddish metallic; the male has bright red spots on the base of wings; the female has dull reddish-brown spots.
Habitat These beautiful damselflies are often common along grassy streams.
Distribution Common throughout eastern North America.
Note The wing base of members of the Calopterygidae, or broad-winged damselflies, is gradually narrowed instead of stalked as in the rest of the species of the other families of damselflies. Damselflies are so named because they are weaker fliers than the dragonflies and, therefore, more graceful and damsellike. Adults hold their wings at an angle over their long slender abdomen.

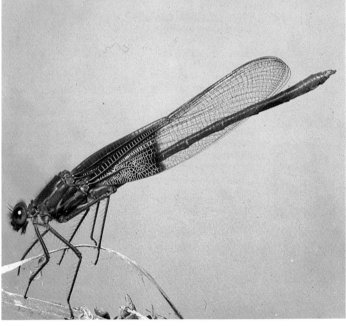

11 CALOPTERYX MACULATA
Black-wing

Family Calopterygidae
Order Odonata
Wingspan 56–60 mm.
Recognition marks Body is metallic blue or green; wings of male are entirely black, female wings are dark gray with a white stigma.
Habitat These species flit along the shores of streams, especially those with abundant aquatic vegetation. They are also found among cattails and around floating vegetation.
Distribution Throughout eastern North America.
Note The females of these species insert their eggs into the stems of aquatic plants, placing them just below the surface of the water. The naiads are often found on the submerged portions of these same plants.

---

12 ENALLAGMA CIVILE
Bluet Damselfly

Family Coenagrionidae
Order Odonata
Wingspan 34–40 mm.
Recognition marks Body is blue with black markings; wings are unmarked.
Habitat They are found in lakes and streams. Very common throughout North America.
Note Most of the damselflies collected are bluets, or members of the genus *Enallagma*. The males of these insects are brightly colored, usually more so than the females. The naiads have gill filaments extending from the apex of the abdomen.

13 PELTOPERLA CORA
Roachlike Stonefly

Family Peltoperlidae
Order Plecoptera
Wingspan 34–49 mm.
Recognition marks Brown to dark brown; wings are lightly to heavily smoky brownish-black.
Habitat Naiads, which resemble cockroaches, occur under stones in lakes and streams, particularly those of cooler waters. Adults emerge from the last naiad skin and may be found on woody stems or other vegetation in late spring and summer.
Distribution This species is common in California and Nevada. Other species of the family are found in western and northern regions of North America.
Note Most species of stoneflies inhabit the cooler portions of the world. They emerge from streams in midwinter and can be collected only at that time. On warm sunny days examine bridge rails and supports for resting adults.

---

14 GRYLLOBLATTA CAMPODEIFORMIS
Rock Crawler

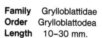

Family Grylloblattidae
Order Grylloblattodea
Length 10–30 mm.
Recognition marks These rare insects are amber yellow, unmarked; wingless. This species is one of the most commonly collected of our ten species.
Habitat It is found among rocks and debris at high altitudes, often near streams at the foot of glaciers.
Distribution Pacific Northwest.
Note Some species of this rare order of insects have been collected recently in caves.

15 TAENIOPODA EQUES
Horse Lubber

Family Acrididae
Order Orthoptera
Length 38–64 mm.
Recognition marks Body is black and shiny; it is marked with margins of yellow to orange; veins of front wings are outlined in yellow; hind wings are rosy-red with black borders.
Habitat Although this species prefers arid regions, it is found as far east as the edge of the range of the eastern lubber grasshopper (*Romalea microptera*) which it resembles. Both species feed on a variety of plants along roadsides. The eastern species may become a pest in gardens.
Distribution Arizona, Texas, and Mexico.
Note This species and entry nos. 16–21 represent a few of the very large family of short-horned grasshoppers (Acrididae). Members of this family have an auditory organ on the first abdominal segment. The males sing (stridulate) during the day by rubbing their femura against the front wings, or sometimes by clicking their front wings together. The females are mute.

16 POECILOTETTIX PANTHERINA
Panther-spotted Grasshopper

Family Acrididae
Order Orthoptera
Length 25–30 mm.
Recognition marks Body is light green; head, pronotum, and legs are marked with small black and white spots; antennae are black, alternate segments are ringed with white.
Habitat This species occurs on various plants belonging to the family Compositae. It is one of several colorfully marked arid region species.
Distribution Arizona and Mexico.
Note The short-horned grasshoppers are the common species of meadows and fields throughout North America. They are usually phytophagous, but not particularly host specific. They will also eat animal matter if it is available. Many species are destructive to field crops.

17 TRIMEROTROPIS ALBOLINEATA
White-lined Grasshopper

Family Acrididae
Order Orthoptera
Length 30–35 mm.
Recognition marks Brownish to rusty-red; wings are yellow; bands on wings not pronounced.
Habitat It is usually seen on trees and shrubs in sandy areas.
Distribution California to southern Arizona.
Note Many species of grasshoppers live in sandy areas where they are masters of camouflage. Their colors blend in with the sand protecting them from predators. Collecting these species is difficult. As they fly, their hind wings flash color. When they drop to the sand, they seemingly disappear from sight. Swinging the net in the general direction of their landing will flush them out, but too late to enclose them in the net. Male grasshoppers, unlike katydids, sing during the day to attract the mute females.

18 MELANOPLUS DIFFERENTIALIS
Differential Grasshopper

Family Acrididae
Order Orthoptera
Length 30–45 mm.
Recognition marks The body is brown to yellow with spotting above; hind femur is marked with black herringbone pattern.
Habitat A common, nonmigrating but very destructive grasshopper found feeding on grass and forage crops.
Distribution Throughout most of North America.
Note A few species of grasshoppers are major pests of grasslands and grass crops, feeding on all parts of the plant that extends above ground. Nymphs as well as adults are capable of eating sixteen times their weight each day. When populations increase to the point of noticeable destruction, control measures, usually chemical, must be instituted. Although this may be effective, it generally results in little profit for the grower and causes considerable environmental pollution.
The genus *Melanoplus* contains a great number of species, more than half the species of the family Acrididae. They are very difficult to identify to species without the use of the technical literature.

19 SPHARAGEMON COLLARE
Mottled Sand Grasshopper

Family Acrididae
Order Orthoptera
Length 30–38 mm.
Recognition marks Body is gray to brown; wings are banded with black; hind tibiae are partly to entirely orange.
Habitat Found in grasslands, meadows, and on the fringes of woodlands. Adults make a crackling sound as they fly by rubbing their front wings together. When handled this and related species spit "tobacco juice" (actually the contents of their stomach) to defend themselves.
Distribution Throughout North America except for the West Coast.
Note Most species of grasshoppers mate in late summer and early fall. The females deposit their eggs in holes dug into the soil by their modified ovipositors. The eggs overwinter and hatch in the late spring or early summer. The nymphs feed on vegetation and molt four to six times until they reach their full size. Wing pads gradually develop and functional wings appear during the last molt.

---

20 OPSHOMAEA VITREIPENNIS
Glassy-winged Toothpick Grasshopper

Family Acrididae
Order Orthoptera
Length 24–30 mm.
Recognition marks Green to yellowish with a faint stripe often present on the side of the abdomen; hind tibia are green.
Habitat This species is found near water on cattails, sedges, and other aquatic vegetation.
Distribution North Carolina south into Florida.
Note This species resembles the katydids but has short antennae. Although this species prefers wet areas, most species of the group are more common in the drier regions of North America. They are generally associated with grasslands and deserts. They often cause great loss to crops and pasture lands, particularly during long dry periods.

21 DACTYLOTUM BICOLOR
Rainbow Grasshopper

Family Acrididae
Order Orthoptera
Length 20–35 mm.
Recognition marks Bluish with bold red and yellow markings; wings are short, not extending over the abdomen.
Habitat This species is found in desert grasslands, especially on gravelly soil. It is rarely found on forage crops.
Distribution Texas and New Mexico, north to Montana.
Note Only nine species of the more than 5,000 kinds of grasshoppers are migratory. They are species of the spur-throated grasshopper family. One or more of the migratory species are responsible for the tremendous crop destruction that occurs cyclically most often in parts of Africa, but also in Europe, Asia, and, in the past, in western United States. These migratory locusts (or grasshoppers) occur in two phases which differ in color, shape, and behavior: a solitary phase, which is more common, and a migratory phase. Through physiological changes the migratory phase occurs following great increases in population resulting from favorable environmental conditions. These include not only an abundance of food, but favorable temperature, humidity, and an increase in rainfall. During the migratory phase locusts fly across the land in great swarms eating all vegetation in their path.

22 SCUDDERIA FURCATA
Fork-tailed Bush Katydid

Family Tettigoniidae
Order Orthoptera
Length 36–40 mm.
Recognition marks Green, sometimes tinged with brown; antennae are long and hairlike; wings extend over and beyond the end of the abdomen.
Habitat Common on grasses, shrubs, and trees, usually found at the edges of meadows, forests, and marshes.
Distribution Occurs throughout the United States.
Note The family Tettigoniidae, the long-horned grasshoppers or katydids, is characterized by their very long antennae, swordlike ovipositor, and their green color. Males stridulate and produce the characteristic "kadydid, kadydidn't" sounds heard on warm summer nights. These sounds are characteristic of each species and may serve as a means of identification. Most females are mute, although some can chirp in reply to the mating calls of the male. The female auditory organs are located on the base of the front tibiae.

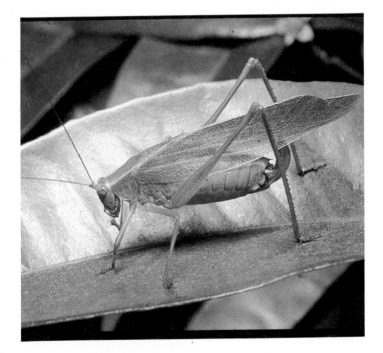

23 INSARA ELEGANS
Mesquite Katydid

Family Tettigoniidae
Order Orthoptera
Length 28–30 mm.
Recognition marks Light green body and darker green front wings marked by eight white bands.
Habitat Found in deserts on mesquite trees, creosote bushes, and other desert plants.
Distribution Southwestern United States.
Note The long-horned grasshoppers and katydids sing particularly in the early evening in late summer and early fall. After mating takes place, the female deposits her eggs on twigs or under bark. The nymphs hatch the following spring and begin feeding. Most katydids are phytophagous and nocturnal. During the day they rest well hidden in green vegetation, and they are easily overlooked by collectors. A few are of economic importance because they feed on ornamental plants and occasionally on forage crops.

24 MICROCENTRUM RHOMBIFOLIUM
Broad-winged Katydid

Family Tettigoniidae
Order Orthoptera
Length 50–65 mm.
Recognition marks Green body; the middle of the front margin of the pronotum has a blunt "tooth"; wing is broad and leaflike.
Habitat Common on many kinds of plants and trees, including ornamentals and crops; often a serious pest.
Distribution Across southern United States, north to Utah, Colorado, Kansas, Indiana, and New York.
Note Many katydids, including this species, can be collected with a sweep net in meadows, on fence rows, and in vegetation along railroad tracks. Nymphs can be kept alive and fed until they reach the adult stage.

Adult specimens should be spread in same manner as butterflies and moths, although usually only the wings on the right sides are set.

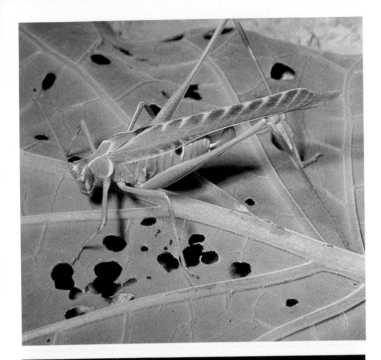

25 ARETHEAE GRACILIPES PAPAGO
Papago Thread-legged Katydid

Family Tettigoniidae
Order Orthoptera
Length 30–33 mm.
Recognition marks Green body, with colored stripe on side of abdomen; legs are long, stiltlike, and very thin; antennae are very long, hairlike, extending well beyond the end of the abdomen.
Habitat Found on grasses and weeds along roadsides, meadows; attracted to lights at night.
Distribution Arizona to California. A similar species occurs in eastern United States.
Note Both the western species illustrated here and the eastern species, *A. phalangium*, are very fragile. Take care when collecting these insects to prevent breaking off legs and antennae even of living specimens. When dried they are very likely to lose their appendages unless carefully handled.

W

26 NEDUBA CARINATA
Carinated Shield-back Katydid

Family Dectidae
Order Orthoptera
Length 20–40 mm.
Recognition marks Brownish body; pronotum is striped or mottled with light tan; wings are short.
Habitat A common bush, shrub, and tree-dwelling species.
Distribution Pacific Coast States and British Columbia.
Note The family Dectidae are often called the shield-backed grasshoppers or katydids. They resemble crickets more than other orthopterans. Their dull color is an effective camouflage when hiding on branches and trunks. Handle with care because some species can inflict a severe bite. More than sixty species of this family occur in the United States, but most species are western.

W

27 STENOPELMATUS FUSCUS
Jerusalem Cricket

Family Gryllacrididae
Order Orthoptera
Length 30–50 mm.
Recognition marks Brownish body, abdominal segments banded with black; space between eyes is very wide; legs are short with many spines.
Habitat These crickets are very common in arid regions. They are nocturnal, ground-dwelling insects.
Distribution British Columbia to Mexico and east to South Dakota and Colorado.
Note They eat both animal and plant materials; they may be destructive to ornamental plants. They are capable of biting when handled. They can stridulate weakly.

28 OECANTHUS FULTONI
Snowy Tree Cricket

Family Gryllidae
Order Orthoptera
Length 12–14 mm.
Recognition marks Pale green and yellow head and antennal bases. Members of the family Gryllidae have long hairlike antennae. The ovipositor is needlelike; cerci relatively long and stout. The body is somewhat flattened, the head large. The front wings of the male have modified areas which form stridulatory organs. Auditory orgahs are located on the front tibiae. These insects are usually brown, black; some are green (tree crickets).
Habitat Found on deciduous trees and shrubs; feed on aphids. The female can damage young stems and twigs by inserting eggs into incisions made in the twigs.
Distribution Throughout the United States and southern Canada.
Note Cricket songs are probably even more familiar than those of katydids because crickets sometimes invade homes, living in basements, singing during the fall and winter. The snowy tree cricket illustrated here makes a sound "treet-treet-treet," repeated at a very high pitch. These insects are found in trees and shrubs throughout the summer.

29 GRYLLUS ASSIMILIS (Complex)
Field Cricket

Family Gryllidae
Order Orthoptera
Length 14–30 mm.
Recognition marks Brown to black; head is large; wings are relatively short; body is cylindrical, somewhat flattened; abdomen has cerci.
Habitat Very common in fields; often seen in grain fields where they may at times be destructive. Crickets nest in the ground in fields and meadows, but sometimes invade houses to hibernate.
Distribution Throughout North America.
Note Males produce an intermittent shrill song so characteristic that almost everyone can identify this species by the sound alone. During one stage of their life cycle, crickets molt (lower right). They are easily reared in captivity (on lettuce, bread, bone meal, and water) and can be used as fish bait, as well as food for lizards, snakes, and turtles kept in captivity. They are also raised commercially and supplied to schools, colleges, and universities for study and research.

Ground crickets belonging to the genus *Allonemobius* and other species of *Gryllus* include some of the common species of crickets in North America. They too are phytophagous and sometimes cause damage to crops. The true house cricket, *Acheta domestica*, paler than the field cricket and originally from Europe, often enters homes and become pests.

30 GRYLLOTALPA HEXADACTYLA
Northern Mole Cricket

Family Gryllotalpidae
Order Orthoptera
Length 20–40 mm.
Recognition marks Brown, some black; front tibiae and tarsi are adapted for rapid burrowing into loose soil and sand.
Habitat Nocturnal, common in mud and soil along margins of lakes and ponds. Adults retreat into burrow, but they can be heard chirping from inside.
Distribution Eastern North America, south to South America.
Note Although common in their range, they are not easy to collect. They can easily escape by burrowing into loose soil.

W

---

31 DIAPHEROMERA FEMORATA
Walkingstick

Family Phasmatidae
Order Phasmida
Length 68–101 mm.
Recognition marks Brownish, sometimes gray or greenish, head has stripes; middle femora of male is usually banded.
Habitat Phytophagous; found in trees and shrubs where they feed at night. Sometimes they become abundant enough to defoliate forests, especially oak trees. This may weaken the trees and allow other pests or plant disease to invade and destroy the trees.
Distribution Eastern North America, south to Florida, and west to Arizona.
Note Walkingsticks are well camouflaged as twigs or sticks. Some tropical species resemble leaves. This, of course, protects them from predation. In addition, however, some species have a defensive fluid which they secrete, spraying would-be predators.
Walkingsticks are difficult to collect because they stand motionless in the presence of large animals, including humans. Beating branches and foliage may dislodge them. Few species fly, but some come to lights at night where they can be easily captured.

F

32 TIMEMA CALIFORNICA
California Timema

Family Phasmatidae
Order Phasmida
Length 30–35 mm.
Recognition marks Green, sometimes brown or even pinkish; body is stout, less sticklike than other walkingsticks.
Habitat This species of walkingstick is found in chaparral, especially on such plants as *Cercocarpus*, *Ceonothus*, and fir.
Distribution California. Five additional species occur in southwestern United States; considered to be rare.
Note Approximately 700 species of walkingsticks (Phasmida) occur throughout the world, but the majority of them occur in tropical regions. Even in the United States, all but two species are confined to the Southern States or the West Coast.

33 FORFICULA AURICULARIA
European Earwig

Family Forficulidae
Order Dermaptera
Length 10–15 mm.
Recognition marks Brown; antennae are filiform; 14–15 segmented; elytra and legs are lighter in color; forceps of male are large, bowed; those of female are nearly straight.
Habitat Nocturnal, usually scavengers, but this species, which was introduced into the United States from Europe in the early 1900s, sometimes becomes a pest, particularly on roses and other garden flowers, and sometimes on fruit and vegetable crops. They overwinter as adults, and in their search for suitable places to hibernate, they may invade homes. Although they are winged, they seldom fly.
Distribution Cosmopolitan.
Note Despite the name, they have never been known to invade the external ear of humans. The abdominal forceps should not be cause for alarm. Although they may pinch slightly, they are too weak to inflict injury.

34 STAGMOMANTIS CALIFORNICA
California Mantis

Family Mantidae
Order Dictyoptera
Length 45–50 mm.
Recognition marks Green, yellowish, or brown; wings of male are brownish with paler mottling and purplish at base; female wings are shorter than the abdomen, brown, purple, and yellowish orange; forelegs have banded tibiae.
Habitat Common on bushes and low vegetation, and often attracted to lights at night.
Distribution Texas and Colorado west to California. Most of the other 1500 or so species are tropical. Many of the species that occur in the United States have been introduced from other areas, and most of the species are confined to the Southern States.
Note These predaceous insects, as all mantids, are skilled at stalking prey. Their ability to rotate their head exceeds that of most insects and gives them a distinct advantage in locating prey. Nymphs as well as adults are not only predaceous but cannabalistic as well. During the courtship stage of mating, the female may toss the male off her back and decapitate him. The headless male then mounts the female and copulation takes place. Apparently the nerves that control the copulatory process are located in the abdominal ganglia of the male. After the female is fertilized, she may consume the rest of the male. Eggs are laid in a mass (lower right photo) which resembles papier-mâché. The shape of the egg mass is characteristic of the species. The winter months are usually spent in the egg stage.
One can easily collect mantid egg cases in most areas of the United States and southern Canada. Harvest them in late fall and keep them in a cold place until spring. Be sure food is available for the nymphs or they will eat one another. Tiny nymphs may eat bits of meat, but will survive better on fruit fly larvae, and soon fruit fly adults. Finally feed them house flies. They require a great amount of food, so if kept several to a cage, they must be fed often.

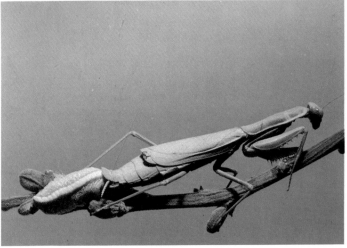

35 BLABERUS CRANIIFER
Death's Head Cockroach

Family Blaberidae
Order Dictyoptera
Length 30–50 mm.
Recognition marks Pronotum is greatly extended over the head; antennae are long and filiform; brown with yellow and black markings; wings extend beyond the end of the abdomen.
Habitat This is a wild cockroach that lives in forest litter as a scavenger. Occasionally it enters buildings and becomes a pest. Although tropical and unable to tolerate cold weather, it is sometimes transported in shipments of food to northern regions. So far it has not become established in the North.
Distribution Tropical America, native in United States only at Key West, Florida.
Note This is the largest cockroach in our region and is therefore often reared and used as an experimental animal in physiology classes. It is necessary to obtain a permit from the United States Department of Agriculture to raise and ship this insect.

36 ARENIVAGA BOLLIANA
Desert Cockroach

Family Polyphagidae
Order Dictyoptera
Length 15–25 mm.
Recognition marks Male is brown with long wings; female is black and wingless; front femora of males are hairy at the base and ventral margin with a row of closely placed, spinelike setae.
Habitat Live in the nests of wood rats; males are attracted to lights at night.
Distribution Texas. There are several additional species of *Arenivaga*, most of which occur in the desert regions of southwestern United States and Mexico. One species lives in palmetto leaves in Florida.
Note These cockroaches and other wild species are generally not collected because of the special methods needed to find them. They are scavengers, living on decaying plant and animal material. They provide a source of food for lizards, snakes, and other desert animals.

37 BLATTELLA GERMANICA
German Cockroach

Family Blattellidae
Order Dictyoptera
Length 8–13 mm.
Recognition marks Adults are light brown; both sexes are winged; two dark longitudinal stripes on the pronotum.
Habitat Common in kitchens and bathrooms of homes and public buildings, especially in areas of high humidity and where food particles are likely to be present. This cockroach, as are all species, is nocturnal. It is probably the most common "domestic" cockroach.
Distribution Throughout North America; probably introduced from Africa on slave ships, or in European supply ships.
Note The complete life cycle takes 3–4 months. The female deposits her eggs in a capsule, or ootheca, which she carries around with her, attached to the end of her abdomen. It is dropped just before hatching. The nymphs must compete for food by themselves.
Cockroaches do not bite. The spines on their legs may cause a minor irritation if handled. Except in the most filthy conditions, cockroaches do not spread disease. In fact there is evidence that they secrete bactericidal substances from their tarsal pads which prevent the transmission of pathogens.

H

---

38 HAPLOEMBIA SOLIERI
Webspinner

Family Oligotomidae
Order Embidiina
Length 4–7 mm.
Recognition marks Elongate, cylindrical, slightly flattened; antennae are filiform; females are always wingless; males are winged or wingless; cerci are short; basal segment of fore tarsi is enlarged to contain a silk-producing gland; legs are short; body is yellow to brown.
Habitat All webspinners, including this species, live in colonies but they are not social in the sense of ants and termites because they do not have castes. The colonies are under bark, stones, or in forest litter near the base of trees. Their silken galleries look like tubes or mats of silk. They feed upon moss, lichens, dead leaves, and bark.
Distribution Southern States from Florida to California.
Note These insects are poorly known even after years of study by Dr. E. S. Ross of the California Academy of Sciences, the world authority on the group. They are, however, easy to raise in vials and jars on dried leaves and some water. Once a colony is established, it will continue indefinitely with little attention.

W

39 ZOOTERMOPSIS ANGUSTICOLLIS
Dampwood Termite

Family Hodotermitidae
Order Isoptera
Length 23–26 mm.
Recognition marks Brownish; wings are gray; soldiers have reddish heads; ocelli are absent; antennae of soldiers have twenty-three segments; 3-segmented cerci; mandibles of soldiers are large and toothed.
Habitat This and related species attack lumber, utility poles, and trunks of dead trees. They do not need ground contact to maintain their colony.
Distribution West Coast States; related species in southern United States and Mexico.
Note Dampwood termites, so-called because they do not form tunnels from the ground but live entirely within the wood itself, can be severe pests and go undetected for a long period of time. The species illustrated here is known to cause considerable damage to buildings and various wood products.
This group of termites have no worker caste. The majority of individuals in a colony are nymphs who work. Eventually they develop into soldiers or reproductives. A new colony is formed by the nuptial pair (upper right photo) which leaves its original nests after developing wings. When they reach a suitable site, they shed their wings and mate. Eggs are laid, hatch, and a new colony is formed. Eventually the queen (lower right photo) becomes greatly enlarged with eggs.

RETICULITERMES HESPERUS
Subterranean Termite

Family Rhinotermitidae
Order Isoptera
Length 6–8 mm.
Recognition marks Brown to blackish; wings are dark; soldier's head is yellow; mandibles are black; head has a conspicuous fontanelle, a pore in the front of the head.
Habitat This is a subterranean termite which needs ground contact from which to build tunnels into wood. The winged reproductive (upper right photo) takes part in colonizing flights, usually during the day following a rainy period. From these a new termite colony is formed. After a short flight they drop to the ground, shed their wings, and dig in. Eventually the worker caste develops and takes over the duties first performed by the reproductives. Once there are enough workers and soldiers (lower right photo) to care for the colony, it will continue to grow.
Distribution Western North America. A similar species, *R. flavipes*, the eastern subterranean termite is found throughout eastern North America.
Note Faulty construction practices account for most of the termite damage in this country. Wood buried at a building site can form the nucleus for a colony. Workers will construct runways across concrete foundations to get to the wood of buildings. Unless barriers are placed on top of foundations and all wood in contact with the soil is chemically treated, termites may cause grave structural damage.

41 ZOROTYPUS SNYDERI
Zorapteran

Family Zorotypidae
Order Zoraptera
Length ±2 mm.
Recognition marks Robust, cylindrical; brown to dark brown or blackish; head is rather small; antennae are short, 9-segmented; thorax has three distinct segments; legs are short, rather stout; wings on thoracic segments are widely separated at the base, hind wings are smaller than front wings, both with reduced venation.
Habitat Frequently found in old sawdust piles; some have been discovered in termite colonies. They are scavengers.
Distribution Florida and the West Indies.
Note Zorapterans might be confused with small termites and some barklice, but the 9-segmented antennae and lack of any caste system help to distinguish them. These are rare insects and little is known about them.

42 ECHMEPTERYX HAGENI
Scaly-winged Psocid

Family Lepdopsocidae
Order Pscoptera
Length 1.5–5 mm.
Recognition marks Brown, head grayish with brown markings; brown scales on thorax; brown scales on forewings.
Habitat Occur on tree trunks and branches. They run rapidly and will take flight to escape capture. Most specimens are females.
Distribution Eastern United States and southeastern Canada.
Note Psocids are studied by only a few specialists. The order is apparently a large one, but the species are hard to collect, small, and appear rather less interesting than the more showy insects. However, they play a large role in nature's economy, principally as scavengers, important in the detritus cycle. Some reports show that psocids are among the first to invade newly formed islands, which indicates that the group is probably actively occupying new niches and forming new species in a rapid state of evolution.

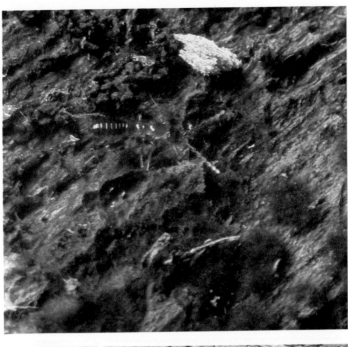

43 LAEMOBOTHRION MAXIMUM
Hawk Louse

Family Laemobothriidae
Order Mallophaga
Length 6.5–11 mm.
Recognition marks Each side of the head has prominent enlargements in front of the eyes near the base of the antennae.
Habitat Ectoparasites of hawks and osprey.
Distribution Throughout North America where their hosts live.
Note Bird lice females cement their eggs onto the feathers of their host. The nymphs hatch and join the adults in feeding on pieces of feathers and on skin secretions. They are also known to feed on mites that also infest the host. These pests are bloodsuckers and cause swelling and blood secretion from the lesion. This furthers the irritation which may then weaken the host.

W

---

44 PEDICULUS HUMANUS
Body and Head Louse

Family Pediculidae
Order Anoplura
Length 2.5–3.5 mm.
Recognition marks Head is narrow; body is flattened; legs have distinct claws; brown to yellow-brown or pale.
Habitat Ectoparasites of humans, these lice live on hairy parts of the body other than the head and pubic area. The eggs, or nits, are glued to hairs or clothing. Lice also cling to clothing and can thus be spread from person to person, as well as by direct body contact. The life cycle is completed in about one month.
Distribution Cosmopolitan.
Note The body louse, or cootie, is a vector of human disease, including epidemic typhus, trench fever, and relapsing fever. The presence of lice lesions on the skin is known as pediculosis and can be a serious problem if the lice are not controlled by some type of insecticide in shampoo or cream. The head louse, a more common variety, is transmitted by combs, brushes, and head rests. The pubic louse, or crab, lives only on pubic hairs and is obtained through direct contact with infected persons.

D

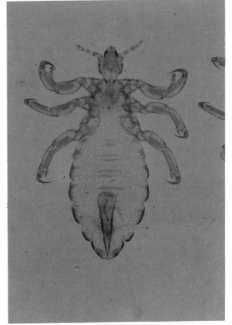

45 SCIRTOTHRIPS CITRI
Citrus Thrips

Family Thripidae
Order Thysanoptera
Length 1–1.4 mm.
Recognition marks Antennae are 8-segmented; maxillary palpi are 3-segmented; wings have fringe of hairs; male is smaller than female.
Habitat Pests of citrus flowers; also on flowers of a variety of shrubs and trees.
Distribution Arizona and California; related species throughout North America.
Note Thrips are common insects usually associated with flowers. Their sucking mouthparts damage the flowers of many ornamentals and stunt the growth of fruit and seeds. They may also be vectors of plant disease. As a group they are generally beneficial because many species are predaceous and help to control certain plant pests.

G

46 BELOSTOMA FLUMINEA
Giant Water Bug

Family Belostomatidae
Order Hemiptera
Length 40–55 mm.
Recognition marks Body is oval, somewhat flattened; brownish; front legs are adapted for grasping prey; hind legs are flattened and serve as swimming paddles; abdomen has terminal breathing tube.
Habitat Some species of this group deposit their eggs on aquatic vegetation, but others glue their eggs to the back of the male where they are carried until they hatch. They are very common in freshwater ponds.
Distribution Eastern and central United States south to Texas.
Note These bugs are easily collected in dip nets, but they can inflict a very painful bite and should be handled carefully. These very large insects are both excellent flyers and swimmers. They are predators of other insects, tadpoles, small frogs, small fish, and other water creatures. They are attracted to electric lights in large numbers and, therefore, are sometimes called electric light bugs.

W

47 PELOCORIS FEMORATUS
Creeping Water Bug

Family   Naucoridae
Order   Hemiptera
Length   5–12 mm.
Recognition marks   Oval, dull yellowish brown; front legs are enlarged and raptorial with long claws on the middle and hind legs; legs are not adapted for swimming but are used to crawl on vegetation; they resemble small Belostomatidae.
Habitat   These predaceous insects are found in streams and ponds among aquatic vegetation; they are inconspicuous until they move. They also hide under stones, making them difficult to find and collect.
Distribution   Very common in eastern United States west to the Mississippi River. Other species are found in southeastern United States, and some in the southwestern states.
Note   The best way to collect these insects is by gathering some aquatic vegetation and bottom muck. Carefully remove the plant material and search through the bottom debris.

48 GERRIS REMIGIS
Water Strider

Family   Gerridae
Order   Hemiptera
Length   4–5 mm.
Recognition marks   Slender, elongated; black; legs are long, stiltlike; wings are usually absent.
Habitat   Commonly found "skating" over the surface of the water of ponds and streams. The hairlike setae on the feet make an impression in the water that resembles boots or skates in outline. These dimples in the water are characteristic of insects of this family only.
Distribution   There are over twenty species in North America, many of which are widely distributed.
Note   Identification of the species is possible only by the use of technical keys and descriptions. Some members of this family are the only truly marine insects known. Members of the genus *Halobates* are wingless and spend their entire lives on the surface of the ocean far out at sea. They lay their eggs on seaweed, floating debris, and sometimes on other aquatic animals. They are predaceous and capture their prey by means of the raptorial forelegs. Their diet includes small insects and crustaceans of various kinds.

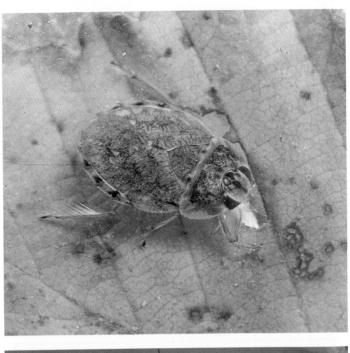

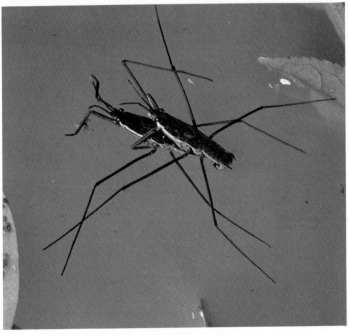

49 NOTONECTA UNDULATA
Backswimmer

Family Notonectidae
Order Hemiptera
Length 10–18 mm.
Recognition marks Dorsal surface of the body is convex, usually light cream, sometimes slightly reddish; ventral surface is flat; hindlegs are long with fringes of hair used for swimming; forelegs are adapted for grasping prey.
Habitat These bugs swim on their backs, holding their legs above the surface of the water, creating an oarlike effect. They are predaceous, feeding on insects and other aquatic organisms in ponds and slow-moving streams. They deposit their eggs on aquatic vegetation.
Distribution Common throughout the United States.
Note Three genera occur in North America, north of Mexico, but the majority of species occur in the Southern States. Their wings are well developed. The adults become pests when they are attracted to swimming pools at night by the lights around pools. Pool covers, use of light traps around pools, and orange lights will reduce the problem. They are very clumsy on land and can bite if handled. They are sometimes known as water bees because their bite is painful and similar to that of a bee sting.

50 CLOSTEROCORIS AMOENUS
Plant Bug

Family Miridae
Order Hemiptera
Length 6–8 mm.
Recognition marks Body is narrow and elongate; eyes are some distance from the pronotal collar; pronotum is triangular, and the collar region is flattened; first segment of hind tarsi is elongated.
Habitat Nymphs and adults of this and related species are plant-juice feeders. Many are host specific, but others are widely distributed and feed on any plant soft enough for them to penetrate the epidermis with their sucking mouthparts.
Distribution Western United States, with related species throughout North America.
Note Several hundred species of Miridae are found in North America. This is the largest family of true bugs with more than 5,000 species in the world. Many are serious pests of forage and field crops in particular, but few plants are immune to their beaks. The species are similar in appearance. They are under 10 mm long and soft-bodied; antennae are 4-segmented; forewing has a cuneus, a triangularly apical piece of the basal part of the wing which is set off from the rest of the front wing, a characteristic of this family in particular. Identification is very difficult and requires technical literature and a great amount of special study. Sweep nets passed over grass and weeds will yield vast numbers of these bugs. They must be carefully mounted on paper points.

51 HORCIAS DISLOCATUS
Yellow Plant Bug

Family Miridae
Order Hemiptera
Length ±6.5 mm.
Recognition marks Reddish orange with large spots on the scutellum; wing membrane is black.
Habitat This species feeds on false Solomon's seal, wild geranium and other plants, especially those in moist, shaded areas.
Distribution Northeastern United States west to Minnesota and south to Texas.
Note The color of this species is exceedingly variable. The insect is very common, with certain color varieties typical of certain localities.

52 DACERLA MEDIOSPINOSA
Ant Bug

Family Miridae
Order Hemiptera
Length 4–6 mm.
Recognition marks Their shape is antlike; the pronotum has a raised posterior margin forming a spinelike projection; yellow; the head is dark brown or black; the abdomen is dark brown; the apical half of the front wings is dark.
Habitat On lupines with ants.
Note Mimicry is not uncommon among the true bugs. Some resemble ants, as in this case. This is undoubtedly the mimic, the ant the model. It is believed that the bug is predatory on aphids and mimics the ant to trick the aphids who are ''friendly'' to the ants. It may be that the bugs like the aphid honeydew and as mimics can sneak in and feast without attracting the attention of the ants.

53 PSELLIOPUS CINCTUS
Assassin Bug

Family Reduviidae
Order Hemiptera
Length 12–13 mm.
Recognition marks Dull orange; head and front lobe of the pronotum are marked with black and white; legs and first two segments of antennae have black and white bands.
Habitat Predaceous upon insects; found on shrubs and other vegetation, particularly in meadows.
Distribution Eastern North America.
Note Assassin bugs (Reduviidae) form a large family, many species of which are common predatory bugs. Most species have either oval or elongated bodies, with elongated heads and stout sucking mouthparts. There is a median longitudinal groove on the underside of the prothorax that is minutely, transversely striated. The beak fits into this groove and by moving the head up and down, rubs against the striations to produce a squeaking sound. The front femora are usually enlarged. Some species are bloodsuckers and attack mammals and even humans. The wheel bug, *Arilus cristatus,* is a very large species with a semicircular crest on the pronotum which resembles a cogwheel. This species can inflict a severe bite. Members of the genus *Tritoma* are bloodsucking insects in southwestern United States and Central America and are vectors of Chagas disease, a form of sleeping sickness.

54 PHYMATA AMERICANA
Ambush Bug

Family Phymatidae
Order Hemiptera
Length 8.5–9.5 mm.
Recognition marks Yellow and brown or yellow and black, sometimes greenish; front femora are greatly enlarged, front legs are raptorial.
Habitat Predatory insects found on a wide variety of flowers where they await bees and other insects as well as spiders. Their coloration matches that of the flowers, providing excellent camouflage.
Distribution Throughout the United States.
Note The family Phymatidae, the ambush bugs, have relatively few species in our area, but some are common and may be found in the flowers' heads of almost every plant, especially toward the end of summer and in the fall.

55   CORYTHUCA CILIATA
Sycamore Lace Bug

Family   Tingidae
Order   Hemiptera
Length   ±5 mm.
Recognition marks   Pronotum and front wings have elaborate lacelike sculpturing; antennae and beak are both 4-segmented; grayish to white.
Habitat   This species occurs most commonly on sycamore trees, often in such large numbers that the leaves turn white from loss of sap and fall off prematurely. It also infests ash, hickory and mulberry.
Distribution   Across southern Canada and northern United States.
Note   This is a moderately large family. This genus alone contains nearly fifty species which are difficult to identify to species without the aid of the technical literature. Many, if not most, of the lace bugs are pests. They deposit their eggs on the leaves of trees and shrubs. Both the nymphs and the adults feed extensively and reproduce rapidly, causing serious damage to the plant. Collect by beating leaves and branches of tree. They also hide in crevices in bark of trees. These small bugs must be mounted on paper points.

---

56   ARADUS ACUTUS
Flat Bark Bug

Family   Aradidae
Order   Hemiptera
Length   5–8 mm.
Recognition marks   Body is oval and very flat; usually dark brown; abdomen extends beyond the wings.
Habitat   Usually on oak.
Distribution   Throughout North America.
Note   These flat bugs are found on or under bark where they feed upon fungus. To collect them, strip off bark, or carefully examine the cracks in bark. When disturbed, they drop to the ground, sometimes making it possible to find them by collecting ground litter and placing it in a Berlese funnel. About seventy-five species of the genus *Aradus* alone occur in the United States. They are difficult to identify to species.

57 LYGAEUS KALMII
Small Milkweed Bug

Family Lygaeidae
Order Hemiptera
Length 8–10 mm.
Recognition marks Red and black with a red spot on the top of the head; red of the wing forms a broad X-shaped area.
Habitat Both this species and the large milkweed bug (see note below) are found in large numbers on the seed pods and flower heads of the common milkweeds. Adults are abundant until the first frost, after which they seek out plant debris, small logs, or even houses under and in which to hibernate.
Distribution Throughout the entire United States.
Note The large milkweed bug, *Oncopeltus fasciatus*, is 17–18 mm (0.66–0.7 in.) in length with a Y-shaped head marking and two broad transverse orange bands across the wings. Both species are easy to rear. The large milkweed bug is often used for physiological studies or demonstrations. The sex of the large milkweed bug can be distinguished by observing the ventral surface: the female has black spots on the two posterior abdominal segments; the male has a black spot on only the last segment.

58 DYSDERCUS SUTURELLUS
Cotton Stainer

Family Pyrrhocoridae
Order Hemiptera
Length 11–17 mm.
Recognition marks Usually bright red and black; front femora are never thickened; head is inserted in the thorax to the eyes; beak is elongated and reaches the abdomen.
Habitat Phytophagous, found on cotton.
Distribution Florida and adjacent southeastern states.
Note Only seven species of this relatively large tropical family occur in the United States. This species is a serious pest and it also carries a fungus which causes the staining of the cotton fibers. It is also commonly found on hibiscus species and solanum species, and sometimes on oranges.

59 DYSDERCUS ANDREAE
St. Andrew's Cotton Bug

Family Pyrrhocoridae
Order Hemiptera
Length 8–11.5 mm.
Recognition marks Bright red with a prominent white "St. Andrew's Cross" marking on the front wings.
Habitat Phytophagous, living on low vegetation; often a pest of cotton, dwarfing the bolls and staining the fibers.
Distribution Georgia, Florida, and the West Indies.
Note Most species of the family Pyrrhocoridae are marked with bright yellow, red, brown, and white, generally thought to be warning colors. All species in our area are confined to the Southern States where they are referred to as "red bugs" or "cotton stainers." When they infest cotton they leave a red stain on the cotton fibers which renders the cotton unsuitable for market.

C

60 ACANTHOCEPHALA TERMINALIS
Leaf-footed Bug

Family Coreidae
Order Hemiptera
Length 10–20 mm.
Recognition marks Dark brown; head is narrower than the pronotum; front wing has many veins in the membrane; hind tibiae are expanded and leaflike.
Habitat Found on trees, shrubs, and weeds; phytophagous.
Distribution Eastern United States west to Colorado and south to Florida and Texas.
Note Members of this family are generally rather large. They are sometimes called squash bugs. The true squash bug is the common *Anasa tristis*, often a serious pest of cucurbits. Over 100 species of this family occur in North America. One of the most spectacular species is the large (±20 mm; 0.8 in.) *Leptoglossus phyllopus*, which has greatly expanded hind tibiae and is a pest of truck crops in the southeastern states. Other species are common on mesquite and other desert plants in the southern arid states. They are often collected in sweep nets. When handled they give off an unpleasant but harmless odor.

W

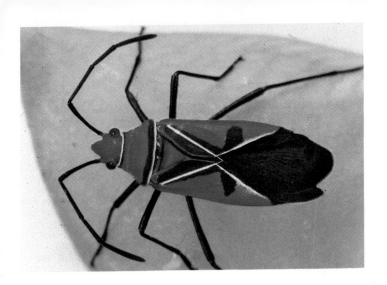

STIRETRUS ANCHORAGO
Shield-back Bug

Family Scutelleridae
Order Hemiptera
Length 8–11 mm.
Recognition marks Blue and white or yellow and orange and red; color markings are variable: note anchor on some (upper right photo), which may be obscure on others (lower right photo).
Habitat Predaceous, feeding on the larvae of beetles, butterflies, and moths.
Distribution Eastern United States west to the Great Plains.
Note These bugs are closely related to the stink bugs, family Pentatomidae. Most species of both families are predaceous, some are phytophagous, and some are both. The eggs are usually barrel-shaped and are laid in groups on the underside of leaves or on stems. Adults and nymphs produce a disagreeable odor from special glands located on the abdomen (of nymphs) and thorax (of adults). Some stink bugs and shield-back bugs are agricultural pests; others are beneficial and attempts have been made to use them for biological control.

62 MEGANTIA HISTRONICA
Harlequin Bug

Family Pentatomidae
Order Hemiptera
Length 9–11.5 mm.
Recognition marks Shiny black or deep blue with prominent red and orange irregular markings.
Habitat Found on cabbage and related vegetables. Eggs are white with two black bands and a white spot. They are deposited directly on the leaves of the plants and resemble rows of small barrels. Adults hibernate during the winter.
Distribution Eastern United States west to Colorado, south to Florida, Texas, and California.
Note The harlequin bug is sometimes called the calico bug or fire bug. It is a serious pest of cruciferous plants, especially in the Southern States. Over 180 species of stink bugs occur in North America north of Mexico. Among those that are pests, in addition to the species described here, is *Acrosternum hilare*, a pest of soybeans, known as the green stink bug, and *Euschistus variolarius*, the one-spot stink bug, which feeds on berries and fruits of various kinds.

C

---

63 PODISUS MACULATUS
Spined Stink Bug

Family Pentatomidae
Order Hemiptera
Length 11–13.5 mm.
Recognition marks Sharp spine on each side of the pronotum; light brown, sometimes marked with purplish red.
Habitat Predaceous, found on tall weeds in alluvial soils along streams and in dense woodlands. The adults are active from May to October. (This species feeds on the larvae of a swallowtail butterfly.)
Distribution Throughout United States.
Note Stink bugs can be collected easily by sweeping in weeds, meadows, along streams and near woodlands. Specimens are usually large enough to be pinned. The disagreeable odor they produce is not harmful.

W

64 PERILLUS BIOCULATUS
Eyed Stink Bug

Family Pentatomidae
Order Hemiptera
Length 8.5–12 mm.
Recognition marks Brightly marked stink bug with the scutellum, corium, and thorax margined with red, yellow, white, or orange, but the color is extremely variable.
Habitat Predaceous. This is an important predator upon the Colorado potato beetles, *Leptinotarsa decemlineata*.
Distribution Widely distributed throughout the United States.
Note This species has been introduced into Europe in an attempt to control the Colorado potato beetle in that area.

65 TIBICEN CANICULARIS
Dog Day Cicada

Family Cicadidae
Order Homoptera
Length 50–60 mm.
Recognition marks The antennae are short and filimentous; the legs are slender; males have sound producing organs at the base of the abdomen on the ventral side. Usually green, with clear membranous wings.
Habitat Adults of this common species appear in the late summer. Males characteristically emit a loud buzzing sound during hot August days, and this usually extends into September. After mating, females deposit eggs in twigs of shrubs and small trees. The eggs may overwinter, or they may hatch and drop to the ground. The nymphs dig into the soil and spend a number of years (in this species usually not more than two years) in the ground feeding on the roots of trees.
Distribution Throughout eastern United States, south to Florida, and west into California.
Note The principle damage done by cicadas is to small trees by the egg-laying process. Cicadas are not easy to collect unless one is lucky enough to find the nymph in its last nymphal skin. If this is placed in a jar on a stick, the adult will soon emerge, the wings will unfold and harden to form a beautiful fresh specimen. Males will soon sing, thus attracting the females.

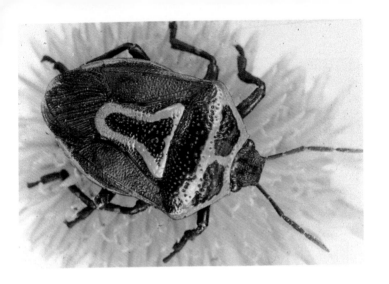

66 MAGICICADA SPECIES
17-Year Cicada

Family Cicadidae
Order Homoptera
Length 19–33 mm.
Recognition marks Black with clear wings and red wing veins; eyes are usually red.
Habitat There are six species of the periodical cicadas, each differing in color, size, song, and life cycle. Illustrated here is the 17-year cicada, so-called because the nymph takes seventeen years to mature and emerge from the soil. Other species which look much like this one take only thirteen years to mature and are called 13-year cicadas. The latter species are generally southern, while the seventeen-year kind are northern. The life habits are very similar to the preceding species but periodical cicadas emerge in a large brood in a particular area from year to year. These brood have been carefully mapped and it is now possible to determine when and where they will emerge. This is important for fruit growers who can thus plan to avoid brood damage to the twigs of the young trees.
Distribution Eastern United States west to Iowa.
Note When brood emerges they are so abundant they can be collected by hand. However, the noise made by the males can cause injury to the ears.

67 UMBONIA CRASSICORNIS
Horned Treehopper

Family Membracidae
Order Homoptera
Length ±5 mm.
Recognition marks Yellow; pronotum is modified into a thornlike projection which is dark at the tip; wing is transparent.
Habitat Phytophagous. These insects are abundant on trees and shrubs of various kinds.
Distribution Florida; related species occur throughout the United States, but they are most abundant in the south.
Note Insects of the family Membracidae are commonly called treehoppers. They are all phytophagous, common on field vegetation, as well as on shrubs and trees. They can generally be recognized by the modifications of the large prothorax. Eggs are deposited on the host plant in slits made in the bark. This oviposition habit may cause damage to the plant in addition to the damage caused by the feeding of the nymphs and adults.

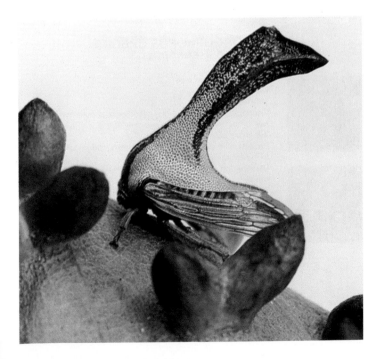

68 SPHONGOPHORUS SPECIES
Sponged Treehopper

Family Membracidae
Order Homoptera
Length ±6 mm.
Recognition marks Yellowish brown; prothorax is greatly enlarged and modified as illustrated; wings are yellowish.
Habitat Phytophagous; common on trees and bushes; these insects are capable of jumping when disturbed even though they do not have enlarged hind femora.
Distribution Southwestern United States, Mexico, and Central America.
Note Various species of the family Membracidae range in size from 5–13 mm (0.2–0.5 in.). These small jumping insects are astoundingly modified in almost grotesque ways. The pronotum extends over the abdomen; some may be humped, others spined, ridged, or ornamented with hooks, spines, or barbs. Tropical species are quite bizarre.

---

69 SPHONGOPHORUS SPECIES
Antlered Treehopper

Family Membracidae
Order Homoptera
Length ±5 mm.
Recognition marks Brown; prothorax is modified with tree-like branches extending anteriorly and posteriorly, covering the entire body.
Habitat Phytophagous, usually inhabitating trees, often high in the foliage out of reach of collectors.
Distribution Southwestern United States, Mexico, and Central America.
Note Treehoppers are common in most areas of the United States and Canada on field vegetation. Although they are not as bizarre as the tropical species, many resemble thorns. One common species is the buffalo treehopper, *Stictocephala bubalus*, a green treehopper about 8 mm (0.3 in.) in length. This species is often a serious pest of ornamentals because of the damage they do to the plants by oviposition.

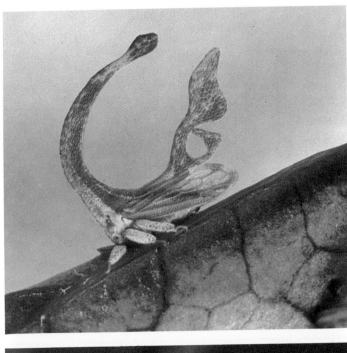

70 PHILAENUS SPUMARIUS
Spittle Bug

Family Cercopidae
Order Homoptera
Length 6–8 mm.
Recognition marks Brownish with paler mottled markings; head is broad; body is somewhat flattened.
Habitat Common in forage crops and grains.
Distribution Pacific Northwest south to California, east to northeastern United States, south to South Carolina.
Note Froghoppers or spittle bugs deposit their eggs on plants. The nymphs suck plant juices and produce a "spittle" that is voided from the anus. Nymphs surround themselves in spittle as a means of protection, but this material is troublesome to growers. It can clot farm machinery by wetting down the plants and entangling the stems in the machine.
Adults (and unfortunately, nymphs) may be collected by sweeping vegetation (but the nymphal spittle makes a mess of the net) in cultivated crops as well as in pastures and meadows.

71 GRAPHOCEPHALA COCCINEA
Redbanded Leafhopper

Family Cicadellidae
Order Homoptera
Length 8–9 mm.
Recognition marks Green with red markings; legs are yellow; head has yellow marking; ventral surface is yellow. Leafhoppers, family Cicadellidae, vary from 3–12 mm; body is wedge-shaped; usually green or brown, but many species are brightly marked with red, yellow, or blue.
Habitat Phytophagous; found on blackberry and various other garden and ornamental plants.
Distribution Common throughout the United States.
Note These species are very similar to the froghoppers, but they differ by having one or more rows of spines on the hind tibiae. There are more than 2500 species in North America north of Mexico, making this the largest family of the Homoptera. They are active species capable of rapid running, jumping, and flying. All species are plant-juice suckers; none are known to suck blood. Many species are of considerable economic importance. The potato leafhopper, *Empoasca fabae,* is a pest of several truck crops. Leafhoppers produce "honeydew" which is emitted from the anus and includes sugar from plant juices. This material is attractive to ants which may tend the leafhoppers as they do certain aphids.

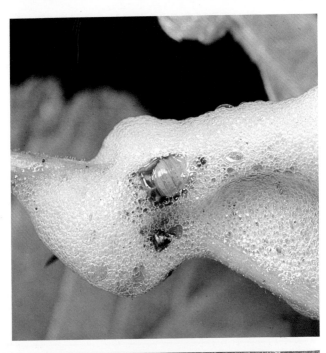

72 DRAECULACEPHALA SPECIES
Vampire Leafhopper

Family   Cicadellidae
Order   Homoptera
Length   5–7 mm.
Recognition marks   Green; front wings reticulate veined on apical third; head is elongated, usually longer than the pronotum.
Habitat   Species of this genus are found especially abundant in low swampy land and feed on coarse grasses and sedges.
Distribution   Species are common throughout eastern North America, with representatives throughout North America including tropical regions.
Note   Leafhoppers are all phytophagous, feeding on a wide variety of plants. This results in the transmission of bacterial and fungal plant diseases which probably cause more crop loss than the attack from the insects.

73 METCALFIA PRUINOSA
Planthopper

Family   Fulgoridae
Order   Homoptera
Length   5–8 mm.
Recognition marks   White, appears to be covered with powder; eyes and parts of the body are light brown.
Habitat   This species is a pest of citrus fruit as well as many other species of woody plants. Note the egg scars on the branch.
Distribution   Throughout eastern North America, west to the Rocky Mountains and south to Texas, New Mexico, Arizona, California, and Mexico.
Note   The family Fulgoridae is characterized by a few large spines on the hind tibiae, the filamentous short antennae that rise below the compound eyes, and a reticulated anal area on the front wings. Our species have the broad head, often with a cephalic horn, and they are usually brownish. Tropical species, however, may be as large as 50 mm (2 in.), have greatly enlarged heads, and are often brightly colored.

This phytophagous group usually does not cause serious economic loss to cultivated crops even though they are widely distributed. They are seldom as abundant as the related leafhoppers and treehoppers. Nymphs and adults produce honeydew and some nymphs also produce waxy, white, taillike filaments from the end of the abdomen.

74 TRIALEURODES VAPORARIORUM
Greenhouse Whitefly

Family Aleyrodidae
Order Homoptera
Length ±1.5 mm.
Recognition marks The fore wing is white, abdomen is pale yellow; thorax and legs, head, and antennae are pale buff, the tip of the head black; eyes are divided; body is covered with mealy white wax. Male is smaller than female. The insects belonging to the family Aleyrodidae are all small, 3 mm (0.1 in.), or less in length, wings and body opaque, in our species, whitish, more or less mealy. The wings of some species are marked with dark spots or bands.
Habitat This is a pest in greenhouses and on house plants; during the summer months they may become garden pests.
Distribution Cosmopolitan.
Note Although these insects are considered to have incomplete metamorphosis, there is a pupal stage. Eggs, nymphs, and adults are found on the underside of the leaves of various plants. The species described here and a few others are important pests. The majority of the species live in the tropics. This insect survives in the north only because it is protected by the temperature of homes and greenhouses.

---

75 APHIS SALICETI
Willow Aphid

Family Aphidae
Order Homoptera
Length ±4 mm.
Recognition marks Rust-red, pink, to apple green; cornicles at end of the abdomen are as long as the filament of the antennal segment six; prominent tubercles on dorsal surface of cauda (tail).
Habitat This is an aphid inhabiting both willow and species of the carrot family, including parsnips and fennel. It is considered to be a serious pest.
Distribution Widely distributed throughout North America.
Note The photo (right) captures ants in the act of tending these aphids, commonly referred to as the ants' "cows." The cornicles produce a honeydew cherished by the ants. In return, the aphids receive protection from the ants who ward off predators. Aphids belong to four different families. It is a very large group of insects, the species of which are difficult to identify without careful study, examination under a microscope, and by referring to the technical literature. The life cycle of various species of aphids differ greatly. Unlike most insects, they undergo stages wherein reproduction takes place parthenogenetically, mainly during the summer months when food is abundant. In the fall, sexual reproduction takes place and eggs are laid, the stage in which most aphids pass the winter.

76 ICERYA PURCHASI
Cottony Cushion Scale

Family Margarodidae
Order Homoptera
Length 6–8 mm.
Recognition marks Scales are reddish brown; the female has a large fluted egg sac which protrudes from the end of the body. This sac contains many bright red eggs.
Habitat Found on different woody ornamental plants, including maple, boxwood, pecan, walnut, and citrus. Unlike most other scales, this species retains its legs and is able to move about on the host plant. The young scales hatch inside the female, then crawl out and wander about the plant. A serious pest, it has been brought under control by a ladybird beetle, the vedalia, *Rodolia cardinalis*, which is an aggressive feeder on the scale. This is a good example of successful biological control of an insect pest.
Distribution North Carolina, Florida, Gulf States, Texas, Arizona, and California.
Note The superfamily Coccoidea is divided into about twenty families. The major families include: Coccidae, the wax or tortoise scales; Diaspididae, armored scales; Lacciferidae, lac insects; Margarodidae, giant coccoids, and Pseudococcoidae, mealybugs. Usually scales are destructive to plants, and they are difficult to control. One species, the cochineal scale, *Dactylopius coccus*, is beneficial because it is a source of cochineal dye.

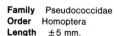

77 PSEUDOCOCCUS CALCOELARIAE
Mealy Bug

Family Pseudococcidae
Order Homoptera
Length ±5 mm.
Recognition marks White to gray; body is covered with waxy secretions.
Habitat Phytophagous; a pest of many cultivated plants, particularly those in homes and in greenhouses; sometimes found on citrus.
Distribution Throughout North America.
Note Mealy bugs are scale insects that secrete a cover of wax giving them a pallid, mealy appearance. Several species are important pests of ornamental plants. They are difficult to control and easily spread by the introduction of infested plants. More than 300 species of the family Pseudococcidae occur throughout the world, but most species are tropical. This species survive on plants raised in a controlled environment.

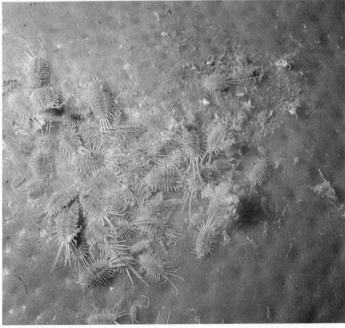

INSECTS WITH COMPLETE METAMORPHOSIS

CHRYSOPA CARNIA
Green Lacewing

Family   Chrysopidae
Order   Neuroptera
Length   9–15 mm.
Recognition marks   Green with pale green wing veins; the wings are transparent, large, extending beyond the abdomen; the body is soft and cylindrical; the antennae are long and filiform; the eyes are golden.
Habitat   Larvae and adults are predaceous upon aphids and other insects including eggs and larvae. They are commonly found on plants that are hosts to other insects. They are nocturnally attracted to lights. When handled they emit a disagreeable odor.
Distribution   Throughout North America.
Note   The eggs (lower left) are laid at the end of a long stalk. The vigorous larvae (lower right) prey upon almost any living thing not too big for them to handle. Newly hatched larvae eat the eggs of other insects. This probably accounts for the stalked eggs of the species because the larvae would eat unhatched eggs within their reach. The larvae have sickle-shaped hollow jaws and are able to grasp their prey, hold it in place, and suck out the contents. The adults (upper right) hatch from a cocoon spun by the larva. These insects and related species are easy to rear, and are especially beneficial in control of moth pests.

79 BRACHYNEMURUS FEROX
Ant Lion

Family Myrmeleontidae
Order Neuroptera
Length 35–40 mm.

Recognition marks Adults are brownish gray to gray; the body is elongate and cylindrical; the antennae are approximately the length of the thorax, and clubbed. These insects resemble dragonflies in size and shape, but differ in that they can fold their wings back over the abdomen and have clubbed antennae. Larvae are somewhat oval, flattened, and have long sickleshaped mandibles.

Habitat The adults are feeble flyers, seldom seen except at lights at night. The larvae, called antlions, are predaceous. They dig a shallow coneshaped pit (lower right) in sand and lie in wait at the bottom, entirely covered by sand except for the poised mandibles, for ants or other insects. The sides of the pit will crumble when the insect struggles to get out, but the larvae mandibles close about the victim and suck its body fluids. The carcass is discarded and the trap is reconstructed.

Distribution Western United States and British Columbia; related species are widely distributed throughout southern United States and Mexico, particularly in sandy areas.

Note The order Neuroptera, probably the most primitive group of insects with complete metamorphosis, is divided into several families which differ greatly in size, shape, and habits. Although these insects have been studied intensely for many years, they remain poorly known.

80 HEMEROBIUS PACIFICA
Brown Lacewing

Family Hemerobiidae
Order Neuroptera
Length 6–12 mm.
Recognition marks The wings are brownish; eyes are dark; they are otherwise very similar to the green lacewings.
Habitat Adults and larvae are predaceous on aphids, mites, and mealy bugs. This species and related species are more common in forests than in fields.
Distribution Western United States.
Note Over fifty species of brown lacewings have been described. The group is mainly western, but some species occur in the east. Among the several families of Neuroptera is Corydalidae, one member of which is the dobsonfly or fishfly. The adult male of the species has very large, but weak mandibles and do not bite. They often appear at lights nocturnally in regions near ponds and streams. Another family, the Sisyridae, or spongillaflies, have aquatic larvae that prey upon freshwater sponges. Members of the family Mantispidae have greatly elongated prothoraxes and raptorial front legs. They can be confused with praying mantids, but are much smaller, brown, and both pairs of wings are membranous. The family Ascalaphidae, or owlflies, have very long clubbed antennae which project in front and are about the same length as the body. Eyes are divided and their body is very "hairy."

W

---

81 CICINDELA REPANDA
Bronze Tiger Beetle

Family Cicindelidae
Order Coleoptera
Length 12–13 mm.
Recognition marks Brownish bronze with somewhat greenish or coppery metallic hue; the margin of the elytra is white, with a variable pattern; the surface of the elytra is granular and punctate.
Habitat On sandy banks and gravel bars of streams and other sandy areas.
Distribution Common throughout United States and southern Canada.
Note Members of the tiger beetle family, Cicindelidae, and especially the genus *Cicindela* are the delight and bane of collectors. They are swift runners and fast fliers. It takes skillful sweeps of the net to catch them, but they are prizes in any insect collection. They are identified to species by color pattern, but these are variable making it necessary to carefully study each specimen in order to name them.

W

82 CICINDELA SPLENDIDA
Splendid Tiger Beetle

Family Cicindelidae
Order Coleoptera
Length 12–15 mm.
Recognition marks Elytral margins are metallic blue or green, strongly contrasting with the disk of the elytra which is brilliantly copper-red or malachite green.
Habitat Usually in sandy areas, particularly in evergreen forests.
Distribution Eastern North America west to the Rocky Mountains.
Note The larvae of tiger beetles are all carnivorous. They make a vertical burrow in the soil, 300 mm (1 foot) deep. The head and thorax is modified to form a plug at the top of the tube. The larva awaits, with open jaws, until a passing insect touches the larva, whereupon the jaws snap closed and a struggle follows. The dorsal surface of the fifth abdominal segment has two pairs of hooks that help prevent larva from being dragged from the hole.

83 OMUS DEJEANI
Dejean's Omus

Family Cicindelidae
Order Coleoptera
Length 15–21 mm.
Recognition marks Black; elytra have numerous very large scattered pits among smaller punctures; rest of the body is nearly smooth.
Habitat In rotten stumps. Adults will bite if handled.
Distribution Common in the Pacific Northwest. Other very similar species occur throughout the western states.
Note Dozens of species of the genus *Omus* have been described, but relatively few are valid names representing natural species. These beetles, except for this species, are relatively rare. Very little is known about their habits or their life history.

84 SCAPHINOTUS ANGUSTICOLLIS
Narrow Snail Eater

Family Carabidae
Order Coleoptera
Length 16–24 mm.
Recognition marks Black with brownish red on elytra and head; pronotum, and elytral margins are somewhat greenish; elytra are slightly sculptured with about twenty striae; both maxillary and labial palpi, each with apical segment enlarged, are spoon-shaped.
Habitat Forests; adults feed on snails and slugs.
Distribution Western coastal area, with relatives throughout North America.
Note Most of the species of the large beetle family Carabidae are predaceous, therefore, beneficial. Other species in the same group as the snail eaters feed on caterpillars. As forest species, they no doubt are important controls of some forest pests.

85 OMOPHRON OBLITERATUM
Hunch-backed Beetle

Family Carabidae
Order Coleoptera
Length 4.5–6.5 mm.
Recognition marks Oval; greenish, marked with light brown; elytra are finely striated; surface has fine punctures.
Habitat Predaceous; they burrow in mud and moist sand along the shores of lakes and streams. They are often found under stones or in holes between roots of plants along the water's edge.
Distribution Southwestern United States; relatives throughout North America.
Note These and many other species of semiaquatic beetles may be forced to the surface and captured by throwing water over the sand bank in which they are burrowing.

86 CHLAENIUS SERICEOUS
Green Ground Beetle

Family Carabidae
Order Coleoptera
Length 13–17 mm.
Recognition marks Elongate-oval, convex; bright green, sometimes with bluish tinge; antennae are usually pale but with a darker apex; ventral surface is nearly black; striae of elytra are fine, distinctly punctate; intervals between striae are flat, densely and finely punctate.
Habitat Adults common along the edges of strreams, lakes, and ponds, or in grass in wet areas.
Distribution Throughout North America.
Note The fifty or so species of the genus *Chlaenius* which inhabit Canada and the United States are mainly in warm temperate areas. The species are varied ecologically; some prefer wet areas while others are found in dry grassy areas. Some species lay their eggs in mud cells which are distinctly shaped and characteristic of the species. The family Carabidae is a dominant family in temperate areas. A day's collecting among stones, under logs, in grassy areas, and along the shores of ponds and streams will reward the collector with a great variety of species.

87 THERMONETUS MARMORATUS
Spotted Water Beetle

Family Dytiscidae
Order Coleoptera
Length 11–13 mm.
Recognition marks Rather convex; black with large yellow spots; upper surface is shiny, smooth, with few punctures; thorax is without lateral margins.
Habitat Aquatic, found in ponds, slow streams, puddles, and animal watering tanks.
Distribution Arizona and California, with relatives throughout western North America.
Note These diving beetles evolved from terrestrial forms but are well adapted to aquatic life. When diving, they take air with them by means of the fine pile covering the surface of the abdomen under the wing covers. When they lift the elytra slightly an air chamber is formed. After the oxygen is expended, the beetle rises to the surface and renews the supply. Both the larvae and the adults are predaceous, feeding on other insects, and sometimes even on small fish. The larvae's jaws are modified into long curved hollow structures. The sharp points pierce and hold their prey which are then sucked dry.

88 GYRINUS LIMBATUS
Whirligig Beetle

Family Gyrinidae
Order Coleoptera
Length 3.5–4.5 mm.
Recognition marks Elongate-oval; black, more or less shiny, with densely bronze reflections.
Habitat Found in "schools" along the margins of lakes, streams, and ponds, They glide across the surface in search of prey. When disturbed they bunch closely together and swim in circles, whence their common name.
Distribution Throughout eastern North America.
Note The family Gyrinidae contains two common genera, *Gyrinus* species are all under 8 mm (0.3 in.) in length. The genus *Dineutus* is larger, all species over 9 mm (0.35 in.). The fifty or more species that occur in the United States and Canada are difficult to identify to species except by technical characteristics of the male genitalia.

---

89 HYDROBIUS FUSCIPES
Water Scavenger Beetle

Family Hydrophilidae
Order Coleoptera
Length 6.5–8 mm.
Recognition marks Oblong, convex; pitch black above, shiny; somewhat paler beneath; thorax is finely punctate; elytra are striated, some stria indistinct at base; striae are closely punctate; intervals flat, not densely punctate.
Habitat Often in debris along the beaches of lakes.
Distribution Common throughout northeastern North America.
Note The water scavenger beetle family, Hydrophilidae, is a group of streamlined beetles with palpi that are longer than the short modified antennae. Most species are found in ponds and streams, but some are terrestrial. The adults feed on decomposing aquatic vegetation, but the larvae are carnivorous and feed on other insects and snails.

90 PLATYPSYLLUS CASTORIS
Beaver Parasite

Family   Leptinidae
Order   Coleoptera
Length   2–3 mm.
Recognition marks   Flattened, louse-shaped; reddish brown to dark brown; antennae are short with an apical club; eyes are absent; elytra are short; wings are absent; legs are short with spines.
Habitat   Ectoparasite of the beaver; the larvae and adults spend most of their life in the fur of the host, feeding on epidermal material or exudates from the skin through lesions caused by biting. The larvae leave the host to pupate in the earth of the beaver lodge.
Distribution   Northern and eastern North America wherever beavers live.
Note   In addition to the beaver parasite beetle, the family Leptinidae contains four species that live in the nests and fur of rodents and insectivorous mammals, or sometimes in the nests of ground-dwelling bees. These species are not particularly modified as ecotoparasites and seem to be facultative, perhaps in the early evolutionary stages of becoming parasites.

91 NICROPHORUS INVESTIGATOR
Sexton Beetle

Family   Silphidae
Order   Coleoptera
Length   18–22 mm.
Recognition marks   Black with orange markings; pronotum is black; elytra have four orange spots; body is elongate-convex.
Habitat   The adults bury carrion, particularly small mammals, snakes, and frogs (see discussion of behavior, p. 31).
Distribution   Western coastal states; relatives throughout North America.
Note   The species of sexton beetles are identified by their orange markings, and by the shape of the thorax and hind legs. There is considerable color variation which has resulted in some confusion of names.

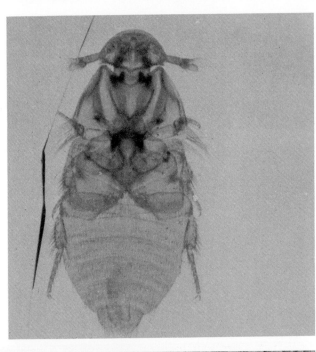

92 SILPHA LAPPONICA
Lapland Carrion Beetle

Family   Silphidae
Order   Coleoptera
Length   10–14 mm.
Recognition marks   Oval, slightly oblong, somewhat flattened; brownish olive; rows of tubercles between elytra ridges; pronotum is yellow.
Habitat   Adults and larvae on carrion.
Distribution   Northeastern North America.
Note   This genus and related genera, known as the "large carrion beetles," form one of many families with some species that are attracted to this material. No doubt they play an important role as a part of the detritus cycle in some ecosystems, but they are nearly entirely absent in the tropics. If the beetles are not present, flies soon consume much of the carrion.

93 STAPHYLINUS VIOLACEOUS
Violet Rove Beetle

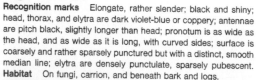

Family   Staphylinidae
Order   Coleoptera
Length   12–14 mm.
Recognition marks   Elongate, rather slender; black and shiny; head, thorax, and elytra are dark violet-blue or coppery; antennae are pitch black, slightly longer than head; pronotum is as wide as the head, and as wide as it is long, with curved sides; surface is coarsely and rather sparsely punctured but with a distinct, smooth median line; elytra are densely punctulate, sparsely pubescent.
Habitat   On fungi, carrion, and beneath bark and logs.
Distribution   Northeastern North America; other species common throughout North America.
Note   The large family Staphylinidae, the rove beetles, have short elytra that expose several abdominal terga. The several hundred North America species range in length from 1–20 mm (0.04–0.8 in.), all very similar in shape. They resemble somewhat members of the order Dermaptera, but without apical abdominal forceps. The family has received the attention of many specialists, but they remain difficult to identify to species. The biology of most of the species remains unknown.

94 HOLOLEPTA POPULNEA
Flat Clown Beetle

Family Histeridae
Order Coleoptera
Length 7–9.5 mm.
Recognition marks Nearly quadrate and flattened; black; surface is sparsely punctate; head is recessed into the thorax; antennae are clubbed, mandibles are prominent.
Habitat Adults and larvae are both found under the bark of recently felled poplar and willow. The larvae are predaceous on other beetle larvae.
Distribution Rocky Mountain region, with related species throughout United States and southern Canada.
Note Members of the family Histeridae, the clown beetles, vary greatly in size and shape. They are almost always black, rarely with red markings. The surface is polished. The elytra are shortened, exposing two abdominal terga. Adults and larvae live in many ecological habitats. Some species are found in excrement, some in decaying animal matter, and others in various plant materials including decaying debris and in fungus. Some are cylindrical and live in burrows of wood-boring beetles, and a few are highly modified in shape, somewhat resembling ants and live in ants' nests.

95 SAPRINUS FIMBRIATUS
Carrion Clown Beetle

Family Histeridae
Order Coleoptera
Length 4.5–5 mm.
Recognition marks Black; thorax and elytra are rather coarsely punctate; elytral striae are short, not reaching apex of elytra.
Habitat On carrion, especially dead fish and frogs along the shore of lakes and streams.
Distribution Southwestern United States.
Note This is one of the largest groups of the family Histeridae. Their "shoe-button" appearance and short elytral stria are spot identification characteristics. The large number of species and their very similar structure make identification to species difficult.

96 LUCANUS ELEPHAS
American Stag Beetle

Family Lucanidae
Order Coleoptera
Length Male 45–60 mm; female 30–35 mm.
Recognition marks Dark brown and shiny, legs and antennae are nearly black. Males have mandibles nearly as long as the body; female mandibles are short, not as long as the head.
Habitat Adults may be found in decaying oak stumps, and sometimes they are attracted to lights at night.
Distribution Northeastern United States.
Note Members of the family Lucanidae, the stage beetles, may be recognized by their scarablike antennae, but the plates of the antennal club cannot be closed. The males of most species have very large mandibles.

97 ODONTOTAENIUS DISJUNCTUS
Peg Beetle

Family Passalidae
Order Coleoptera
Length 30–36 mm.
Recognition marks Black and shiny, somewhat flattened; head has a short bent horn, the "peg." Elytra have numerous deep stria; surface is finely punctate.
Habitat Adults and larvae live in decaying logs and stumps.
Note Although the family Passalidae, the peg beetles, is represented by many species in the tropics, only one species occurs commonly in the United States. The larvae and adults communicate by stridulatory squeaking, the larvae by rubbing specially modified hind legs against the side of the body, and the adults by rubbing the abdomen against the wing covers.

98 CANTHON IMITATOR
Dung Roller Beetle

Family Scarabaeidae
Order Coleoptera
Length 10–18 mm.
Recognition marks Black to bronze or green; pronotum and elytra are coarsely granular; clypeus is sharply, deeply emarginate.
Habitat Adults gather fresh dung which they form into a ball, in the center of which the female lays an egg. Then both sexes roll this food store to a suitable location and bury it. The larva hatch and feed on the dung, there being a sufficient supply to feed the larva until it reaches maturity.
Distribution Southern United States
Note The large dung-rolling beetles, members of the genus *Canthon* occur throughout North America, but they are more abundant in the southern regions. Species of several genera of scarabs feed on dung. In some regions this is an important part of the detritus cycle, a process necessary to return nitrates and other necessary nutrients to the soil.

99 PLEOCOMA HIRTICOLLIS
Rain Beetle

Family Scarabaeidae
Order Coleoptera
Length 18–28 mm.
Recognition marks Oval, slightly elongate, black, shiny above, chestnut below, with yellowish, hairlike setae; males are smaller than females with larger antennal clubs, winged and with an erect horn on the front of the head between the eyes; females may be reddish brown with much smaller antennal clubs and wingless.
Habitat The genus *Pleocoma*, the rain beetles, have approximately thirty species, all confined to the Pacific Coastal region and Utah. Each species has a very restricted range, often confined to a single canyon.
Distribution California.
Note Adults appear in October and November. They do not feed. They have a very long life cycle, lasting nine to thirteen years. The larvae feed on roots. The wingless females emerge from the pupal cases and dig a tunnel to the surface. They remain at the mouth of the tunnel until the males fly to the burrow for mating. Collectors often find the males flying at night during or just after rains. Both sexes may be captured by following the males to the female burrow.

100 LICHNANTHE RATHVONI
Rathvon's Scarab

Family Scarabaeidae
Order Coleoptera
Length 11–16 mm.
Recognition marks Black with head, pronotum, and part of the thorax greenish and shiny; elytra are brownish; long, erect black hairlike setae on ventral side.
Habitat Larvae feed on decaying leaves and other organic debris near streams. Adults are attracted to light at night.
Distribution Pacific Northwest.
Note The larvae of many scarabs are usually grublike, white, with brown heads, C-shaped. They are root feeders and may cause considerable damage to crops and to ornamental plants. They are difficult to control because of their hidden life deep in the soil.

W

---

101 POLYPHYLLA DIFFRACTA
Unlined Giant Chafer

Family Scarabaeidae
Order Coleoptera
Length 22–28 mm.
Recognition marks Elytral stripes are broken and ragged, sometimes totally absent so that the entire body and elytra appear to be brown or black, rarely showing paler elytral stripes.
Habitat Oak and pinon pine canyons.
Distribution Southwestern United States.
Note The genus *Polyphylla* is a large genus with about twenty-two species in our area. Most of them have striped elytra (see next entry). Little is known of the life history of the species.

W

102 POLYPHYLLA DECIMLINEATA
Ten-lined Giant Chafer

Family Scarabaeidae
Order Coleoptera
Length 25–25 mm.
Recognition marks Brown, elytra are black; each elytron has four white stripes; yellow and white scales on the body, each located in a puncture.
Habitat Adults (upper right) feed on needles of pine. The grub-like larvae (lower right) feed on roots of grasses.
Distribution Western United States.
Note Species of this genus occur throughout the United States except in the humid Midwest from Ohio to Iowa and the Mississippi Valley.

Many scarabs, especially those of the tropics (see entry 112) have large horns on head and thorax, used in combat during mating contests. The females attract the males, probably by means of pheromones. Horns are used not to injure the opponents, but rather to lift them up and turn them over so that they are temporarily helpless. If combat occurs in a tree, the scarab may use its horns to raise its opponent and drop it over the edge. The famous naturalist, William Beebe, spent much time observing and photographing this phenomenon.

103 MACRODACTYLUS UNIFORMIS
Large-clawed Scarab

Family Scarabaeidae
Order Coleoptera
Length 8–11 mm.
Recognition marks Dull yellowish brown to reddish brown; integument is covered with yellow scales.
Habitat Abundant on wild grape vines, especially along the borders of marshy areas, streams, and lakes.
Distribution Western North America.
Note This species is very similar to the eastern North American *Macrodactylus subspinosus*. The rose chafers, as these are sometimes called, are pests of ornamental roses. Unless the infestation is particularly severe, it is easily controlled by hand picking them from the rose bushes. This must be done daily, however, because the adults fly from bush to bush and new infestations may come from surrounding wild areas.

---

104 HOPLIA DISPAR
Brown Chafer

Family Scarabaeidae
Order Coleoptera
Length 7–8.5 mm.
Recognition marks Color varies from bright orange to light green, rarely irridescent blue, green, or golden, due to the color of the dense round scales that clothe the body; claws of the front and middle tarsi are unequal in length, the outer one larger and bifid at the tip.
Habitat Adults are found on various flowers during the day. They hide under boards and debris at night.
Distribution Pacific Northwest; other species occur throughout North America.
Note One species, *H. callipyge*, the grapevine hoplia, is destructive to grapes and many other plants.

105 POPILLIA JAPONICA
Japanese Beetle

Family Scarabaeidae
Order Coleoptera
Length 18–29 mm.
Recognition marks Metallic blue-green with reddish brown or coppery elytra; abdomen has patches of white hairlike setae.
Habitat This is a very destructive beetle imported from Asia. Eggs are laid in the soil in grassy areas. The larvae feed on the roots of grass and other plants. Adults emerge from midsummer to early fall and infest many plants, particularly members of the rose family, damaging both the leaves and the flowers.
Distribution It has spread slowly across much of eastern United States since its introduction in 1913.
Note The species is controlled by a fungus disease known as Milky Disease and by various parasitic wasps and flies. For effective control, large areas must be treated, or reinfestation from surrounding regions results in continued damage to crops and ornamentals. This and the following five species belong to the scarab subfamily Rutelinae (see note, entries 109 and 110).

106 PELIDNOTA PUNCTATA
Spotted June Beetle

Family Scarabaeidae
Order Coleoptera
Length 20–25 mm.
Recognition marks Dull yellowish brown with black on head, two black spots on pronotum, and three on each elytron; legs are black; ventrally darker greenish brown to black.
Habitat Adults feed on grape leaves; larvae feed on roots of trees.
Distribution Eastern United States.
Note This large scarab is often seen flying to porch lights or walking on sidewalks. It is attractive and harmless. Unfortunately it is not easy to raise, but adults kept in captivity will feed on fruit and live for several weeks.

107 PLUSIOTIS BEYERI
Beyer's Scarab

Family Scarabaeidae
Order Coleoptera
Length 28–32 mm.
Recognition marks Light green with purple legs; elytra have vague striae.
Habitat Adults feed on oak at lower elevations.
Distribution Arizona.
Note This species is rare in the sense that it is restricted to certain areas in Arizona canyons. This, the following species, and two others are the only representatives of the large genus *Plusiotis* in our area. Many species occur in Mexico and Central America. They are among the most beautiful of beetles. WARNING: This species should not be collected. It is in danger of extinction.

108 PLUSIOTIS GLORIOSA
Glorious Beetle

Family Scarabaeidae
Order Coleoptera
Length 25–28 mm.
Recognition marks Bright green with silver stripes on the elytra.
Habitat Adults feed on juniper leaves at elevations over 4,000 feet. They are attracted to ultraviolet lights at night. By day their color camouflages them by blending in well with their host plant. This is often called the most beautiful beetle in North America.
Distribution Texas to Arizona and northern Mexico.
Note This is the best known of our species of *Plusiotis*. The immature stages remain unknown.
WARNING: This species is endangered and should not be collected.

W

109 PARACOTALPA URSINA
Bear Beetle

Family Scarabaeidae
Order Coleoptera
Length 14–16.5 mm.
Recognition marks Head, pronotum, and ventral surface are metallic blue-black, elytra are reddish brown; body has long whitish hairs; head and pronotum have coarse punctation.
Habitat Adults feed on blossoms, buds, and leaves of various trees, particularly those of the rose family.
Distribution Southern California.
Note The many species of the large subfamily Rutelinae of the family Scarabaeidae are often crop pests. Most of the species are colorfully marked. More than sixty species occur throughout the United States, and many more are known from the American tropics.

110 PARACOTALPA GRANICOLLIS
Hairy Bear Beetle

Family Scarabaeidae
Order Coleoptera
Length 13.5–17.5 mm.
Recognition marks Head, pronotum, and ventral surface are metallic green; elytra are brownish red; legs are black; body has long whitish hairs; head and pronotum have large confluent punctures.
Habitat Adults are reported as pests of apple blossoms in some areas; they also feed on buds and leaves of peaches.
Distribution Pacific Northwest.
Note The largest genus of the subfamily Rutelinae is the genus *Anomala*. It is closely related to this species, with over thirty species in the United States and Canada. Their color is extremely variable so that identification to species is dependent upon a variety of technical characters.

111 BOTHYNUS GIBBOSUS
Carrot Beetle

Family Scarabaeidae
Order Coleoptera
Length 11–16 mm.
Recognition marks Reddish brown, paler ventrally; punctures on elytra all much coarser than those of the thorax; head has small, transverse toothed ridges.
Habitat Larvae feed on roots of various grain crops. The adults are found on a variety of garden plants including carrots, beets, and potatoes, but rarely do any serious damage. The adults are attracted to lights at night.
Distribution Throughout North America.
Note This and the following species belong to the large subfamily Dynastinae. Tropical regions have many species, including some of the largest known beetles. Some of these have horns (see *note*, entry no. 102).

G

112 DYNASTES TITYLUS
Hercules Beetle

Family Scarabaeidae
Order Coleoptera
Length 40–60 mm.
Recognition marks Usually greenish gray with brownish to black irregular spots on the elytra, sometimes uniformly dark brown; male has three horns on the thorax: the middle one, which is ventrally covered with yellow, is the largest and bends down and meets a similar, upwardly bent horn on the head; female has only a slight tubercle on the head.
Habitat The larvae live in rotting logs and stumps, particularly in pine. The adults have an offensive odor. They sometimes congregate in the fall on ash logs.
Distribution Southeastern United States, north to Indiana and New Jersey, west to Texas.
Note One of the world's largest insects, *Dynastes hercules*, is closely related to this species. It lives in the West Indies and northern South America. Other species are called rhinoceros and elephant beetles. (See entry no. 102 for further information about horned beetles.)

W

113 COTINUS MUTABILIS
Green June Beetle

Family Scarabaeidae
Order Coleoptera
Length 24–28.5 mm.
Recognition marks Head is a shiny, somewhat metallic green; pronotum is a deep green with a tawny lateral stripe; elytra are usually a pale red-brown with the sutural margins greenish; ventral surface and legs are bright metallic green; body has yellow or pale hairlike setae.
Habitat Adults feed on ripe fruit, buzzing loudly as they fly from branch to branch. Larvae feed on roots.
Distribution Abundant from Texas to Arizona, with many related species throughout the United States, but most abundant in the Southern States.
Note This scarab is a member of the subfamily Cetoniinae, the largest of the family. It includes the biggest of all insects, the goliathus beetle, *Goliathus goliathus*, of West Africa, which is as large as a mouse.

---

114 TRIGONOPELTASTES DELTA
Flower Scarab

Family Scarabaeidae
Order Coleoptera
Length 7–10 mm.
Recognition marks Head is black; pronotum is black with a triangular spot on the disc, outlined in fine yellow pile; elytra are brownish, variegated with black; venter is covered with a dense yellow pile. The "delta" on the pronotum is typical of this species, but the elytral markings vary.
Habitat Adults are common on a wide variety of flowers. They are attracted to lights at night.
Distribution Southeastern United States, from Ohio to Florida, and west to Arkansas and Texas.
Note The genus *Cremastocheilus* is related to these beetles, but are members of a different tribe. All thirty-three species are associated with ants; hard-bodied scarabs have tufts of golden trichomes at posterior corners of the thorax which seem to attract the ants. The larvae of the beetles live in the ants' nest, apparently on the organic debris. The adults are not particularly favored by the ants, however. Their hard bodies protect them from injury by the ants.

115 TRICHIOTINUS AFFINIS
Flower Beetle

Family   Scarabaeidae
Order   Coleoptera
Length   9–10 mm.
Recognition marks   Head, thorax, ventral side of body, and legs greenish black; elytra are greenish with reddish brown stripes; sides have whitish transverse bars; a short whitish bar is often present behind the scutellum.
Habitat   Adults occur on a variety of flowers where they feed on pollen. The larvae live in decaying wood.
Distribution   Throughout eastern North America.
Note   The genus *Trichiotinus* contains eight species in the United States and Canada, all similarly marked. They have large claws and hairy bodies.

---

116 EUBRIANAX EDWARDSI
Water Penny

Family   Psephenidae
Order   Coleoptera
Length   4–6 mm.
Recognition marks   Body is dark brown; head is hidden beneath the pronotal expansion; each claw has a membranous appendage at its base which is nearly as long as the claw; male has antennal segments with lateral appendages; those of the female are filiform.
Habitat   Adults are found on bushes hanging over the surface of streams. Larvae are "water pennies" found in streams creeping over stones in flowing water and resemble a round disk almost as broad as long. The pupa is also aquatic. A related species, *Psephenus lecontei,* is also called a water penny, and is found throughout much of the United States.
Distribution   California.

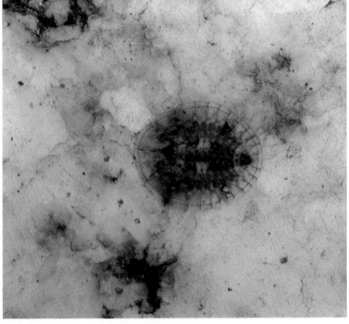

117 HIPPOMELAS SPHENICA
Metallic Wood-boring Beetle

Family Buprestidae
Order Coleoptera
Length 18–25 mm.
Recognition marks Blackish with a brassy reflection; pubescence sparse and extremely short; prothorax is one-half wider than it is long; elytra are finely punctate.
Habitat Larvae bore into the heartwood of many species of trees. Adults occasionally come to lights at night. They may be collected by beating limbs and foliage of forest trees.
Distribution Southwestern United States.
Note Members of the large family Buprestidae are usually woodboring beetles in the larval stage. Some are leaf miners, stem borers, or gall makers. They are usually of a metallic color. Adults are strong flyers and make a loud buzzing sound as they fly, but do not open their elytra in flight, unlike other beetles. Many species are of economic importance, particularly those whose larvae bore into the heartwood of fruit trees.

F

118 BUPRESTIS GIBBSI
Flat-headed Borer

Family Buprestidae
Order Coleoptera
Length 14–20 mm.
Recognition marks Elytra are greenish to purple with three pairs of yellow spots, the anterior pair elongate and extending around the sides of the elytra, the two posterior pairs transverse.
Habitat Adults are found on oak. The larvae probably bore in oak heartwood. They are known as flat-headed borers because of their large flattened head and thorax.
Distribution Pacific Northwest.
Note Buprestidae often come to newly felled trees in forests. They are rapid fliers and usually must be captured with the aid of a net. Some species are attracted by the smoke of forest fires and are known to have special sense organs on their antennae to detect smoke. Buprestidae are widespread.

F

119 BUPRESTIS ADJECTA
Pine Borer

F

Family Buprestidae
Order Coleoptera
Length 13–18 mm.
Recognition marks Body is entirely metallic green to blue-green, with somewhat coppery sides; tips of the elytra are acute, each with two small apical teeth.
Habitat Adults are beaten from pine and spruce branches; the larvae infest pine and spruce wood.
Distribution Western North America.
Note The species of the genus *Buprestis*, particularly the golden buprestid *B. aurulenta*, are among the most destructive forest pests. The adults are beautifully colored beetles. They are particularly attracted to pitchy wood and lay their eggs on fire scars or the exposed pitchy wood of pines, spruce, firs, and other conifers. These beetles may even attack flooring and woodwork of homes, barns, and other wooden buildings, eventually completely destroying them. The larvae take many years to mature.

120 CHRYSOBOTHRIS FEMORATA
Flat-headed Apple Tree Borer

O

Family Buprestidae
Order Coleoptera
Length 7–16 mm.
Recognition marks Dark bronze with sheen of green, copper, or brass; raised areas of elytra are sparsely punctate; each of front tibiae of male has a row of small acute teeth.
Habitat Larvae infest poplar, maple, walnut, willow, oak, elm, apple, pear, and many other trees.
Distribution Eastern and Central North America.
Note A closely similar species, *C. mali*, replaces this species in the West. Many of the wood-boring beetle larvae are referred to either as flat-headed or round-headed borers. This refers to the shape of the head and thorax. The flat-headed borers are members of the family Buprestidae. The round-headed borers are members of the family Cerambycidae, the long-horned beetles.

121 ACMAEODERA SCALARIS
Cactus Buprestid

Family Buprestidae
Order Coleoptera
Length 5-10 mm.
Recognition marks Head, pronotum, and elytra are clothed with setae; black, but a large area of the elytra is yellow.
Habitat Adults are common on cactus blossoms and may be beaten from branches of shrubs and trees. The larvae are wood borers.
Distribution Southwestern United States and Mexico.
Note The genus *Acmaeodera* contains about 150 North American species. They are almost always marked with yellow and sometimes with additional red spots. The scutellum is not visible when elytra are closed. The larvae, so far as is known, all bore into the wood of trees and shrubs. About eighteen species are of economic importance, damaging various species of western trees and shrubs.

122 ALAUS OCULATUS
Eyed Click Beetle

Family Elateridae
Order Coleoptera
Length 28-45 mm.
Recognition marks Black and mottled with small patches of white; thorax has two large "eye" spots about as close together as their width; elytra are distinctly striated.
Habitat Adults live beneath loose bark of stumps or logs, or in wood piles. Larvae lie in decaying wood and are often found in the trunks of old apple trees.
Distribution Throughout eastern North America.
Note This is one of the most common of the showy marked members of the family Elateridae. As with all species of this family, it has a jumping mechanism composed of a prothoracic projection that fits into a socket on the middle part of the thorax. When placed on its back, any click beetle can flex its prothorax against the socket and catapult itself several inches into the air in an attempt to right itself. This ability has earned these beetles their common names of click beetles or snap beetles.

123 ALAUS MELANOPS
Small-eyed Click Beetle

Family Elateridae
Order Coleoptera
Length 20–35 mm.
Recognition marks Dull black with few white markings; "eye" spots on thorax are smaller and more oval than those of the preceding species.
Habitat Adults are found under the bark of rotting logs; larvae usually inhabit the same wood.
Distribution Pacific North America.
Note The genus *Alaus* contains eight North American species, recognizable by the "eye" spots on the pronotum. Related to them are others of the subfamily Pyrophorinae, which have deep grooves on the underside of their body for the insertion of their antennae or legs, or in some, grooves for both. Others of this group have large, plumose antennae, and still others, members of the genus *Chalcolepidius* (see entry 125) and related genera, are brightly marked with white, brown, green, and blue.

124 PYROPHORUS SCHOTTI
Lantern Click Beetle

Family Elateridae
Order Coleoptera
Length 20–22 mm.
Recognition marks Brown; hind angles of the pronotum have small reddish spots that in living specimens are luminescent.
Habitat Adults are active at night. In flight the thoracic light organs glow and the abdominal light organs cast a light over the ground. These latter organs are hidden when the elytra are closed. The amount of light produced is considerable, enough so that a few in a jar will provide a reading lamp. The larvae are carnivorous and also luminescent. They sometimes are beneficial because they prey upon grubs.
Distribution Extreme southern United States and Mexico.
Note Five species of *Pyrophorus* occur in our area. They are difficult to identify to species except by means of male genitalia.

125 CHALCOLEPIDIUS WEBBI
Black and White Click Beetle

Family Elateridae
Order Coleoptera
Length 36–38 mm.
Recognition marks Smooth, polished, black, clothed rather densely with small, recumbent, and flattened hairlike setae; dark bluish; lateral edges of the pronotum rather broadly and elytra very narrowly clothed with dense white recumbent pubescence, the white border abruptly limited.
Habitat Larvae bore in wood of ponderosa pine and others, usually above 5,000 feet elevation. Pupation takes place in the wood after the larvae chew open exit holes. The adult emerges from the solid wood with just enough room for the final push to their freedom.
Distribution Southwestern United States and northern Mexico.
Note Related species in tropical America are brightly marked with various colors.

126 AMPEDEUS APICATUS
Black-tailed Click Beetle

Family Elateridae
Order Coleoptera
Length 9–12 mm.
Recognition marks Black; elytra reddish orange with apical black patch not reaching sides or suture except near apex; pronotal vestiture is light yellow.
Habitat Larvae in decaying wood; adults on flowers.
Distribution Western North America.
Note The larvae of Elateridae are called wireworms. Some of them damage crops, e.g., potato tubers. Others are pests of beets, tobacco, wheat, and other crops.

127 ZARHIPIS INTEGRIPENNIS
Glowworm Beetle

Family Phengodidae
Order Coleoptera
Length Male 18–20 mm; female 30–50 mm.
Recognition marks Female: pale yellow or tan, resembles a larva, lacks wings, body is elongate; abdomen has luminescent lateral spots. Male: pale yellowish brown; antennae are plumose; elyra are short, apices are pointed, apical half is much narrower than basal portion.
Habitat The luminescent larvae are predaceous on small arthropods. They live in leaf litter under forest trees or under bark.
Distribution California.
Note The small family Pyrochroidae is represented in our area by about twenty species. More are found in tropical regions. The species are very similar to each other in appearance. One or more species occur throughout most of North America. Look for them at night, especially when it is warm, rainy, or very humid. Males are attracted to lights at night. Members of this family, a few species of Elateridae (see entry no. 124) and nearly all of the family Lampyridae are the only terrestrial luminescent animals.

128 ELLYCHNIA CALIFORNICA
Western Firefly

Family Lampyridae
Order Coleoptera
Length 10–14 mm.
Recognition marks Black or rusty black; disk and side margins of thorax are black; between them is a reddish and yellow space or line; elytra are finely granulate-punctate, and covered with a fine, recumbent yellowish pubescence.
Habitat Common in spring on tree trunks in woods, especially maple at or near flowing sap; attracted to moth bait; also found on flowers.
Distribution Throughout North America.
Note The fireflies are also called lightningbugs. Several species are usually common in most regions. Their ability to regulate their light flashes is unique and the flash pattern is usually characteristic of the species. Experts can identify these insects by their flash pattern alone. The flash is used by a female, resting on the ground, to attract a male of her own species who will answer with a similar flash and fly to the female.

129 PHOTINUS PYRALIS
Common Eastern Firefly

Family Lampyridae
Order Coleoptera
Length 10–14 mm.
Recognition marks Pitchy brown; thorax has dull yellow margins, the convex disk roseate with a central black spot; elytra have pale suture and narrow side margins. The light organs are always larger in the males.
Habitat Adults predaceous; larvae luminescent and predaceous.
Distribution Throughout eastern North America.
Note Firefly light is produced by a mixture of chemicals similar to enzymes, resulting in "cold" light, that is, a chemical reaction that produces nearly all light and very little heat.

---

130 PHOTURIS PENNSYLVANICA
Woods Firefly

Family Lampyridae
Order Coleoptera
Length 12–15 mm.
Recognition marks Head and thorax are dull yellow; thorax has a red disk with a narrow median dark stripe; elytra are brown or pitchy black with pale narrow side margins, suture, and narrow stripe on the disk. Thorax and elytra are densely and rather roughly punctate. Members of this genus can be recognized by their large eyes, slightly exposed head, and antennae which are longer than one-half the length of the body. The light organs in both sexes occupy the whole of the fifth and following segments.
Habitat Adults are found in forests rather than in fields as most members of the family.
Distribution Throughout the United States.
Note The light organs of fireflies are used in biochemical assays. They are gathered from wild populations because so far no one has been able to raise fireflies in captivity.

131 CHAULIOGNATHUS PENNSYLVANICA
Goldenrod Soldier Beetle

Family Cantharidae
Order Coleoptera
Length 9–12 mm.
Recognition marks Head and ventral parts are black; thorax is yellow with a broad black spot on the basal half; elytra are yellow with an oblong-oval blackish spot on the apical third (sometimes more extended); ventral abdominal segments are margined behind with yellow.
Habitat Adults are abundant in the fall on flowers of goldenrod and other composites. They feed on pollen and nectar. Larvae are carnivorous and feed on other insect larvae.
Distribution Eastern United States, south to Texas.
Note This is a common representative of the rather large family, Cantharidae, the soldier beetles. They resemble the fireflies except that their head is exposed and they lack light-producing organs.

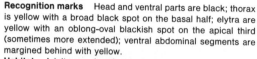

132 LYCUS FERANDEZI
Net-winged Beetle

Family Lycidae
Order Coleoptera
Length 10–18 mm.
Recognition marks Dull brownish yellow; elytra appear approximately in apical fourth or more, antennae except at extreme base; palpi, tibiae, and tarsi are black; the head varies from partly to entirely black; elytra of the male are broad, those of the female are narrower.
Habitat Adults and larvae are predaceous.
Distribution Southwestern United States.
Note The family Lycidae, the net-winged beetles, contains about eighty species. The adults fly during the day and are usually found on the leaves of flowers of plants where they prey upon other insects. Their bodies contain a very toxic chemical which protects them from predators.

133 ANTHRENUS VERBASCI
Varied Carpet Beetle

Family Dermestidae
Order Coleoptera
Length 2–3 mm.
Recognition marks Convex, oblong-oval; thorax is black, the disk sparsely clothed with yellow scales, the sides more densely covered with white scales; elytra are black with a large basal ring and two transverse zigzag bands of white scales, bordered by yellow ones; ventral surface has fine, long, grayish yellow scales.
Habitat Adults are common on flowers. They may enter homes, lay eggs, and produce destructive larvae. These and other species will eat wool carpets and sometimes infest stored food products.
Distribution Cosmopolitan.
Note The family Dermestidae, the skin and larder beetles, are pests of stored materials. The kapra beetle, *Trogoderma granarium*, a serious pest of stored grain, belongs to this group. This beetle is not established in North America, but only because of the continued search of imported goods by the United States Department of Agriculture entomologists.

S

---

134 COLLOPS VITTATUS
Two-lined Collops

Family Malachiidae
Order Coleoptera
Length 5–8 mm.
Recognition marks Pitchy blue-black; the sides of the pronotum, margin, and suture of the elytra are marked with orange-red or yellowish red; the disk of the elytra is dark bluish; disk of the pronotum usually has a large dark spot; basal segments of male antennae are greatly enlarged.
Habitat Adults are predaceous or feed on pollen; larvae are predaceous.
Distribution Throughout North America.
Note Although the family Malachiidae is rather large, with about 500 species in the United States and Canada, the group is poorly known and rather rare in collections. Some species are very beneficial as predators on various crop pests. They are common in cotton fields in the South, but are not yet used as a natural control.

W

135 TRICHODES ORNATUS
Ornate Checkered Beetle

Family Cleridae
Order Coleoptera
Length 5–15 mm.
Recognition marks Elytra have red to yellow basal, median, and subapical bands which vary to small spots on otherwise metallic bluish black body.
Habitat Adults are found on flowers of cactus, yucca, composites, and many other plants where they feed on pollen or prey upon other insects. Larvae prey upon solitary bees and wasps.
Distribution Throughout all of North America.
Note The bright colors of species of the family Cleridae, the checkered beetles, make them interesting additions to any collection. Most of the species are predaceous, both as larvae and adults, feeding on other insects. A few species infest stored animal products; some feed on carrion, and many are found gathering pollen. The hairlike setae on their bodies trap pollen and transfer it to other flowers. It is doubtful that these beetles are the primary pollinators for any species of plant.

136 TRICHODES HORNI
Horn's Checkered Beetle

Family Cleridae
Order Coleoptera
Length 7–10 mm.
Recognition marks Body is slender; pronotum is black with greenish luster; elytra are yellowish brown and bordered with dull black; abdomen and legs are yellowish brown.
Habitat Adults and larvae predaceous. Nocturnal species hide during the day in cracks, under loose bark, or under dried leaves.
Distribution Southwestern United States.
Note The members of the family Cleridae are considered to be of economic importance because of their predaceous habits. They are often important in the control of wood-boring and bark beetle larvae. Many species are nocturnal and will come to lights at night. Many others must be hand picked or beaten from flower heads. When the adults are disturbed, they will crawl into flower heads and some will feign death. A few feed on the eggs of lubber grasshoppers.

The cosmopolitan red-shouldered and red-legged ham beetles, *Necrobia ruficollis* and *N. rufipes,* feed on smoked meat, cheese skippers (larvae of certain flies that infest cheese), blowflies, and carrion. They are cannibalistic as well.

137 CUCUJUS CLAVIPES
Red Cucujid

Family Cucujidae
Order Coleoptera
Length 10–14 mm.
Recognition marks Adults (upper right) are bright red to scarlet; body is very flat. The size, shape, and color of this species clearly separate it from all other beetles. Larvae (lower right) are also very flat and characteristic of the species.
Habitat Both adults and larvae are found under loose bark of tulip-poplar, and other deciduous trees, but they are rare.
Distribution Southern Canada, eastern United States, south to North Carolina, west to the Rocky Mountains.
Note Most species of this family are flat, and most are very much smaller than the beautiful species illustrated here. They generally live under bark. However, several species infest stored food products. Although these beetles can be controlled by using chemicals, it is much easier to throw away all infested flour, cereals, and spices. New supplies should be stored in metal or glass containers to prevent further infestations from any remaining eggs that might hatch in cupboards.

138 CYPHEROTYLUS CALIFORNICA
Pleasing Fungus Beetle

Family Erotylidae
Order Coleoptera
Length 16–18 mm.
Recognition marks Black; elytra are yellowish gray with numerous small, irregularly placed black spots.
Habitat Adults are found in fungus, or in fungus-rotted wood. They are attracted to some household products such as powdered milk.
Distribution Southwestern United States.
Note The pleasing fungus beetles, family Erotylidae, are rather small, with only fifty species in the United States and Canada. Most species are smaller than the one shown here. They infest fleshy fungi, decaying wood, or old moldy stored grain.

W

139 OLLA ABDOMINALIS
Ash-gray Ladybird Beetle

Family Coccinellidae
Order Coleoptera
Length 3–6 mm.
Recognition marks Ashy gray to pale yellow with black spots on the pronotum and elytra.
Habitat Adults and larvae feed on aphids.
Distribution Throughout North America.
Note The ladybird beetles, or ladybugs as they are often called, are probably the most beneficial of all beetles because they feed on other insects, particularly plant bugs (Homoptera) which are very destructive plant pests.

B

140 HIPPODAMIA CONVERGENS
Convergent Ladybird Beetle

Family Coccinellidae
Order Coleoptera
Length 4.5–6.5 mm.
Recognition marks Head, legs, and pronotum of adults (upper right) are black, the latter with white edges and the pronotal disk with two convergent white lines; elytra are red, each with six black spots, the anterior three smaller than the posterior three.
Habitat Common on stems and foliage of weeds and cultivated plants where both larvae and adults feed on aphids and other plant bugs.
Distribution Abundant throughout North America.
Note The adults congregate in the fall to hibernate (lower right). They sometimes form great masses on plants. When the temperature drops to freezing, they crawl under boards, leaves, and into cracks and crevices, and overwinter in the adult stage. When it becomes warmer in the spring they emerge, breed, and lay eggs. In the summer both adults and larvae can be seen feeding on other insects, living together on the same host plant. Attempts have been made to rear this species and others as a means of controlling garden pests. Although they are beneficial, the expense of handling them is far greater than the crops that are saved.

141 COCCINELLA NOVANOTATA
Nine-spotted Ladybird Beetle

B

Family   Coccinellidae
Order   Coleoptera
Length   5–8 mm.
Recognition marks   Head and pronotum are black with pale yellowish margins; elytra are orange to reddish yellow, each with four black spots; scutellum is black, the spot extending onto the elytra.
Habitat   Adults (upper right) and larvae (lower right) are predaceous, especially feeding on aphids in field crops.
Distribution   Throughout northern North America, south to Georgia and Texas.
Note   The spots that mark the elytra of many ladybird beetles vary considerably within the species, and color patterns alone are insufficient for the identification of all specimens of a species. Size, shape, and various technical characters including the structure of the male genitalia must also be noted.

Not all ladybird beetles are beneficial. Some, such as Jacques' beetle, *Subcoccinella vigintiquatuorpunctata*, a European species recently introduced into the United States on flowers, feed on various wild plants and are spreading throughout eastern United States. The Mexican bean beetle, *Epilachnia varivestis*, is a pest of beans, and *E. borealis*, the squash beetle, is a pest of squash.

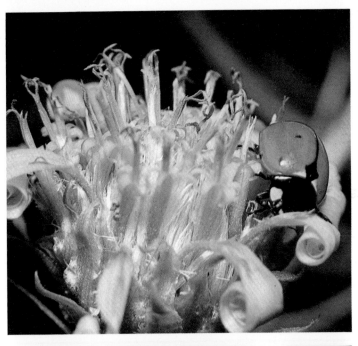

142 CYCLONEDA POLITA
Casey's Ladybird Beetle

Family Coccinellidae
Order Coleoptera
Length 4–5 mm.
Recognition marks Head of male is white; female head has a median black spot; pronotum is black except for front and side margins which are pale, with a median anterior region black to varying widths; elytra are blood red, with a small paler area on each side of the scutellum, very rarely entirely yellow.
Habitat Adults and larvae predaceous.
Distribution Rocky Mountains and west to the Pacific Coast.
Note This species and two others of the genus, *C. sanguinea*, and *C. munda*, are very similarly marked. Their combined ranges cover all of North America. The three species are easily mistaken, but they do not interbreed, leaving little doubt about their distinctness.

143 GLYPTASIDA COSTIPENNIS
Desert Darkling Beetle

Family Tenebrionidae
Order Coleoptera
Length 15–20 mm.
Recognition marks Moderately convex; black; surface is rough and opaque; prothorax is more than twice as wide as it is long with rounded sides; surface is coarsely and confluently punctate throughout.
Habitat Adults frequent desert areas, usually active at night, but they do not come to light.
Distribution Southwestern United States.
Note The large family Tenebrionidae, the darkling beetles, in North America is best represented in the West. The great variation in size and shape of the species makes this group difficult to define and to recognize. Most species are black, some have white markings, and a very few are marked with red. Very often their body is rough and irregular in shape, and their integument is usually very hard. The biology and habits of most species are little, if at all known. Most of the desert species are fungus feeders, but some are known to gather and store seeds. All species of this family, in common with several related families, have one less tarsal segment on the hind tarsi than on the front and middle legs.

144 COELUS CILIATUS
Round Darkling Beetle

Family Tenebrionidae
Order Coleoptera
Length 5.5–7.5 mm.
Recognition marks Oval; dark brown to black; sides of body have long, pale, hairlike setae; surface of the body is shiny and coarsely punctate.
Habitat Common in the sand of ocean beaches.
Distribution Pacific Coast.
Note The classification of the family Tenebrionidae is complicated and the identification of the species is difficult. The literature on the family is widely scattered.

145 NOSERUS PLICATUS
Rugged Darkling Beetle

Family Tenebrionidae
Order Coleoptera
Length 14–18 mm.
Recognition marks Body is elongate and very hard and black, with a rough surface; apical segments of the antennae are fused; elytra are fused; hind wings are absent.
Habitat Adults and larvae live under oak bark.
Distribution California.
Note This species belongs to a very distinct section of the family Tenebrionidae. Some of the beetles of this group are so rugged that they can remain alive in captivity for months without food or water. Often they are seen in Mexican curio shops where they are sold as jewelry, decorated with rhinestones and bits of colored cloth glued to their backs.

146 ELEODES ARMATA
Desert Skunk Beetle

Family Tenebrionidae
Order Coleoptera
Length 15–35 mm.
Recognition marks Black with a smooth body; apex of elytra are attenuate; anterior angles of prothorax are acute, prominent, and toothed; femora have long acute teeth.
Habitat A common desert species, the adults are scavengers. The larvae feed on roots of grasses and other plants.
Distribution Common from Arizona to California.
Note The genus *Eleodes* is a very large and difficult group. Of the more than 100 species that occur in the United States, this is one of the few species that can be easily recognized by its shape and the presence of femoral spines. One species, *Eleodes opacus*, the plains false wireworm, is of economic importance because its larvae damage wheat seeds and young plants, particularly during droughts.

---

147 ALOBATES PENNSYLVANICA
False Mealworm

Family Tenebrionidae
Order Coleoptera
Length 20–23 mm.
Recognition marks Elongate-oval and convex; black; surface is barely shiny; pronotum is nearly square; elytra are marked with five rows of punctures.
Habitat Adults and larvae are found throughout the year beneath bark and logs where they feed upon other insects.
Distribution Throughout the United States.
Note Several species of Tenebrionidae are stored-product pests. The large species, *Tenebrio molitor*, is known in the larval stage as the yellow mealworm and infests stored grain and grain products. Larvae are used as fish bait and fish food in aquaria. Some very small species (4–5 mm; 0.15–0.2 in.), members of the genus *Tribolium*, are common pests of flour.

148 DENDROIDES CONCOLOR
Fire-colored Beetle

Family Pyrochroidae
Order Coleoptera
Length 9–13 mm.
Recognition marks Elongate and slender; head, antennae, and elytra are black; thorax and legs are reddish yellow; antennae of each segment have a lateral branch, that of the male longer than the branch of the female; eyes are very large; males' eyes almost touch dorsally.
Habitat Adults live on flowers or vegetation. Larvae live under bark. They are carnivorous.
Distribution Throughout eastern North America.
Note The small family, Pyrochroidae, the fire-colored beetles, contains only fifteen species in our region. Most species are found around dead or decaying trees. They are attracted to lights at night.

149 MORDELLA ATRATA
Tumbling Flower Beetle

Family Mordellidae
Order Coleoptera
Length 3–6 mm.
Recognition marks Dark velvety black; base of elytra and body are ventrally covered with a somewhat iridescent pubescence; base of the dorsal exposed portion of the abdomen is covered with silvery gray pubescence.
Habitat Often found on wild-rose blossoms.
Distribution Throughout North America.
Note Members of the family Mordellidae, the tumbling flower beetles, are all of similar wedge shape and easily recognized by their pointed abdomens. They are called tumbling flower beetles because of their habit of dropping from the flowers when disturbed. They are able to jump as well. The adults are flower feeding, and are often abundant on umbelliferous flowers. Most larvae are carnivorous. Some are in rotting wood, others are leaf and stem miners; a few are parasites of wasps.

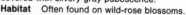
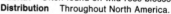

150 CYSTEODEMUS WISLIZENI
Desert Blister Beetle

Family Meloidae
Order Coleoptera
Length 10–15 mm.
Recognition marks Pronotum has short lateral spines; elytra are greatly inflated, resembling a large spider; dark metallic blue to purplish; surface has dense, deep, coarse, partly confluent punctures.
Habitat Adults sometimes found on flowers, usually found crawling on the desert floor.
Distribution Southwestern United States.
Note The large family Meloidae, the blister beetles, are soft-bodied, usually elongate, with the head bent and with a narrow neck. The tarsi are heteromerous, i.e., the first two pairs have five segments each and the hind pair have only four segments. (See Tenebrionidae, entry no. 143.) Their common name refers to the body fluids which contain cantharidin, which when released and upon contact with human skin will cause blisters. (See also note, entry no. 151.)

151 LYTTA VULNERATA
American Spanish Fly

Family Meloidae
Order Coleoptera
Length 12–20 mm.
Recognition marks Body elongate; head and thorax are shiny; elytra have somewhat raised reticulations; head, except between the eyes, and pronotum, except for a pair of spots in the middle, are orange; elytra, abdomen, and legs are black.
Habitat Adults are attracted to lights at night. The larvae are found in wild bee nests.
Distribution Throughout western North America.
Note This species is a close relative of the European "Spanish fly," *Lytta vesicatoria*. Cantharidin extracted from these beetles is used as a diuretic and as an aphrodisiac.

152 PYROTA PALPALIS
Fire Blister Beetle

Family Meloidae
Order Coleoptera
Length 10–15 mm.
Recognition marks Shiny surface with only small and inconspicuous punctures dorsally; head, prothorax, venter, and legs are pale red or rusty brown; pronotum sometimes has a pair of small black spots in the center; elytra are usually whitish yellow with three wide black bands.
Habitat Adults are found on flowers feeding on pollen and nectar. The larvae probably lie in the nests of solitary bees.
Distribution Southwestern United States and Mexico.
Note Several species of Meloidae are important plant pests, particularly members of the genus *Epicauta* which feed on members of the potato plant family. One species is called the "old-fashioned potato bug" because it was a pest of potatoes before the Colorado potato beetle (see entry no. 182) invaded our potato fields.

153 NEMOGNATHA LURIDA
Nectar-sucking Blister Beetle

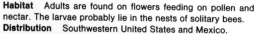

Family Meloidae
Order Coleoptera
Length 7–15 mm.
Recognition marks Shiny; surface has small but distinct and moderately dense punctures; dorsally reddish brown to yellow with the scutellum reddish or black; tips of elytra may be sometimes black or entire elytra may be black; body is clothed with moderately dense, erect pubescence.
Habitat Adults feed on nectar and pollen.
Distribution Throughout western United States from the Mississippi River to the Pacific Coast.
Note Many species of blister beetles, Meloidae, are predators on the eggs of bees and grasshoppers. They have a free-living larval stage, known as a triungulin, so named because of the three slender appendages at the end of each leg. These larvae attach themselves to bees that visit flowers. The triungulins ride back to the bees' nest where they transform into legless larvae that feed on pollen, honey, and bees' eggs. Other triungulins wander over the ground until they find the buried egg pods of grasshoppers. These species are beneficial as a control of grasshopper pests, although this is at least partly offset by the feeding habits of their adults.

154 STYLOPS VANDYKEI
Bee Parasite Beetle

Family Stylopidae
Order Coleoptera
Length 1–1.5 mm.
Recognition marks Male is black; antennae and legs are brownish, sometimes with yellowish abdominal segments. Females resemble larvae and are parasitic on bees, usually *Andrena* bees.
Habitat The female remains throughout her life in her insect host, usually bees, wasps, grasshoppers, or plant bugs, only her head protruding. Males locate the female for mating. After mating the eggs develop within the female and hundreds of larvae are released, falling to the ground or on flower heads. These larvae have legs and resemble the triungulins of Meloidae. They locate and attach themselves to a new host. The males eventually develop wings and the cycle is repeated.
Distribution Various species occur throughout North America.
Note These parasitic insects somewhat resemble parasitic beetles of the family Rhipiphoridae, which in turn are relatives of the family Meloidae, the blister beetles. The Stylopidae, however, are greatly modified due to a parasitic mode of life. Their body form is much different from all other beetles and their exact relationships are still a matter of speculation. They are sometimes placed in a separate order, Strepsiptera.

---

155 STENODONTES DASYTOMUS
Shade-tree Longhorn

Family Cerambycidae
Order Coleoptera
Length 23–27 mm.
Recognition marks Reddish brown to dark brown or blackish; antennae are rather short, reaching only to the basal third of the elytron in the male, shorter in the female; margins of the prothorax are serrated, disk has large polished spots without punctures.
Habitat Adults remain on the trunks and trees they infest as larvae. The larvae bore into the heartwood of various living trees such as willow, oak, boxelder, and sycamore.
Distribution Throughout southern United States.
Note Most species of the family Cerambycidae have very long antennae, usually longer than the length of the body. The more primitive species, such as the one described here, have short antennae. They are also flattened in contrast to the more or less cylindrical body of the other species. Many species are very colorfully marked.

156 PSYRASSA TEXANA
Slender Texas Longhorn

Family Cerambycidae
Order Coleoptera
Length 11–13 mm.
Recognition marks Slender, tapered body, uniformally chestnut brown; head is coarsely but sparsely and irregularly punctate; thorax is shallowly punctate, clothed with sparse, long, erect hairlike setae; elytra are coarsely and somewhat densely punctate, clothed with a few scattered, long, erect hairs; antennae are longer than the body in males, shorter in the females.
Habitat Adults beaten from acacias and attracted to lights at night. Larval host is unknown.
Distribution Texas. Related species occur in eastern and southern United States and in Mexico.
Note The larvae of one species is a twig pruner, girdling twigs of oak, hickory, and other trees, causing them to fall to the ground in the spring.

157 ENAPHALODES NIVEITECTUS
Barklike Longhorn

Family Cerambycidae
Order Coleoptera
Length 23–27 mm.
Recognition marks Brown or reddish black; sparsely pubescent except for dense patches of white pubescence on head, pronotum, and most of the elytra; head is coarsely, sparsely punctate between the eyes; antennae are longer than the body, each segment with a spine; pronotum is coarsely and densely punctate; elytra coarsely but not densely punctate, punctures finer toward apex, apices prominently bispinose.
Habitat Adults on branches and trunks of oak. Larvae bore in oak.
Distribution Southern Arizona.
Note This genus contains eight species distributed throughout the United States. Most species infest oak and a few other trees, particularly nut trees.

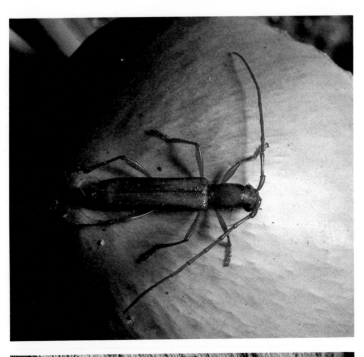

158 ROSALIA FUNEBRIS
Banded Alder Borer

Family Cerambycidae
Order Coleoptera
Length 23–28 mm.
Recognition marks Elongate, somewhat flattened, sides nearly parallel; black with patches and bands of dense white or bluish white pubescence; antennae of the male are longer than the body, of the female somewhat shorter than the body; surface of head and pronotum are finely, closely punctate; elytra are roughly punctate, more coarsely at the base.
Habitat Adults are found near their host plant after emerging. Larvae infest alder, oak, willow, and other trees, often causing serious damage.
Distribution Pacific Coast of North America.
Note This species and many of its relatives are brightly marked and prizes for any collector. Some of the species are attracted to lights at night, but a beating net must be used to collect them. Often this is done at night when the adults are more likely to be active.

159 XYLOTRECHUS INSIGNIS
Willow Longhorn

Family Cerambycidae
Order Coleoptera
Length 12–18 mm.
Recognition marks Cylindrical; male is reddish brown with coarse brown and yellow vestiture; head has a conspicuous V-shaped frontal ridge; surface is roughly punctate; elytra have yellow pubescence forming a pair of basal spots and transverse, subapical, and apical bands. Female is larger and black, with a broad yellow band at the base and apex of the pronotum; elytra have five transverse bands, incomplete basally, complete apically.
Habitat A pest of willow, poplar, and other trees.
Distribution Pacific Coast; related species throughout North America.
Note This species represents a large group of tiger-striped long-horned beetles. Some of the larvae cause considerable damage to lumber and nut trees by boring that weakens the trees, causing them to break in windstorms and making them susceptible to plant diseases.

160 CLYTUS BLAISDELLI
Douglas Fir Borer

Family Cerambycidae
Order Coleoptera
Length 9–11 mm.
Recognition marks Elongate and moderately slender; black, with legs and antennae reddish, and body distinctly margined with a band of yellow or whitish hairlike setae; pubescence pattern of elytra consists of an oval, slightly oblique spot on the shoulder, a transverse band at the apical third, and a vague apical patch; antennae are only about half as long as the body.
Habitat The larvae infest Douglas fir.
Distribution This and related species are found locally throughout North America.
Note Other species of this genus infest a wide variety of trees including pine, maple, beech, oak, basswood, and others. The larvae of long-horned beetles are known as round-headed borers, in contrast to the flat-headed borers which are the larvae of the metallic wood-boring beetles, family Buprestidae.

161 CALLONA REMOSA
Mesquite Longhorn

Family Cerambycidae
Order Coleoptera
Length 30–38 mm.
Recognition marks Male is brown; femora are frequently reddish orange except at base and apex; elytra are green with brassy reflections; dorsal surface is bare, ventral surface has pubescence; antennae are somewhat shorter than the body; pronotum is coarsely, densely punctate; elytral surface is crinkled. Female is somewhat larger than the male and completely black; antennae reach to beyond the middle of the elytra.
Habitat Adults are found on mesquite near their emergence holes. The larvae bore into mesquite where they feed on the wood, making a gallery in the sapwood about one inch below the surface. As they grow the gallery is enlarged. Waste material is discarded through a small opening at surface that is otherwise kept plugged to prevent ant invasions.
Distribution Southern Texas and northern Mexico.
Note This species belongs to the tribe Purpuricenini which contains many colorful species.

162 TRAGIDION ANNULATUM
Wasplike Longhorn

Family Cerambycidae
Order Coleoptera
Length 15–32 mm.
Recognition marks Males are dark brown or reddish brown, elytra are dull brownish yellow margined at base with brown; pubescence is golden on elytra except at base and other parts of the body are black with bluish or violet reflections; antennae are longer than the body; they are broadly ringed with orange or brownish yellow. Female is black, with reddish orange elytra, broadly margined with black at the base; antennae are shorter than the body.
Habitat Adults are found on various flowers. The larvae bore into the branches of *Baccharis sergilioides* which grows at elevations between 2,000 and 5,500 feet.
Distribution Southwestern United States and Mexico.
Note Other species of this genus breed in mesquite, oak, yucca, and agave. *Tragidion coquus* occurs throughout eastern United States; the remaining species are mostly in the arid Southwest.

163 DENDROBIAS MANDIBULARIS
Horse-bean Longhorn

Family Cerambycidae
Order Coleoptera
Length 17–32 mm.
Recognition marks Moderately broad and slightly convex; body is shiny, without pubescence; black or reddish black; elytra are yellow with a dark base and usually with an arched median band that divides the yellow area, but which is sometimes reduced or broken; suture and lateral margins sometimes mostly dark; mandibles very large in male; antennae very long, extending beyond length of body.
Habitat Adults sometimes come to lights at night. Larvae infest horse-bean, willow, and citrus trees.
Distribution Southwestern United States and Mexico.
Note This is one of the most attractive of the long-horned beetles, subfamily Cerambycinae. However, many other species in this subfamily have color combinations that delight the eye.

164 DESMOCERUS PALLIATUS
Elderberry Longhorn

Family Cerambycidae
Order Coleoptera
Length 18–26 mm.
Recognition marks Elongate and subcylindrical; metallic bluish except for yellow basal half of elytra which has two black spots; surface is rather finely and densely punctate, coarser on elytra; antennae extend to about middle of the elytra in both sexes; male antennae are slightly longer than female antennae.
Habitat Adults are often found flying around elderberry bushes where they feed on the flowers. Larvae bore in the roots or base of the stems of the elderberry. When they are mature, they work their way into the hollow pith of the branches and excavate a pupal cell. The adult emerges in the spring and early summer.
Distribution Eastern North America.
Note This eastern species is very distinct and cannot be confused with any other long-horned beetle. Two related species occur along the West Coast.

165 NECYDALIS CAVIPENNIS
Hornet Longhorn

Family Cerambycidae
Order Coleoptera
Length 13–24 mm.
Recognition marks Reddish brown to black; surface is dull; pubescence is dense and golden; antennae are stout, black, and much shorter than the body; elytra are very short, the apices narrowed; legs are elongate.
Habitat Adults are found by beating oak branches. Larvae bore in several species of oaks, eucalyptus, and other trees.
Distribution Arizona and California.
Note All of the seven species of this genus have short elytra. Some of them are slender and resemble ichneumonid wasps. Others might be confused with rove beetles. They are easily separated, however, by the large, heart-shaped third tarsal segment. All but one of the species live on the West Coast. The eastern species is *Necydalis mellita* which flies and sounds like a large bee.

166 CENTRODERA SPURCA
Stump Borer

Family   Cerambycidae
Order   Coleoptera
Length   19–30 mm.
Recognition marks   Stout; pale brownish, shiny surface; tips of mandibles, eyes, and two marginal spots at the middle of the elytra are black; head is densely punctate; pubescence is sparse; male antennae are longer than the body; pronotum and elytra have coarse punctures; female antennae are shorter than the body.
Habitat   Adults are collected by beating branches and nocturnally at lights. Larvae live in soil and feed in rotting stumps and roots.
Distribution   Western United States.
Note   This species and the following entries, nos. 167–170, are representatives of the very large subfamily Lepturinae. These colorful long-horned beetles are often found on flowers. Some species resemble bees or wasps. They are difficult to identify to species.

167 STENOCORUS VESTITUS
Flower Lepturine

Family   Cerambycidae
Order   Coleoptera
Length   Male 9–16 mm; female 11–21 mm.
Recognition marks   Male elongate; elytra are broad at the base, tapering posteriorly; black, with brownish yellow elytra, and usually pale appendages and abdomen; pubescence is dense, recumbent, and usually golden; surface is generally densely punctate; antennae are about as long as body; female is broader, with less tapering elytra; antennae extend to about middle of elytra.
Habitat   Frequently on flowers of many kinds. Larvae breed in Douglas fir.
Distribution   Pacific Coast states.
Note   Species of this genus vary considerably in shape. The genus is one of many similar genera, with over 200 species and subspecies. They are difficult to identify to species without the use of the technical literature.

168 STENOCORUS NUBIFER
Variable Flower Lepturine

Family Cerambycidae
Order Coleoptera
Length Male 9–17 mm; female 12–21 mm.
Recognition marks Male body is strongly tapered posteriorly; all black to brownish yellow with head black, pronotum, legs, and ventral surface pale; elytra often have pale shoulders or pale stripes; pubescence varies from very sparse to dense and recumbent; surface is finely punctate; antennae are about as long as the body. Sides of the elytra in females are less tapered than those of males; antennae extend a little beyond the middle of elytra.
Habitat Adults frequent flowers of many kinds.
Distribution Western United States.
Note This species is extremely variable as are other species of this group, adding to the difficulty of identification. More information is needed about their life histories, host plant preferences, and distribution patterns.

169 CORTODERA SUBSPILOSA
Western Mountain Flower Longhorn

Family Cerambycidae
Order Coleoptera
Length Male 7–11 mm; female 8–13 mm.
Recognition marks Male elytra are slightly tapered; black, often with elytra, legs, antennae, and abdomen brownish yellow; pubescence is usually dense, long, and erect; punctation is usually fine and dense; antennae are shorter than the body; female is stouter; antennae extend to about the middle of elytra.
Habitat Adults fly about many species of flowers.
Distribution Northwestern North America; other species throughout western North America.
Note The twenty species of this genus in North America are recognized by their slender antennae, oval eyes without an indentation near the antennae, and the short head. The species are rather small. They can be identified only by using technical features.

170 STENOSTROPHIA TRIBALTEATA
Tiger-spotted Flower Lepturine

Family Cerambycidae
Order Coleoptera
Length 7–12 mm.
Recognition marks Sides are tapered in male; female is more robust; black with appendages often pale; elytra has four yellow transverse bands; elytral pubescence is dense, short, and recumbent, yellow and black; punctations are fine and shallow; antennae are shorter than the body. The two-colored pubescence is distinctive to this species.
Habitat Adults are near flowers of many kinds.
Distribution Western North America.
Note The three species of the genus *Stenostrophea* in North America may be recognized by the distinctive yellow and black transverse bands on the elytra. They are smaller than most Lepturines.

W

171 MONEILEMA ARMATA
Black Cactus Longhorn

Family Cerambycidae
Order Coleoptera
Length 13–33 mm.
Recognition marks Elongate; black; surface is shiny; head is sparsely punctate with small and medium punctures intermixed; thorax is slightly wider than long, the surface minutely punctate on disk, larger punctures along the base and beneath the lateral spine; elytra are sparsely, irregularly punctate to within one-third of the apex, the remaining portion densely punctate.
Habitat Adults feed on cactus and their larvae bore into the plant.
Distribution Colorado, New Mexico, and Texas.
Note This is a large genus with about thirty species, all western, and all cactus feeders. The adults first appear in May or June and emerge continuously until the end of September. During the day, the adults hide on the lower part of the cactus where they are protected from the hot rays of the sun. After copulation takes place on the plant, the female lays her eggs in the fresh wound at a point where a branch has been gnawed off. The larvae bore into the cactus. Pupation takes place within the plant. The second generation of adults gnaw their way out.

W

172 NEOPTYCHODES TRILINEATUS
White-fringed Longhorn

Family Cerambycidae
Order Coleoptera
Length 21–35 mm.
Recognition marks Elongate-ovate, rather slender, slightly flattened; reddish brown to black, the elytra sometimes lighter; head has a broad white stripe and a double orange stripe; pronotum has three white stripes; each elytron has two white stripes and a disk, each with two rows, more or less distinct, of very small orangish dots, which sometimes fuse to form two lines; surface is covered with yellowish gray scales; ventrally black with moderately long, fine, yellowish hairlike setae, and irregular patches of dense, yellowish white scales.
Habitat Larvae feed on fig, alder, and mulberry.
Distribution South Carolina to Florida, west to Arizona and Mexico.
Note This species is a member of the large tribe Monchamini with twenty-four species in the United States. The species are often brightly marked and they all have extremely long antennae, sometimes more than twice the length of the body.

---

173 MONOCHAMUS CAROLINENSIS
Carolina Sawyer

Family Cerambycidae
Order Coleoptera
Length 13–23 mm.
Recognition marks Elongate, robust, subcylindrical; brownish; elytra are irregularly mottled with patches of brown; pubescence is black, gray, or white; males have extremely long antennae, sometimes four and one-half times as long as those of the female and never less than one and one-half times the length of the body.
Habitat Larvae bore in pine, spruce, and fir. Adults are attracted to lights at night.
Distribution Southeastern United States.
Note Eleven species belong to the genus *Monochamus*, the largest genus of the Monochamini in the United States. This tribe is a part of the subfamily Lamiinae, a large and poorly studied group.

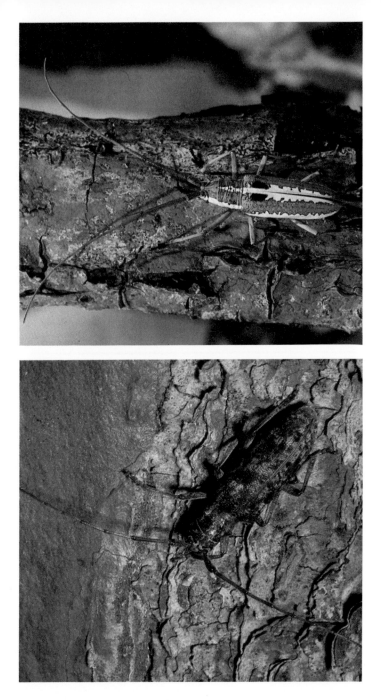

174 LOCHMAEOCLES MARMORATA
Marbled Sawyer

Family Cerambycidae
Order Coleoptera
Length 21–29 mm.
Recognition marks Elongate-ovate, robust, subcylindrical; dark brown, covered with whitish pubescence; head has white and orange pubescence; pronotum sometimes has indistinct orange markings on each side; elytra has extreme base and usually an oblique, broken band at middle of denser white, with small, irregular reddish orange spots, usually outlined in white, scattered over the disk; antennae of male about twice the length of the body, of female only slightly longer than the body.
Habitat Adults are twig girdlers. The larvae feed on bark and sapwood.
Distribution Southern Arizona.
Note This species belong to the large tribe Onciderini with over 250 New World species. However, it is mostly tropical with only seven species reaching the United States. A common species similar to this, *Oncideres cingulata*, the common twig girdler, is a pest in eastern United States where it damages hickory, persimmon, elm, poplar, sour gum, honey locust, dogwood, apple, and pear.

175 COENOPAEUS PALMERI
Cactus Longhorn

Family Cerambycidae
Order Coleoptera
Length 18–24 mm.
Recognition marks Black, densely covered with fine, dark brown pubescence; pronotum and elytra are usually marked with ashy or yellowish gray pubescence in spots, or occasionally over the entire area, sometimes forming bands; antennae about as long as the body in both sexes, all segments broadly annulate with ashy pubescence at base.
Habitat Adults sometimes come to lights at night. Larvae are wood borers.
Distribution Southwestern United States.
Note The presence of at least some dark brown pubescence on the upper surface will distinguish this extremely variable species from the other species in the genus, *C. niger*.

176 OBEREA BIMACULATA
Raspberry Cane Borer

Family Cerambycidae
Order Coleoptera
Length 8–12 mm.
Recognition marks Elongate, slender, cylindrical; black, shiny body; pronotum yellow with two round black spots on the disk, often have a small black spot in front of the scutellum; lower sides of thorax black; head and thorax rather sparsely, deeply, and coarsely punctate; elytra has rows of coarse punctures.
Habitat Adults are collected by sweeping vegetation along the margins of marshes. Larvae bore in the canes of raspberries and blackberries.
Distribution Northeastern United States.
Note The genus *Obera* contains about twenty-five species in the United States. The larvae all bore into the stems and twigs of many trees and shrubs.

177 TETRAOPES BASALIS
Milkweed Longhorn

Family Cerambycidae
Order Coleoptera
Length 12–15 mm.
Recognition marks Stout, short; head, prothorax, and elytra are red; ventral surface, tibiae, and tarsi are black; marked with round black dots: four on pronotum, one on scutellum, and three on each elytron; antennae are black and annulate; pronotum is finely, irregularly punctate; elytra are finely punctate at base, obsolete apically; antennae of males are nearly as long as body; female antennae are somewhat shorter.
Habitat Adults feed on milkweed; larvae bore into stems and roots of the same plant.
Distribution Widely distributed throughout the United States.
Note There are about twenty-eight species of this genus, all of which feed on various species of milkweed. The eyes, for no apparent reason, are divided, making four eyes instead of the normal two, the upper and lower portions of which are widely separated.

178 LEMA SEXPUNCTATA
Six-spotted Lema

Family Chrysomelidae
Order Coleoptera
Length 3–7 mm.
Recognition marks Brownish orange to deep reddish brown on elytra with six black spots on disk; very rarely the whole disk is black.
Habitat Adults and larvae feed only on the day flower; the adults eat only the epidermis of the leaves. The larvae eat holes in the leaves or the entire tissue of the same plant.
Distribution Throughout eastern North America, south into Mexico.
Note This genus contains twenty-three species distributed throughout eastern and southern United States. When disturbed, the beetles drop to the ground and run away or fly to other plants. The eggs are laid underneath the leaves. The larvae carry excrement on their backs. They become full-grown at the end of the fourth instar, drop to the ground, and form a cocoon in a concealed spot, under leaves or trash.

179 SAXINIS KNAUSI
Knaus' Saxinis

Family Chrysomelidae
Order Coleoptera
Length 3–4 mm.
Recognition marks Dark metallic blue to green, with orange-red shoulder spots.
Habitat Adults and larvae occur on a variety of plants, particularly *Ceanothus* species and redroot.
Distribution Central United States west of the Mississippi River, south to New Mexico and Arizona.
Note *Saxinis omogera,* the blue baboon beetle, is very similar to this species. It is found throughout eastern North America, west to Arizona. The genus *Saxinis* contains ten very similar species.

180 CHRYSOCHUS COBALTINUS
Blue Milkweed Beetle

Family Chrysomelidae
Order Coleoptera
Length 6.5–11.5 mm.
Recognition marks Oblong-convex; shiny, cobalt blue, occasionally has a greenish tinge or varies to black; ventrally bluish black to black; head and thorax have coarse, very sparse, deep punctures intermingled with minute ones; elytra are finely and irregularly punctate.
Habitat Adult and larvae common on dogbane and less common on milkweed.
Distribution Western North America.
Note The eastern species, *Chrysochus auratus*, the green milkweed beetle, is very similar but is metallic green. It feeds on the same plants.

---

181 ZYGOGRAMMA EXCLAMATIONIS
Sunflower Beetle

Family Chrysomelidae
Order Coleoptera
Length 7–8 mm.
Recognition marks Oval, convex; head is brown; pronotum is brown with a white anterior margin; sutural and adjacent stripe of elytra are dark, both reaching the apex.
Habitat Adults and larvae feed on sunflowers.
Distribution Western North America.
Note The genus *Zygogramma* contains thirteen species, one, *Z. suturalis* is found in eastern United States. It differs from the species illustrated by having only two very broad dark stripes on each elytron. It lives on ragweed and goldenrod.

182 LEPTINOTARSA DECEMLINEATA
Colorado Potato Beetle

Family Chrysomelidae
Order Coleoptera
Length 5.5–11 mm.
Recognition marks Oval, convex, stout; dull yellow to orange-red; thorax has two short black divergent stripes on disk and six small spots on each side; elytra have sutures and five narrow black stripes on each side, the second and third united near the apex; knees and tarsi are blackish.
Habitat Adults (upper right) feed and lay eggs on potatoes, tomatoes, and related plants. The larvae feed along with the adults on the same plants (lower right).
Distribution North America, Europe, and parts of Asia.
Note This notorious pest is only one culprit in a genus of twelve species. Most members of the genus feed on wild species of plants belonging to the potato family. One common southeastern species, *L. juncta*, feeds on horse nettle. However, another, a western species, *L. rubiginosa*, feeds on indian arrow, a member of the plant family Compositae. The species illustrated here has spread on potatoes from southwestern United States to most parts of the world. It is not now as severe a pest as formerly, but outbreaks continue to cause loss to potato growers.

183 CHRYSOMELA SCRIPTA
Cottonwood Leaf Beetle

Family Chrysomelidae
Order Coleoptera
Length 5.5–9 mm.
Recognition marks Elongate-oval; blackish with a greenish tinge except on elytra; head is dark; antennae are either black or have pale middle segments; pronotum varies from entirely dark to pale anteriorly with reddish spot; each elytron has a narrow sutural stripe and seven elongated dark spots on a dull yellow background; spots vary in size and shape from specimen to specimen.
Habitat Adults and larvae feed on willow and poplar.
Distribution Throughout North America.
Note The genus *Chrysomela* contains nineteen species with great variation in color patterns. Our species all feed on willow, poplar, or alder trees. Certain species are restricted to one or another of these food plants; others will breed on both willow and poplar, but the alder species never breed on the other plants. Oddly enough, in captivity, some species will feed on plants that they avoid in nature. This genus is a good example of the close relationship certain insects have with plants. Species evolution comes about through their adaptation to certain species of plants, an example of one form of co-evolution.

184 CALLIGRAPHA WICKHAMI
Wickham's Calligrapha

Family   Chrysomelidae
Order   Coleoptera
Length   7–8 mm.
Recognition marks   Oval, convex; reddish brown; pronotum has pale anterior and lateral margins with two pale median spots; elytra are pale, marked with irregular patterns of reddish brown: tarsal claws widely separated.
Habitat   Adults and larvae host plant unknown, probably feed on various shrubs.
Distribution   Texas.
Note   The genus *Calligrapha* has about thirty-five species which are all rather similar in appearance. They feed on various trees and shrubs. Most of the species are eastern but they are represented in the western states also. *C. rowena* is a common species found on dogwood. It is also attracted to lights at night. These beetles look like the species illustrated here but the elytral markings are a metallic reddish brown.

---

185 DIABROTICA UNDECIMPUNCTATA UNDECIMPUNCTATA
Spotted Cucumber Beetle

Family   Chrysomelidae
Order   Coleoptera
Length   6–7.5 mm.
Recognition marks   Basic color is greenish yellow; head, much of the legs and antennae and the central part of the under surface are black; elytra have eleven black spots.
Habitat   Adults feed on the foliage of cucumbers, corn, and many other plants. The larvae feed on the roots of corn and grasses.
Distribution   Eastern North America, west to Colorado and Arizona.
Note   The genus *Diabrotica* has ten species assigned to it. As noted above, the larvae feed on roots. Those that feed on corn as larvae are known as corn root worms. The most important of these pests is this species in the South where it is called the southern corn root worm and formerly had a different scientific name until it was learned that the color difference is merely a geographical variation.

186 DIABROTICA UNDECIMPUNCTATA HOWARDI
Western Spotted Cucumber Beetle

Family Chrysomelidae
Order Coleoptera
Length 5.5–7 mm.
Recognition marks Body, legs, and antennae are entirely black; otherwise this resembles the preceding subspecies.
Habitat Adults feed on citrus as well as many other plants. The larvae are pests on the roots of many forage and truck crops.
Distribution Pacific Coast.
Note Eggs of this beetle are deposited on or near the food plant and just below the surface of the ground when the soil is loose. The larvae burrow into the soil and attack the roots of various plants. They do extensive damage to crops. There may be one or two generations depending upon the length of the growing season in the area in which they live.

---

187 PHYSONOTA ARIZONAE
Arizona Gold Beetle

Family Chrysomelidae
Order Coleoptera
Length 11–13 mm.
Recognition marks Elongate-oval; pale greenish yellow; pronotum has three dark longitudinal marks, the median one four to six times longer than it is wide; abdomen is yellow with a short transverse dark mark on each segment near the lateral margin.
Habitat Adults and larvae feed on the flowers of burr sage and gentians. Other species occur on the leaves and flowers of a variety of plants, particularly morning glory and sweet potato.
Distribution Arizona, and related species throughout North America, but absent in the Pacific Northwest.
Note *Physonota unipunctata* is very similar, but black and yellow below. Common throughout eastern North America on flowers and leaves of hawthorn, horse mint, and rosin weed. The characteristic tortoise shape of the species of the subfamily Cassidinae is an easy identification feature. In life their colors are brilliant, but they soon fade in collections. The larvae have a forklike appendage which is extruded from the rear and bent forward over the back to form a "parasol" to protect themselves. The cast larval skins as well as their own feces are carried about with them, providing shade as well as camouflage.

188 CALLOSOBRUCHUS MACULATUS
Cowpea Weevil

Family Bruchidae
Order Coleoptera
Length 2.5–4.5 mm.
Recognition marks Antennae are serrated, with apical segments longer than they are wide; pale brown; dark to black apical segments; legs are pale brown; head, thorax, and elytra have intermixed brown and whitish pubescence on black head and thorax and brown elytra; each elytron has a large lateral spot with a black apex, but the color is variable.
Habitat Larvae live in black-eyed cowpeas. Adults are often found on flowers.
Distribution Throughout eastern North America and nearly cosmopolitan.
Note The species of the family Bruchidae vary considerably in their habits but depend almost entirely upon seeds for their development. Most of the larvae live in the seed pods of Leguminosae, the pea plant family, but other plants may be involved. Usually they are host specific, that is, the majority of the individuals live on a single species of plant. Interesting plant–host relationships result. The seed weevil life cycle is geared to that of the host plant. The female lays her eggs when the plant blossoms. The larvae infest the developing seed pods and mature as the seeds mature. Some species are continuous breeders, however, and are therefore able to live successfully in stored dried seeds.

C

189 RHYNCHITES BICOLOR
Rose Curculio

Family Circulionidae
Order Coleoptera
Length 5–6.5 mm.
Recognition marks Body is convex and broad; head has a moderately long snout; elytra, thorax, and head behind the eyes are bright red; ventrally black; the legs are blackish. Beaks of males are longer and more slender than those of the females.
Habitat On blossoms and leaves of roses; sometimes a pest.
Distribution Throughout the United States, but most abundant northward.
Note The snout beetle family, Curculionidae, contains many hundreds of species that do damage to crops and ornamental plants throughout the world. The group is easily recognized by the long beak present in most species. The chewing mouthparts are small and located at the end of the beak. The antennae are attached on the beak, often about midway.

G

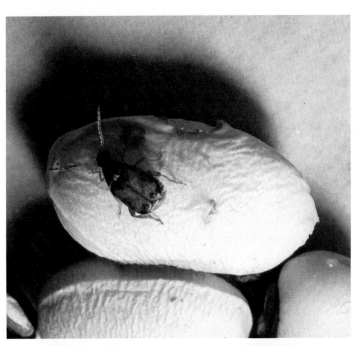

190 OPHRYASTES ARGENTATUS
Silver Twig Weevil

Family Curculionidae
Order Coleoptera
Length 9.5–15.5 mm.
Recognition marks Body is convex; snout is short and broad; antennae are inserted toward the apex of snout; color is usually pearly gray with brown intervals on elytra, but varying to nearly uniformly black in some specimens.
Habitat Usually found by beating deadwood and shrubbery.
Distribution Southwestern United States.
Note This insect belongs to a large group of weevils that are difficult to identify to species. Many are of economic importance.

W

191 CURCULIO PROBOSCIDEUS
Larger Chestnut Weevil

Family Curculionidae
Order Coleoptera
Length 8–11 mm.
Recognition marks Body is elongate-ovate; beak is very long, sometimes longer than the body; dark brown, densely covered with golden or clay-yellow scalelike setae; thorax has darker stripes; abdomen has brownish black spots.
Habitat Larvae feed inside of chestnuts (now rarely), and chinquapins. When the nut falls, the larvae leave and burrow into the soil to pupate.
Distribution Eastern North America.
Note These beautiful nut and acorn weevils are abundant in forests. Their extremely long proboscis may look dangerous but they do not bite. The many species attack chestnuts, hickories, pecans, hazelnuts, and acorns, often in disastrous numbers.

F

192 ODONTOCORYNUS DENTICORNIS
White-scaled Flower Weevil

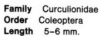

Family Curculionidae
Order Coleoptera
Length 5–6 mm.
Recognition marks Oblong and stout; black with sparse white scales above, denser below.
Habitat Adults are found on various composites, often on goldenrod.
Distribution Throughout central United States.
Note This species is more or less typical of the large number of weevil species. The family Curculionidae is the largest family of animals. One genus alone, *Apion*, has over 1100 species. Because of these great numbers, species are very difficult to identify. The biology of most species remains practically unknown. They are all phytophagous and, consequently, of considerable economic importance.

W

---

193 SCYPHOPHORUS ACUIPUNCTATUS
Agave Weevil

Family Curculionidae
Order Coleoptera
Length 12–15 mm.
Recognition marks Body is stout and broad; surface is sparsely punctate; beak is stout and deflexed; elytra are lightly striated.
Habitat Feed on agave.
Distribution Southwestern United States.
Note Probably the most infamous of all beetles, and particularly weevils, is the cotton boll weevil, *Anthonomus grandis*. This species invaded Texas from Mexico about 1892 and has spread throughout the cotton states. In the past it threatened the entire cotton industry because of the severe damage the larvae do to the boll or developing cotton flower by feeding on pollen and the tender tissues, causing a deformed flower and preventing the development of the seeds and, therefore, the cotton fibers themselves. This weevil is very hard to control because both larvae and adults hibernate away from the cotton fields. They are always present to infest the crop. Vast amounts of chemicals are needed to prevent their development and damage to the cotton.

W

194 PANORPA CONFUSA
Scorpionfly

Family Panorpidae
Order Mecoptera
Length 10–12 mm.
Recognition marks Reddish brown; wings are transparent, slightly yellowish, with large apical spots and smaller spots toward the base. This species is typical of the members of this family and shows the "scorpion" pose.
Habitat Woodlands.
Distribution Southeastern United States.
Note Hangingflies resemble craneflies (order Diptera) and do not have the scorpionlike males. They belong to the family Bittacidae. Their hind legs are raptorial and are used to capture prey.

---

195 CTENOCEPHALIDES FELIS
Cat Flea

Family Pulicidae
Order Siphonaptera
Length Approximately 1 mm.
Recognition marks Dark brown body with spines; combs of spines on head and on pronotum. Similar to dog flea, but the latter has a high, rounded forehead in comparison with this species which has a low, sloping forehead.
Habitat Both the cat flea, illustrated here, and the dog flea, *Ctenocephalides canis,* are temporary ectoparasites of dogs and cats, often interchangeably. The larvae of both species live in nests or around the areas where cats and dogs sleep, i.e., in rugs, cracks in the floor, and so on.
Distribution Wherever cats and dogs live except when the pet is kept in a fumigated building.
Note Fleas of various species are serious pests of domestic animals, wild animals, and humans. The so-called "sand flea" that attacks man is either a cat flea or a dog flea. Some species are vectors of disease and human infestations of fleas can cause serious dermatosis. Fleas are difficult to identify except by specialists. The available literature is helpful if time is spent learning the morphology and its nomenclature. Host data is essential.

196 PSYCHOGLYPHA SUBBOREALIS
Caddisfly

Family Limnephilidae
Order Trichoptera
Length Approximately 20 mm.
Recognition marks Wings are yellow-brown with a red stigma and a silvery streak which runs across the wing. Antennae are about as long as the body.
Habitat Near sunny pools; adults fly by day. Larvae in ponds with vegetation.
Distribution This species is abundant throughout northern North America from Alaska to California and Utah in the west, and from Ontario and Michigan east to Maine.
Note The case-making habit and the structure of the cases of caddisflies have fascinated naturalists for centuries. The larva illustrated here (lower right) belongs to a species of the genus *Nectopsyche*, but is illustrative of a typical caddisfly larval case. It is interesting that there is a correlation between the case structure and the classification of this order. The more primitive members make a sacklike silk net (Philopotaniidae); others make a silk tube retreat in which they hide when not searching for food (Psychomyiidae and Polycentropodidae); still others spin a net to trap food particles (Hydropsychidae). Some caddisflies do not make a case or a net, but simply cling to stones (Rhyacophilidae). The remainder make use of all sorts of material to contruct a case and are usually rather characteristic for each family.

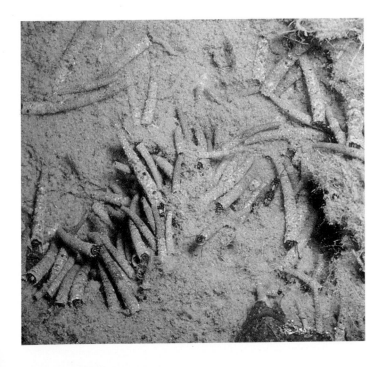

197 TINEA PELLIONELLA
Case-making Clothes Moth

Family Tineidae
Order Lepidoptera
Length Wingspan is 15–18 mm.
Recognition marks Front wings are dark gray mottled with darker gray; hind wings darker at apex.
Habitat This, and several other species of the family are of economic importance as pests of stored products, including fabrics. About 130 species of this family occur in the United States and Canada. In addition to the pest species, others live in rotten wood, fungi, and organic debris.
Distribution The clothes moths are cosmopolitan.
Note The clothes moth (*Tineola bisselliella*) is smaller and the wings are lighter in color. It is sometimes seen flying in closets, but also flies outdoors. Stored clothing must be clean and protected by using moth balls or placed in cedar chests. Larvae make a case out of bits of cloth. They move this around by protruding their head and legs from the case. Their food is woolen clothing and furs.

198 ATTEVA PUNCTELLA
Ailanthus Webworm

Family Yponomeutidae
Order Lepidoptera
Length Wingspan is 25–30 mm.
Recognition marks Front wings are reddish with four bands of pale spots surrounded by black borders.
Habitat Larvae live in webs on ailanthus and feed on leaves.
Distribution Common from New York south to Florida and west to Mexico.
Note Other members of this large family are marked with black spots on a white background. They are called Ermine Moths (*Yponemeuta padella*). A few species are important pests. Some are leaf miners, others feed upon flowers, fruit, and seeds. Various species live throughout United States and Canada. These "micro" Lepidoptera and many others come to lights at night. They are difficult to identify, but a great many of them are colorful and deserve the attention of the serious collector. Many species can be reared from organic matter of various kinds, for example, decaying wood, fungus, rotten fruit, leaf litter, and so on, as well as from various stored products.

199 MELITTIA GLORIOSA
Vine Borer

Family Sessiidae
Order Lepidoptera
Length Wingspan is 40–45 mm.
Recognition marks Front wings are pale green; hind wings are transparent, without scales except on veins; hind legs have a heavy fringe of orange scales.
Habitat Larvae bore into the bark, stems, and roots of many different plants.
Distribution Common in Arizona. This species represents a fairly large family of moths found throughout the United States and Canada.
Note The squash borer (*Melittia curcurbitae*) is a common pest of squash and other curcubites. The peach tree borer (*Synanthedon exitiosa*) is a serious pest of young peach trees. Other species have similar habits. The adults of many species resemble bees and wasps, both in appearance and in flight. Some species even pretend to sting. These brightly colored day-flying moths are often found around flower beds. They are strong flyers so it takes considerable skill with the net to capture them.

200 PARATRYLONE MELANE
Brown Skipper

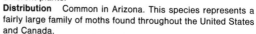

Family Hesperiidae
Order Lepidoptera
Length Wingspan is 28–34 mm.
Recognition marks Dark brown dorsally; reddish brown ventrally. Male has orange spots on the front wings; females have transparent spots. This species is similar to those of the genus *Poanes* which are very common throughout the United States.
Habitat Larvae of the giant skippers bore into Yucca stems. Many other skipper larvae feed on monocotyledonous plants (Lilfy family, grasses, and others) and the remainder feed on a variety of plants.
Distribution Throughout North America.
Note Skippers are considered to be very different from butterflies although they resemble them more than they do moths. Most species are diurnal and visit flowers. They are generally a drab brown without bright markings except that many are marked with a few white or orange spots, particularly at the apex of the front wings. Some uncommon species, such as the giant skippers (subfamily Megathyminae), are rather large, with wingspans up to 80 mm. Most skippers have a wingspan of under 35 mm. A few species have tails on the hind wing similar to those of the luna moth. Over 250 species occur in the United States and Canada. The adults are all strong flyers, visit flowers, and thus cross-pollinate many of the flowers.

201 PYRGUS OILEUS
Checkered Skipper

Family Hesperiidae
Order Lepidoptera
Length Wingspan is 26–32 mm.
Recognition marks Males are bluish gray; females are blackish; wings have checkered white spots, including sub-marginal and marginal series on both wings and in the center, but absent at the base.
Habitat Larvae feed on mallows (Malvaceae).
Distribution Southeastern United States.
Note This is a good example of the several species of "checkered" skippers. A few of these species have almost white wings. Most species occur in southern United States and in tropical America.

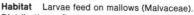

202 PYRRHOPYGE ARAXES
Large Brown Skipper

Family Hesperiidae
Order Lepidoptera
Length Wingspan is 45–60 mm.
Recognition marks Antennal club is curved back, a unique feature of this genus; head is partly to entirely yellowish; abdomen is sometimes banded with yellow; wings have white marginal spots; front wings have several large white spots. This is the only United States species with bent antennal clubs.
Habitat Larvae feed on oak.
Distribution Southern United States and Mexico.
Note This species represents a separate subfamily, Pyrrhopyginae, most species of which are found only in tropical America. The species are large, usually with a wingspan over 45 mm.

203 PAPILIO MACHAON
Old World Swallowtail

Family Papilionidae
Order Lepidoptera
Length Wingspan is 80–85 mm.
Recognition marks Hind wing has a dark area along the inner margin not extending into the discal cell area, and tails only two or three times as long as wide. (A closely related species, *P. oregonius* has tails much longer.)
Habitat Unknown, but in Europe larvae feed on Umbelliferae. Oviposition has been reported on *Artemisia arctica* (Compositae).
Distribution Alaska and Canada and in the northern part of Europe. Rare.
Note This species is one of about twenty-eight species of swallowtail butterflies, so-called because they almost always have tails on the hind wings. Among the most beautiful of butterflies with over 500 species worldwide, most of them tropical, they are highly prized by collectors. One common species, the pipevine swallowtail (*Battus philenor*), lacks tails on the hind wings. This species is widely distributed in the United States. The larvae feed on wild ginger, pipevine, and other plants. It is mimicked by the red spotted purple (*Limenitis astyanax*) (see illustration 250).

204 PAPILIO CRESPHONTES
Giant Swallowtail

Family Papilionidae
Order Lepidoptera
Length Wingspan is 100–140 mm.
Recognition marks Black with a yellow "X" on the front wing and basal and subapical bands on hind wing. Distinguished from *P. thoas* by the larger spots forming in the lower left leg of the "X" on the front wing. This is the largest butterfly in the United States and Canada.
Habitat Larvae feed on a variety of trees and plants including citrus, prickly ash, and hop trees. The osmeterium (see larvae, next species) is orange.
Distribution Eastern North America to Mexico.

205 PAPILIO GLAUCUS
Eastern Tiger Swallowtail

Family Papilionidae
Order Lepidoptera
Length Wingspan is 100–120 mm.
Recognition marks Yellow with black stripes; apex of hind wings has blue spots from inner margin to tails, or in some populations, across entire apex. No other single tailed swallowtail has as much yellow at the base of the front wing, except for the following species (see description of *P. rutulus* for differences).
Habitat This is a very common eastern species often seen in gardens in cities as well as abundant in fields.
Distribution Throughout eastern North America.
Note The larvae feed on many different kinds of trees including ash, basswood, tulip tree, birch, poplar, cherry, maple, apple, etc. The larvae are protected, as are all of the Papilios, by a protrusible forked scent organ, the osmeterium, located on the head, that secretes a foul smelling substance.

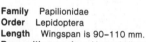

206 PAPILIO RUTULUS
Western Tiger Swallowtail

Family Papilionidae
Order Lepidoptera
Length Wingspan is 90–110 mm.
Recognition marks Very similar to the preceding species, except ventrally the hind wings lack marginal orange spots.
Habitat Larvae feed on willow, alder, sycamore, and aspen.
Distribution Western North America east to the edge of the Rocky Mountains.

207 PAPILIO EURYMEDON
White Tiger Swallowtail

Family Papilionidae
Order Lepidoptera
Length Wingspan is 75–90 mm.
Recognition marks Wings are black with white background, otherwise similar to the preceding species; tails are narrow, usually entirely black or very narrowly white on inner margin. The only other white swallowtail is the zebra swallowtail which has very long tails with white margins on both edges.
Habitat Larvae (lower right) feed on mountain laurel, New Jersey tea, hawthorn, alder, currant, and other plants.
Distribution Western North America.
Note Large false eyes on the mature larve are presumed to be warnings of their chemical protection.

208 COLIAS PHILODICE
Common Sulphur

Family Pieridae
Order Lepidoptera
Length Wingspan is 30–50 mm.
Recognition marks Yellow with wings marked dark brown on top; each front wing has a dark spot and each hind wing has an orange spot; wings ventrally without dark margins; black spot of front wings open; hind wing with double orange spots which are open; each wing with a submarginal row of small dark spots.
Habitat Larvae feed on alfalfa, clover, vetches, and other legumes.
Distribution All of North America except Arctic, desert, and tropical Florida.
Note The family Pieridae contains many species, most of which are yellow or white, marked with black and orange. They are usually called "whites" or "sulphurs." In fact, the common name, "butterfly," indicates this yellow or yellow-orange color of the insects. This common name was probably first applied to yellow European members of this family. They are very abundant and are often found at mud puddles. The several species illustrated here are distinctively marked and may be separated on the basis of their color patterns. In addition to these there are many other common forms such as the cabbage butterfly (*Pieris rapae*), one of our most abundant and widespread species, generally recognized by everyone.

209 COLIAS EURYTHEME
Alfalfa Butterfly

Family Pieridae
Order Lepidoptera
Length Wingspan is 40–65 mm.
Recognition marks Similar to the preceding; generally larger; orange instead of yellow above and with wider dark wing margins.
Habitat Larvae feed on alfalfa, clover, and other legumes.
Distribution Most of North America, but not as far north as *C. philodice*.

210 COLIAS CESONIA
Dog Face

Family Pieridae
Order Lepidoptera
Length Wingspan is 45–60 mm.
Recognition marks Yellow with black margins of front wings forming the outline of a dog's face with a black spot in the yellow as an eye; hind wings very narrowly margined with black.
Habitat Larvae feed chiefly on false indigo or lead plant (*Amorpha fruticosa*) but also other legumes including clover, alfalfa, and soy beans.
Distribution Throughout most of United States and south to Argentina.

---

211 ANTEOS CLORINDE
Clorinde

Family Pieridae
Order Lepidoptera
Length Wingspan is 80–90 mm.
Recognition marks White with irregular yellow spot in the middle of the margin of the front wing.
Habitat Larvae feed on *Cassia spectabilis*.
Distribution Known from Arizona, Texas, and Mexico. This species has been recorded in Kansas and Colorado.
Note This is a rare species, i.e., it lives a secluded life and collectors see it only rarely. Every species must have populations in the wild abundant enough so that mates can be found easily. If not, they would soon become extinct. Another species of *Anteos*, *A. maerula* is similar to this species and much more commonly collected. It is entirely yellow; it lives in Florida and Texas, and has been collected as far north as Nebraska.

212 PHOEBIS PHILEA
Orange Barred Sulphur

Family Pieridae
Order Lepidoptera
Length Wingspan is 65–70 mm.
Recognition marks Yellow with an irregular orange spot on anterior middle of front wing; hind wings have orange apical margins gradually merging with yellow basal.
Habitat Larvae feed on *Cassia* species.
Distribution Gulf Coast, straying north to Nebraska.
Note There are several other species of these large sulphurs, all of them confined to the southern part of the United States.

---

213 EUREMA NICIPPE
Sleepy Orange

Family Pieridae
Order Lepidoptera
Length Wingspan is 40–50 mm.
Recognition marks Orange with black wing margins resembling a sulphur (*Colias*), but much smaller. This is one of the many small Pieridae, but the only orange species in the genus.
Habitat The species flies in a rapid zigzag fashion and it is not easy to capture. Males are often abundant around mud puddles. The larvae feed on *Cassia*, clover, and other legumes.
Distribution Throughout eastern United States and west to California.
Note Other common species in this genus are yellow or white, variously marked with black wing margins, and sometimes with short, broad tails on the hind wings.

214 ANTHOCHARIS SARA
Orange Tip

Family   Pieridae
Order   Lepidoptera
Length   Wingspan is 45–50 mm.
Recognition marks   White body; front wing has prominent orange tip margined by black. Hind wing ventrally (lower right) mottled with brown. These markings are absent in some males. Yellow females are also known.
Habitat   Larvae feed on hedge mustard, rock cress, water cress, nasturtium, and various species of mustards.
Distribution   Western United States.
Note   Five species of the genus *Anthocharis* occur in the United States, all but one western. They usually have orange tips on the front wing, but there is considerable variation from white to yellow and with entirely black wing tips.

W

215 CHLOROSTRYMON MAESITES
Maesites Hairstreak

Family   Lycaenidae
Order   Lepidoptera
Length   Wingspan is 18–20 mm.
Recognition marks   Brilliant purplish blue above; ventrally (lower right) brown; hind wing below has an apical patch extending three-fourths the distance to the front margin of the wing; females are dark brown above with base of front wing and most of the hind wing dark blue; ventrally dark green.
Habitat   Unknown.
Distribution   Southern Florida.
Note   The family Lycaenidae contains many species, mostly small, many of them very rare. Most species are blue or brown colored with delicate, streaked markings, hence their common name, "hairstreaks" (Theclinae). Others are copper colored and popularly called "coppers" (Lycaeninae). The small blue species are simply referred to as "blues" (Plebejinae). The life cycles of many of the blues, especially members of the genus *Plebejus* (see *P. acmon*, entry 224), are very complex and involve interesting relationships with ants.

216 INCISALIA FORTIS BAYENSIS
San Bruno Elfin

Family Lycaenidae

Order Lepidoptera

Length Wingspan is 22–24 mm.

Recognition marks Light brown above with brownish orange at lower edge of hind wing; basal half of wing and outer margins reddish brown, irregularly separated from the brown remainder by a pale irregular narrow pale line; hind wings each have a short, blunt tail; antennae have alternately black and white segments, antennal clubs are dark brown.

Habitat Larvae feed on *Sedum spathulifolium* (Crassulaceae).

Distribution San Bruno Mountains, San Francisco Peninsula, San Mateo County, California. Several other similar subspecies occur in California, Oregon, and in Colorado.

Note This subspecies and five others are, at this writing, on the United States Department of Interior's list of endangered species. The others are: Lange's metalmark (*Apodemia mormo langei*); mission blue (*Plebejus icarioides missionensis*); el segundo blue (*Philotes battoides battoides*), and Smith's blue (*Philotes enoptes smithii*). In addition, the xerces blue (*Glaucopsyche xerces*) is known to be extinct. The last specimen was taken in 1943 in California.

217 ATLIDES HALESUS
Great Purple Hairstreak

Family Lycaenidae

Order Lepidoptera

Length Wingspan is 37–50 mm.

Recognition marks Iridescent bluish green to purple on the thorax and basal half of the wings; underside of front wings are nearly plain brown except for a small patch of blue; ventrally all of the wings have a crimson spot near the base and the hind wings each have three rows of greenish spots near the apex. Males have a large scent patch (see note) on the upper side of the front wing.

Habitat Larvae feed on mistletoe, live oak, western sycamore, and desert ironwood.

Distribution Apparently breeds only in southern United States but strays as far north as New York, Illinois, and Oregon.

Note The males of many species of butterflies have special scales on their wings termed *androconia*, or scent pads. They secrete an odor apparently attractive to the females. These scales are often on the front wings in patches or pads. They also occur on the hind wings of some butterflies, sometimes as a stripe.

218 STRYMON MELINUS
Gray Hairstreak

Family Lycaenidae
Order Lepidoptera
Length Wingspan is 18–20 mm.
Recognition marks Hind wing has two tails; dull velvety green or brown above; ventrally, two bright red spots near the tails.
Habitat Larvae feed on a great variety of plants including the buds, flowers, and pods of hairy bush clover and the developing seeds of hops, beans, and cotton.
Distribution Southern Canada, throughout United States, and south.
Note Many species of Lycaenidae have so-called "target" spots on the apex of their wings, as do many kinds of Lepidoptera, that apparently attract the attention of predators. They aim their attack toward these spots but often end up with a small piece of the wings as the butterfly flies away otherwise unharmed.

219 LYCAENA GORGON
Smartweed Copper

Family Lycaenidae
Order Lepidoptera
Length Wingspan is 25–32 mm.
Recognition marks Males are bright coppery purple; hind wings of both sexes have a series of submarginal bright orange spots or crescents on the ventral side.
Habitat Larvae feed on species of smartweed (Polygonaceae).
Distribution Mountains of Oregon and California.

220 LYCAENA RUBIDUS
Meadow Copper

Family Lycaenidae
Order Lepidoptera
Length Wingspan is 28–32 mm.
Recognition marks Males are metallic copper dorsally, pale cream ventrally; females have either orange or yellow in discal portion of each wing dorsally; submarginal area of wings is orange.
Habitat Adults visit flowers of composites at the edge of mountain meadows and along streams, especially in sagebush regions. The larvae feed on dock.
Distribution Western mountains of Canada and the United States.

221 LYCAENA HELLOIDES
Purplish Copper

Family Lycaenidae
Order Lepidoptera
Length Wingspan is 28–32 mm.
Recognition marks Males are similar to the preceding species but purple; hind wings have orange submarginal band; females are yellow above, also with orange submarginal band on hind wing.
Habitat Larvae feed on dock, knotweed, baby's breath, and other plants.
Distribution Throughout United States.

222 BREPHIDIUM EXILIS
Western Pigmy Blue

Family   Lycaenidae
Order   Lepidoptera
Length   Wingspan is 16–18 mm.
Recognition marks   This is the smallest species of butterfly known; males are dorsally brown; margin of wings are black and bases have an extensive purple area; ventrally grayish white at bases of wings to dark tan apically; females are lighter in color.
Habitat   Larvae feed on various Chenopodiacease and on *Petunia parviflora*.
Distribution   Western United States as far north as Oregon and south into South America.
Note   The genus *Brephidium* is also represented in the eastern part of the United States by the only other species, the Eastern Pigmy Blue (*B. pseudofea*), but does not range north of Georgia. It is found almost always around tidal flats. Adults lack basal blue area on wings.

---

223 EVERES AMYNTULA
Western Tailed Blue

Family   Lycaenidae
Order   Lepidoptera
Length   Wingspan is 20–28 mm.
Recognition marks   The dorsal color of this species varies from brood to brood, from light blue to a brownish blue; the females are darker; ventrally they are a very light bluish white with black spots and one submarginal orange spot on the hind wing. This is the only genus of the subfamily Plebejinae that has tails.
Habitat   Larvae feed on cultivated clover and many other legumes. They are attended by ants and the pupae stridulate.
Distribution   Throughout the United States from the Rocky Mountains to the West Coast. The only other species in the genus, *E. comyntas*, replaces this species in the East.

224 PLEBEJUS ACMON
Acmon Blue

Family Lycaenidae
Order Lepidoptera
Length Wingspan is 22–25 mm.
Recognition marks Males are bright blue above (upper right); front wing has a narrow black apical margin; hind wing has a submarginal orange stripe; females are brown above, sometimes front wing has bluish base; hind wing has broader orange or yellow subapical stripe; both sexes are bluish white underneath (lower right) with black spots and orange subapical stripe.
Habitat Larvae feed on various legumes.
Distribution Western United States east to Kansas, Nebraska, and Minnesota.
Note The larvae of the species of *Plebejus* are attended by ants. The "honey glands" of the larvae, located on the seventh abdominal segment, secrete a sweet liquid that attracts ants. This has resulted in the protection of the larvae from parasitic infestation by flies and wasps. Some species of Lycaenidae have become dependent on ants for transportation to their food plant. The pupae of the genus *Everes* are protected by the ants and draw attention by squeaking or stridulating.

225 ADELPHA BREDOWII
Western Sister

Family Nymphalidae
Order Lepidoptera
Length Wingspan is ±75 mm.
Recognition marks Brown above with white stripe across wings and distinctive orange-yellow patch on apex of front wing, separated from the margin by a narrow brown area; ventrally lighter brown with blue markings. This species is similar to *Limenitis lorquini* but in that species the orange patch is not separated from the margin by a dark band.
Habitat Larvae feed on oak.
Distribution Throughout much of southwestern United States.
Note The brush-footed butterflies (family Nymphalidae) form a large group of about 125 species in United States and Canada. Although mostly drab species, they are usually distinctively marked and some have bright colors. Their front pair of legs are greatly reduced and nonfunctional, resembling a small brush, hence their common name. The wings of the majority of the species are rounded in the normal fashion, but some have irregularly shaped wings which resemble leaves or bark. A selection of species are illustrated here to show the variety of forms. This is the largest family of butterflies.

226 LIMENITIS ARTHEMIS
White Admiral

Family Nymphalidae
Order Lepidoptera
Length Wingspan is 60–70 mm.
Recognition marks Dorsally have a broad white band across each wing on a brown base color; orange spots on base of wings; submarginal rows of orange spots; marginal rows of white and bluish spots; ventrally dark brown with similar markings and some additional orange spots.
Habitat Larvae feed on various trees, including birch, willow, and poplar.
Distribution Eastern United States, west to Rocky Mountains.
Note This species will hybridize with the red spotted purple and others of the genus *Limenitis*.

227 LIMENITIS ASTYANAX
Red Spotted Purple

Family   Nymphalidae
Order   Lepidoptera
Length   Wingspan is 60–80 mm.
Recognition marks   Dorsally, black and pale blue or green with three or four red spots in a row near margin of front wing; ventrally, brown with a submarginal row of red spots; two red spots at the base of front wings and four at base of hind wings. This is a mimic of the pipevine swallowtail (*Battus philenor*).
Habitat   Larvae feed on wild cherry, willow, poplar, and other trees.
Distribution   Throughout eastern United States.

---

228 LIMENITIS ARCHIPPUS
Viceroy

Family   Nymphalidae
Order   Lepidoptera
Length   Wingspan is 60–75 mm.
Recognition marks   Orange with black veins. This species mimics the monarch (*Danus plexippus*, see illustration 264). It differs from the monarch by the presence of the narrow black band across each hind wing.
Habitat   Larvae feed on willow, poplar, oak, and apple.
Distribution   Throughout United States.

229 LIMENITIS LORQUINI
Lorquin's Admiral

Family Nymphalidae
Order Lepidoptera
Length Wingspan is 60–65 mm.
Recognition marks Dark blue, it resembles the western sister (*Adelpha bredowii*) but is smaller; the orange-yellow patches on the front wings reach the margin.
Habitat Larvae feed on willow, cottonwood, and poplar.
Distribution West Coast east to Colorado.
Note The "admirals" are very common butterflies of the northern regions, both in the United States and Canada. One additional species, Weidemeyer's admiral (*L. weidemeyerii*), not illustrated here, occurs in the western mountains. It closely resembles the white admiral (*L. arthemis*).

W

---

230 PRECIS COENIA
Buckeye

Family Nymphalidae
Order Lepidoptera
Length Wingspan is 50–55 mm.
Recognition marks Dorsally dark brown with a conspicuous peacocklike eyespot located on each front wing and a large and smaller one on each hind wing; front wings have small orange spots and a dull, whitish band; hind wings have a narrow, but conspicuous band of yellow-orange; ventrally, much the same markings except that the eyespots are greatly reduced.
Habitat Larvae feed on plantain, snapdragon, and other plants.
Distribution Throughout the entire United States.
Note The only other species of peacock butterflies, as these are known, occurring in our area is *P. evarete* which is found only in southern Florida and southern Texas. There are many tropical species of this group.

W

231 CHLOSYNE NYCTEIS
Silvery Checkerspot

Family Nymphalidae
Order Lepidoptera
Length Wingspan is 30–50 mm.
Recognition marks Wings are tawny orange, lighter on the underside, and marked with black and some white; hind wings are silvery white on underside, but have orange markings.
Habitat Larvae feed on sunflowers and other Compositae.
Distribution Southern Canada, eastern United States west to Wyoming and Arizona.
Note This and the next species are representatives of a large and varied genus of butterflies which are difficult to identify unless they are dissected and the structures of the male genitalia are examined.

232 CHLOSYNE THEONA
White-patched Butterfly

Family Nymphalidae
Order Lepidoptera
Length Wingspan is 30–38 mm.
Recognition marks Dark brown with very wide transverse rows of brownish orange spots, brownish yellow in the center; row of white submarginal spots on each wing.
Habitat Larvae feed on *Leucophyllum texanum*.
Distribution Western Texas and southeastern New Mexico, into Mexico.
Note This species is representative of several very similar species in this group. There are many subspecies showing geographical variation in their color patterns.

233 EUPHYDRYAS CHALCEDONA
Chalcedona Checkerspot

Family Nymphalidae
Order Lepidoptera
Length Wingspan is 50–65 mm.
Recognition marks Wings are black to brown with light yellow spots; color is variable.
Habitat Larvae feed on various Scrophulariaceae.
Distribution Very common in Oregon south to California, Arizona, and into Mexico.
Note There are six species in the genus *Euphydryas*, very similar in coloration, and widely distributed throughout the United States.

---

234 VANESSA ATLANTA
Red Admiral

Family Nymphalidae
Order Lepidoptera
Length Wingspan is 45–50 mm.
Recognition marks Upper surface is purplish black with lightly shaded areas bright orange and white apical spots; under surface of the hind wings is marbled and marked with wavy lines of intricate pattern and by a green-dusted submarginal series of obscure eyespots.
Habitat Larvae feed on nettle and hops.
Distribution Throughout all of North America.
Note There are five species in the genus *Vanessa*, all of which are distinctively marked and very widely distributed.

235 SPEYERIA DIANA
Diana

Family   Nymphalidae
Order   Lepidoptera
Length   Wingspan is 80–100 mm.
Recognition marks   Male (upper right) is brown with the outer third of the wings orange; female (lower right) is black with blue spots.
Habitat   Larvae feed on violets at night and hide in the leaves during the day.
Distribution   Common in southeastern United States.
Note   Most of the seventeen species of the genus *Speyeria* are western and difficult to identify. This species is a typical example. They are also called fritillaries and silverspots. In southern Texas and Central America you may see species of calico butterflies (genus *Hamadryas*), resting head down with outspread wings on the trunk of small, lichen-covered trees. When disturbed, these insects fly away clicking their wings together quite audibly. Eventually, they will return to the same resting spot. The audible clicking is a means by which males stake out territory, similar to the way birds sing to defend their territories and to show intruders that they are trespassing.

236 NYMPHALIS ANTIOPA
Mourning Cloak

Family   Nymphalidae
Order   Lepidoptera
Length   Wingspan is 55–85 mm.
Recognition marks   This butterfly cannot be confused with any other species because of its uniformly brown, nearly black wings and the series of submarginal blue spots with the straw-yellow marginal bands on both pairs of wings; underside is similar but without blue spots.
Habitat   Larvae feed on willow, poplar, elm, and hackberry. Adults overwinter and fly on any warm day of the year.
Distribution   Common throughout North America.
Note   Four species of *Nymphalis* occur in the United States. The other three species are known as tortoise shells because of the marking on the under side of the wings which resembles that of certain tortoises.

W

---

237 LETHE PORTLANDIA
Pearly Eye

Family   Satyridae
Order   Lepidoptera
Length   Wingspan is 45–55 mm.
Recognition marks   Yellowish brown with three black eyespots on the front wings and five on the hind wings dorsally; spots on the ventral surface are distinctly eyed; front wing has conspicuous pearly violet markings.
Habitat   Larvae feed on various kinds of grasses.
Distribution   Northeastern United States, west to the Great Plains.
Note   This is only one example of the wood nymphs, satyrs, and arctics (family Satyridae). About fifty species are recorded in Canada and the United States. Members of this family can be recognized by the round eyespots of various sizes and by the drab brown color.

W

238 HELICONIUS CHARITONIUS
Zebra Butterfly

Family Heliconiidae
Order Lepidoptera
Length Wingspan is 75–85 mm.
Recognition marks Wings are elongate, very dark brown to black with bold, transverse yellow stripes; hind wings have a row of yellow spots.
Habitat Larvae (lower right) feed on passion flower vines. Adults fly in densely wooded areas, or at the edge of such areas.
Distribution Florida and along the Gulf to Louisiana, and strays north to South Carolina, west to Kansas.
Note The small family Heliconiidae is confined to the New World tropics with only four species in our area. The larvae feed on species of passion flower vines which are poisonous, and pass that substance on to the adults. Their striking markings warn predators that they should be avoided. Because of this protection, they are mimicked by many unrelated species.

239 DANUS PLEXIPPUS
Monarch

Family Danaidae
Order Lepidoptera
Length Wingspan is 95–105 mm.
Recognition marks Brownish red shading to dark yellow at the base; veins and wing tips black, white spots in black wing tips; hind wings lack black line across wing (which distinguishes this model from the mimic, the viceroy).
Habitat The larvae feed on milkweed. The larval foodplant is poisonous and both the larvae and the adults are poisonous to birds, the adults receiving the poison through the larvae. These butterflies are also called milkweed butterflies.
Distribution Southern Canada and throughout the United States.
Note The striking pupa (below) is one of the several types of pupae found among the various kinds of butterflies. This unprotected immobile stage is also poisonous and avoided by all predators. The family Danaidae is worldwide in distribution, but only four species live in North America. The most famous and widely recognized is the monarch. Most larvae of the species of this family feed on milkweeds; there are many species in this family of plants. Thus the common name of the family is aptly the milkweed butterflies.

The migratory habits of the monarch have attracted much attention and have been widely studied by lepidopterists. For many years individual butterflies have been marked, released, and recovered in various parts of the continent. In this manner much has been learned about their flight patterns. When they migrate they have the habit of congregating in large numbers in trees (upper right) to "sleep." Butterflies will return to some of these trees year after year. If marked specimens are found in the trees entomologists can learn where they came from. Only recently, however, entomologists have been able to discover the location of the final winter resting grounds in Mexico. In the spring these adults again migrate north, laying eggs as they go. Two or three generations, each lasting from four to six weeks, are produced, the adults dying off and the young taking over. In the fall it is the young replacements that migrate south, flying entirely by instinct.

A few other species of butterflies (for example, the snout butterfly, *Libyrheana bachmannii,* lower right) migrate, but none as precisely as the monarch.

241 SYNCHLORA AERATA
Green Looper

Family Geometridae
Order Lepidoptera
Length Wingspan is 15–22 mm.
Recognition marks Grass green, mottled with white scales; each wing has a transverse white line; palpi are reddish.
Habitat Larvae feed on various flowers and young seeds of low plants such as raspberry, compositae, and others.
Distribution Widely distributed in eastern North America.
Note The geometer moths (family Geometridae) is a large family of rather fragile moths, usually easily recognized by the characteristic shape of the adult as is shown by this species. The pattern of the front wings is usually continued on the hind wing, another good recognition characteristic.

The larvae are called inchworms, measuringworms, spanworms, or loopers (depending on the region). The one illustrated here (lower right) is not the larva of the green looper, but it is typical of the larvae of this family. Notice how it resembles a twig, a feature that affords it protection from many predators. These larvae frequently spin a strand of silk down which they descend from a tree or bush. At times they are abundant, and they crawl along in a looping manner. They are harmless to people, but they are often agricultural and forest pests. Two famous species in this family are the fall cankerworm (*Alsophila pometaria*) and the spring cankerworm (*Paleacrita vernata*), both pests of shade trees. The females of these particular species are wingless.

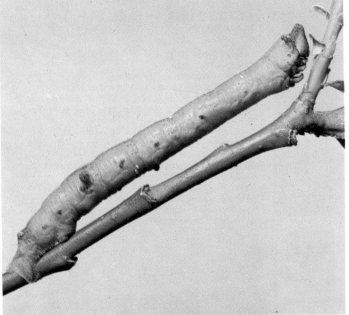

242 MALACOSOMA SPECIES
Tent Caterpillars

Family Lasiocampidae

Order Lepidoptera

Length Adults have a wingspan of about 28–38 mm.

Recognition marks Most species are recognized by the rich yellow-brown color with two dark lines across the front wings, sometimes uniting to form a broad band.

Habitat The larvae of many species form an extensive community tent of silk as illustrated here. They spend the night in these silken shelters and forage out from them by day. They are pests of many cultivated trees including apple, wild cherry, and others. Not all species make tents (for example, the forest tent caterpillar, *M. dissttria*) even though they are called "tent" caterpillars.

Distribution Various species are found throughout North America.

Note Members of the family Lasiocampidae are commonly called the lappet moths. About thirty-five species occur in the United States and Canada.

---

243 ACTIAS LUNA
Luna Moth

Family Saturniidae

Order Lepidoptera

Length Wingspan is 100–120 mm.

Recognition marks Body is white; wings are green and marked with brown and white; hind wings have long tails. This species cannot be confused with any other North American species.

Habitat The larvae feed on the leaves of many kinds of trees and shrubs. The cocoons are found on the ground among leaves.

Distribution Throughout southeastern Canada and eastern United States.

Note The beautiful giant moths that belong to the family Saturniidae are the delight of all students of insects. Sixty-five species occur in North America. A few of the striking species are pictured on the following pages.

244 HEMILEUCA EGLANTERINA
Sheep Moth

Family Saturniidae
Order Lepidoptera
Length Wingspan is 65–70 mm.
Recognition marks Usually dark brown marked with brownish yellow or somewhat brick colored, but varies from almost entirely dark yellow to very dark brown. The adults of this species are extremely variable in color. Males have plumose antennae, females filiform. Adults are diurnal, flying at midday.
Habitat Larvae feed on willow, aspen, birch, choke cherry, wild rose, manzanita, buckthorn, and many other plants.
Distribution Throughout western North America.
Note The genus *Hemileuca* contains eighteen species and several subspecies in the United States and Canada.

245 AGAPEMA GALBINA
Greasewood Moth

Family Saturniidae
Order Lepidoptera
Length Wingspan is 55–65 mm.
Recognition marks Brown with white markings darkened by brown scales; each wing has medium-sized eyespots with an inner orange ring and a narrow white center.
Habitat Larvae feed on greasewood (*Laria* species).
Distribution Western Texas, New Mexico, and Arizona.
Note The genus *Agapema* contains four species in the United States and Canada.

HYALOPHORA EURYALUS
Ceanothus Silkmoth

Family   Saturniidae
Order   Lepidoptera
Length   Wingspan is 105–110 mm.
Recognition marks   Reddish brown; each wing has white, elongated eyespots; front wing has small, multicolored marginal eyespot. The lighter color distinguishes this species from the one described in following entry. However, this species will readily cross breed in captivity with the species that follow.
Habitat   Larvae feed on the many trees and shrubs, particularly *Ceanothus* species. Notice that all of the dorsal tubercles of the larva (lower right) of this species are yellow (compare with the next species).
Distribution   British Columbia and the West Coast States, Idaho, Nevada, Montana, Utah, and south into Mexico.
Note   Moths of the genus *Hyalophora* are relatively easy to rear in captivity. They are often used for physiological and development experiments. Much of our knowledge of insect hormones has been learned by these experiments.

247 SATURNIA MENDOCINO
Mendocino Saturniid

Family Saturniidae
Order Lepidoptera
Length Wingspan is 45–65 mm.
Recognition marks Rich brown with dark brown spot on each wing, that of the front wing particularly, surrounded by white; moderate dark brown band across the hind wings.
Habitat Larvae (lower right) feed on manzanita, ceanothus, and other plants.
Distribution California.
Note Two additional species of the genus *Saturnia* occur in North America. They are confined to California also, and are very rare.

W

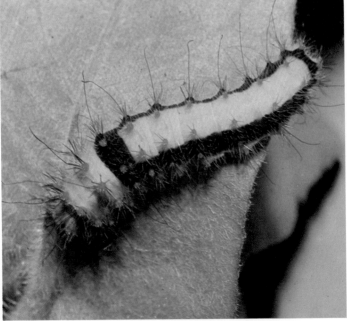

248 HYALOPHORA CECROPIA
Cecropia Moth

Family Saturniidae
Order Lepidoptera
Length Wingspan is 80–130 mm.
Recognition marks Very similar to the preceding species, but darker; crescents on wings vary from white to reddish, bordered with red and black.
Habitat Larvae feed on a great variety of trees and shrubs. These larvae are green with a bluish tint; two rows of blue tubercles along each side, two rows of yellow ones along the back, and two pairs of red ones on the thorax.
Distribution Southern Canada and eastern United States, west to the Rocky Mountains, and south to Arizona.
Note There are a total of four species in this genus in the United States and Canada.

249 ROTHSCHILDIA JORULLA
Rothschild's Saturniid

Family Saturniidae
Order Lepidoptera
Length Wingspan is 100–110 mm.
Recognition marks Similar in appearance to the cercropia moth, but with teardrop-shaped white spots on each wing; eyespots of front wing margin are obscure.
Habitat Natural food plants of larvae are uncertain because of confused identifications in the records. However, the species has been reared on a wide variety of plants such as willow, ash, lilac, and privet.
Distribution Arizona and southern Texas in only a few localities, but is found in Mexico and Central America more abundantly.
Note Only three species of the genus *Rothschildia* occur in North America and these are known only from our southern border states.

ANTHERAEA POLYPHEMUS
Polyphemus Moth

Family Saturniidae
Order Lepidoptera
Length Wingspan is 100–130 mm.
Recognition marks Reddish brown to cinnamon; each wing
has a large round eyespot; no definite eyespot on the outer
margin of the front wings.
Habitat Larvae (lower right) feed on a wide variety of trees
and shrubs. They are easy to rear.
Distribution Southern Canada and throughout the United
States. This is the most common and widespread Saturniid
moth.
Note Only one species of *Antheraea* occurs in North
America. Two additional subspecies are recognized. Several
other genera of Saturniid moths not shown here occur in various regions of Canada and the United States.

W

251 EUMORPHA PANDORUS
Pandora Sphinx

Family Sphingidae
Order Lepidoptera
Length Wingspan is 110–115 mm.
Recognition marks Beautiful greenish tinged front wing with a narrow pink dash.
Habitat The adults fly at dusk and later. The larvae feed on grape, Virginia creeper, and other plants.
Distribution Throughout eastern United States.
Note This is a large family of easily recognized moths. They all have the characteristic streamlined shape of this species. About 115 species live in Canada and the United States. Some of the species have clear wings and shorter, stocky bodies.

252 SMERINTHUS CERISYI
Willow Sphinx

Family Sphingidae
Order Lepidoptera
Length Wingspan is 55–65 mm.
Recognition marks Front wings have an irregular outer edge; brown with dark brown and light gray markings; hind wings are pink or rose with prominent dark eyespots, without a center bar.
Habitat Larvae feed on willow and poplar.
Distribution Southern Canada and northern United States, south in western mountains to Arizona.
Note Most sphinx moths have a very long proboscis used to suck nectar from flowers. Sometimes these dayflying moths are mistaken for hummingbirds. They have been reported to visit hummingbird sugar feeders.

253 MANDUCA SEXTA
Tobacco Hornworm

Family Sphingidae
Order Lepidoptera
Length Wingspan is 110–120 mm.
Recognition marks Wings are dark, mottled with gray; abdomen has six orange-yellow spots on each side.
Habitat Larvae (lower right) feed on tobacco, tomato, potato, and other solanaceous plants.
Distribution Throughout eastern United States.
Note This species is easy to rear in school laboratories. It is available commercially in kits for this purpose.

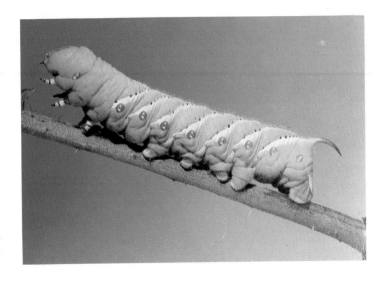

254 ECTYPIA CLIO
Clio Moth

Family   Arctiidae
Order   Lepidoptera
Length   Wingspan is 45–50 mm.
Recognition marks   Entirely white except for black veins on front wings, and slight markings on hind wings; abdomen is pale yellow with a dorsal median row of black spots.
Habitat   The food plant of this rare moth is uncertain.
Distribution   Southern California.
Note   Members of the family Arctiidae are often called tiger moths because of their bright colors, usually in the form of stripes. The adults and larvae are poisonous to birds and other predators. The colors are warnings.

255 GNOPHAELA VERMICULATA
Pericopid Moth

Family   Arctiidae
Order   Lepidoptera
Length   Wingspan is 40–45 mm.
Recognition marks   Brown with yellow markings on the wings. This is representative of a small group of these moths that are less colorfully marked than most.
Habitat   Food plants are not known.
Distribution   Southwestern United States.
Note   Most of the larvae of the tigar moths are densely clothed with hairlike setae. This offers some protection from predators because of the difficulty in grasping these woolly creatures.

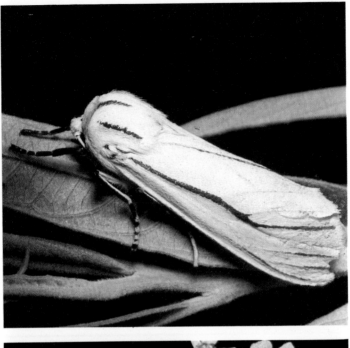

256 PLATYPREPIA VIRGINALIS
Ranchman's Tiger Moth

Family Arctiidae
Order Lepidoptera
Length Wingspan is 50–60 mm.
Recognition marks Front wings are black with large pale yellow spots; hind wings are yellow with black markings varying to almost entirely black with some submarginal yellow spots.
Habitat Larvae food plant not recorded.
Distribution Western United States.
Note A very similar species, *Hyphoraia parthenos*, occurs in northeastern United States and southern Canada.

W

---

257 APANTESIS PHYLLIRA
Southern Tiger Moth

Family Arctiidae
Order Lepidoptera
Length Wingspan is 28–32 mm.
Recognition marks Front wings black with distinct cream stripes; the "M" at the outer fourth does not have fine stripes between the cross bars; hind wings reddish orange with large black marginal and submarginal spots.
Habitat Larvae feed on watermelon, tobacco, and other low plants.
Distribution Southern United States.
Note This species is very similar to *A. virgo* which is larger and has more stripes on the front wings and large basal black spots on the hind wings. *A. parthenice* is almost exactly like this species but it has several additional fine white lines on the front wings. These two species are common throughout the northern United States. There are many additional species in this genus.

C

258 OZODAMIA BARNESII
Barnes' Tiger Moth

Family Arctiidae
Order Lepidoptera
Length Wingspan is 25–30 mm.
Recognition marks Very similar to the preceding species but hind wings are almost entirely black except for an irregular subapical orange spot. Notice also that the hind margin is slightly extended.
Habitat Larvae food plant not recorded.
Distribution Arizona.
Note Related to these species, but not illustrated here, is the banded woollybear caterpillar, famous as a weather prophet. The adults are buff to light brown with darker stripes and spots. The larvae are covered with stiff hair, chestnut in the center, but both ends are black. These familiar woollybears are seen crawling across highways in the fall, searching for a place to hibernate through the winter. It is said that the relative amount of black fur on the ends foretells the length of the coming winter: the more black, the longer the winter. Actually, the wetter the season or the younger the caterpillar, the more black it will have.

---

259 UTETHEISA BELLA
Bella Moth

Family Arctiidae
Order Lepidoptera
Length Wingspan is 35–45 mm.
Recognition marks Front wings are yellow with transverse white stripes; each has a row of small black dots within the stripe; hind wing is pink with a narrow irregular black border.
Habitat Larvae feed on rattlebox (*Crotalaria* species), lespedeza, and other legumes.
Distribution Eastern United States, west to Kansas and Texas.
Note Sometimes insects are imported for the biological control of weeds. By propagating a species that is host specific for a certain plant, it can become a "pest" of a pest plant. One such case is the importation of the cinnabar moth (*Tyria jacobaeae*), an Arctiid, to control the klamath weed, also an imported pest now established in California as a rangeland weed. This plant is poisonous to cattle, but it is too expensive to use chemical weed killers on the plant. The moth is bringing the weed under control.

260 LYCOMORPHA PHOLUS
Lycid Mimic

Family Arctiidae
Order Lepidoptera
Length Wingspan is 25–30 mm.
Recognition marks Resembles a lycid beetle; wings are orange at the base, black apically.
Habitat Larvae feed on lichens.
Distribution Common and widely distributed throughout the United States.
Note Related species in the genus are found on Compositae. Their resemblance to Lycidae (order Coleoptera) affords them protection because the lycid beetles (see illustration 132) are very poisonous to predators of all sorts.

261 HYPHANTRIA CUNEA
Fall Webworm

Family Arctiidae
Order Lepidoptera
Length Wingspan is 25–42 mm.
Recognition marks Front wings entirely white to heavily speckled with black spots; hind wings are white; abdomen is white to dark.
Habitat Larvae make a large nest in many different kinds of trees, particularly apple, ash, and oak. The nests enlarge and become very objectionable in the early fall.
Distribution Eastern United States from central New York to Florida.
Note This species is seldom a pest in the United States, but because of the unsightly nests, most people believe they are doing serious damage to the trees. They have been exported to Europe and Japan. There they are severe pests of forest trees.

262 AUTOGRAPHA CALIFORNICA
Alfalfa Looper

Family   Noctuidae
Order   Lepidoptera
Length   Wingspan is 35–40 mm.
Recognition marks   Gray on brown with pale markings, and one or more silver spots.
Habitat   Larvae feed on cabbage and other low succulent plants. They are called loopers because they lack some of their prolegs, causing them to walk in a looping fashion as do the larvae of the Geometridae.
Distribution   Generally distributed throughout North America.
Note   The family Noctuidae is the largest family of Lepidoptera. Many species are of great economic importance. Although there are many attractive species, as a group they tend to be dully colored. Because of the great number of species, they are difficult to identify without the use of technical literature.

C

263 HELIOTHIS ZEA
Corn Earworm

Family   Noctuidae
Order   Lepidoptera
Length   Wingspan is 35–45 mm.
Recognition marks   Reddish brown with dark spots and both pale and dark stripes.
Habitat   Larvae feed on corn, tomatoes, cotton, and tobacco, as well as many wild plants. They are generally considered to be a severe pest of corn because of the damage done to the ears, rendering them unfit or of poor marketing quality.
Distribution   Generally distributed in North America.
Note   The larvae of Noctuidae are usually called cutworms, so-named because they feed at about ground level on the plant and cut into, and often through, the plant stem at the base. Species that infest crops are, of course, the cause of considerable economic loss. Other Noctuid larvae are leaf feeders, and still others stem borers. A few are leaf miners.

C

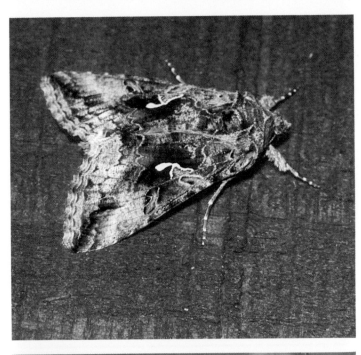

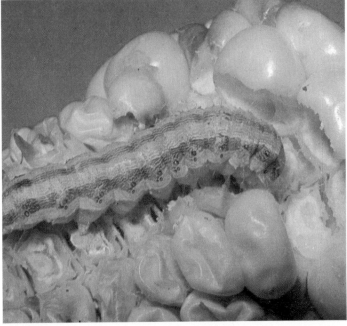

264 ACANTHOLYDA ERYTHROCEPHALA
Pine Webworm

Family   Pamphiliidae
Order   Hymenoptera
Length   8–15 mm.
Recognition marks   Robust; hind margin of pronotum nearly straight; antennae slender, many-segmented; body bluish; head brown.
Habitat   Larvae feed on pine, larch, spruce, and fir.
Distribution   Throughout northeastern United States; introduced into North America from Europe in 1925.
Note   The larvae of sawflies may roll up leaves to create a shelter and to feed. Other species feed openly on the needles and look very much like caterpillars of moths. Sometimes they use silk to tie together leaves for a shelter. The family to which this insect is assigned contains about ninety species in North America. The term "sawfly" refers to about seven families of Hymenoptera. The adults of some species have an ovipositor with serrations which is used to cut into bark where they deposit eggs. The larvae of sawflies may be distinguished from those of caterpillars by the number of abdominal prolegs. Caterpillars never have more than five, while the sawfly larvae have six to eight pair.

265 UROCERUS CALIFORNICUS
Horntail

Family   Siricidae
Order   Hymenoptera
Length   32–36 mm.
Recognition marks   Black; antennae are yellow; legs have yellow bands; patches of yellow on the side of the head; wings are amber; ovipositor is slightly shorter than the length of the body.
Habitat   The larvae infest fir, Douglas fir, and sometimes pine.
Distribution   Throughout western North America. A similar species, *U. albicornis* occur across Canada and northern United States.
Note   Horntails are usually brown or black with yellow markings and with darkened wings. The ovipositor is long and stout which accounts for their common name. The pronotum is wider than long. The larvae have a distinct head capsule, chewing mouthparts, and well developed legs. Various species infest both conifers and deciduous trees that have been injured by fire, lightning, or disease. Larvae may remain in lumber that is used for building, and when the adults emerge they can cause considerable damage by boring through plaster, hardwood floors, rugs, and so on. Seventeen species occur in the United States and Canada.

266 MACROPHYA TRISYLLABA
Sawfly

Family Tenthredinidae
Order Hymenoptera
Length 10–11 mm.
Recognition marks Black, marked with white at antennal apex; clypeus, labrum, mandibles at base, anterior portion of thorax, scutellum, front legs beyond basal third of femora, tarsal segments at base, middle femora at apex, middle tibiae in part, middle tarsal segments, hind femora beneath, and apical margins of abdominal segment (upper right).
Habitat Larvae infest elderberry (lower right).
Distribution Northeastern North America.
Note The family Tenthredinidae is the largest family of sawflies with about 800 species in North America, north of Mexico. The larvae feed on leaves where they produce galls or mine the leaves. A number of species, among them the larch sawfly, *Pristiphora erichsonii*, are serious pests. This species feeds on the needles of older twigs, and where the attack is heavy, the entire tree may be defoliated and die.

The birch leaf-mining sawfly, *Heterarthrus nemoratus*, is an introduced species first recorded in the United States in 1905, but it has since spread throughout northeastern North America. Its hosts are various species of birch, with gray, paper, yellow, and European white birch being the preferred species. The full-grown larvae are somewhat flattened and whitish, the head and segments of the thoracic legs brownish.

Other species in this family are pests of elm, alder, pears, oak, willow, spruce, and many other trees. The caterpillars of these species are often marked with black spots on yellow bodies. They tend to raise the hind part of the body when disturbed, the opposite of the reaction of most moth caterpillars. Sawflies do not sting. Their ovipositor is modified only for cutting into plant tissue to deposit eggs.

267 CEPHUS CINCTUS
Wheat Stem Sawfly

Family Cephidae
Order Hymenoptera
Length 9–11 mm.
Recognition marks Black with yellow banding on the abdomen.
Habitat The larvae feed on the stems of wheat. They bore into the wheat, eventually killing the plant. They bore to the base of the stem and thus are spared during the wheat harvest. The mature larva spends the winter in the stubble unless it is killed by plowing.
Distribution Southern Canada and northern United States.
Note The small family Cephidae contains eleven species in the United States and Canada. In addition to the one pictured here, the black grain stem sawfly, *Trachelus tabidus* is a pest from Michigan to New York, south to Maryland and Virginia. This is an introduced species that infests only cultivated grains. The more primitive Hymenoptera are seldom seen by the casual collector. Sweeping cultivated fields and searching through forests with an aerial net is the only way to add these species to the collection.

---

268 RHYSSA LINEOLATA
Ichneumon

Family Ichneumonidae
Order Hymenoptera
Length ±15 mm.
Recognition marks Black, antennae have small annulations of white; abdomen reddish orange.
Habitat Oviposition is in wood by means of a long ovipositor. The female bores into wood and deposits her egg in the larva of an insect, particularly beetle larvae and sawfly larvae.
Distribution Throughout northern North America.
Note Ichneumon wasps, family Ichneumonidae, are all parasites of holometabolous insects, rarely parasites of spiders and pseudoscorpions. Most species are host specific. They range in size from 3 to 40 mm, but many have extremely long ovipositors, sometimes much longer than the length of the body. Over 8,000 species of these extremely beneficial insects occur in the United States and Canada. Much more could be done to control insect pests by using these insects for biological control than is now being done.

APANTELES SPECIES
Parasitic Wasp

Family Braconidae
Order Hymenoptera
Length 2–4 mm.
Recognition marks Black, legs and antennae brownish black; wings without markings, but in some species they may be dusky (upper right).
Habitat The larvae of most of the species of the large genus *Apanteles* are internal parasites of Lepidoptera larvae, mostly of cutworms and spanworms (lower right).
Distribution Members of the genus *Apanteles* are widely distributed throughout North America. Most areas have many species.
Note Members of this genus and of the family Braconidae in general are difficult to identify to species. They are small and very similar in appearance. It is necessary to know the insect host as well. Like Ichneumons, species of braconids are very beneficial in controlling insect pests as well as the populations of many beetle and moth species. Parasitic wasps, which includes many families, are among the largest group of insects. As parasites, they differ from the parasitic worms that infest mammals. The wasp always kills its victim. Their life and development is usually inside the host larva and is atuned to the growth and development of the host. The parasite consumes the vital organs of the host in ascending order of importance. The larval host has continued to feed throughout its normal growth period and it usually attains its full growth. However, by the time it should form a pupa, the parasite has taken over, and instead of a moth or beetle emerging, the parasite leaves as an adult. The term "parasitoid" has been applied to this phenomenon instead of the usual word parasite.

Sometimes more than one parasite may infest the host, or the parasite may even multiply in the embryonic stage so that one original egg of the parasite may produce a great many adults. Some species of wasps are parasitic on other wasp parasites. Instead of the original parasite emerging, the parasite of the parasite appears. This phenomenon is called hyperparasitism.

270 BLASTOPHAGA PSENES
Fig Wasp

Family Agaonidae
Order Hymenoptera
Length ± 1 mm.
Recognition marks Females are winged, males are wingless; black; front and hind legs thickened, middle pair slender; antennae are filiform but apical segments are somewhat thickened; head of the female has a dorsal, longitudinal groove.
Habitat This introduced species pollinates the commercial fig. The Smyrna fig is grown extensively in California, but it produces fruit only when pollinated by pollen from the wild fig or the caprifig, a task which is accomplished only by this species of fig wasp.
Distribution California and Florida where figs are grown.
Note The interesting symbiotic relationship between the fig and this wasp is one of the most remarkable associations among living things. The fig wasp develops in a gall in the wild fig or caprifig flowers. The wingless male emerges first and mates with a female. She in turn collects pollen in the male flowers of the caprifig and pollinates the flowers of all three varieties of figs. She only successfully oviposits in the shorter flowers of the caprifig which is why these wild figs are necessary for the survival of the commercial Smyrna fig.

---

271 NEUROTERUS CLAVENSIS
Oak Gall

Family Cynipidae
Order Hymenoptera
Length ± 2 mm.
Recognition marks Humpbacked; abdomen has two segments visible dorsally, the other segments telescoped beneath; wings have very reduced venation; black.
Habitat This species makes galls on oaks, particularly *Quercus gambelii*, gambel's oak.
Distribution Southwestern United States.
Note The gall wasp family, Cynipidae, and several related families form a very large superfamily, the Chalcidoidea, composed of many thousands of species. They are probably the most difficult of all insects to identify, because of the very small size, the need of host data and life history studies, and the lack of specialists to study these wasps. Gall wasps insert their eggs into the tissues of plant buds, stems, or roots. The activity and secretions of the larvae of most cynipids will cause the plant to develop an abnormal growth, a characteristically shaped enlargement called a gall as seen in the illustration. The gall itself is usually much easier to identify than the insect. Those interested in these insects should collect mature galls and wait for the adults to appear.

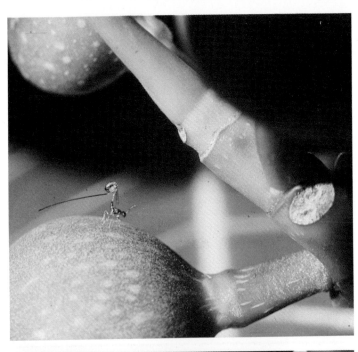

272 GASTERUPTION ASSECTATOR
Wild Carrot Wasp

Family Gasteruptiidae
Order Hymenoptera
Length 11–12 mm.
Recognition marks Black; wings are transparent with dark veins; hind tibiae are club shaped; front wings held folded lengthwise similar to social wasps.
Habitat Adults are found on umbelliferous flowers in open fields in late summer. The larvae are predators in the nests of other wasps and bees.
Distribution Throughout southern Canada and United States.
Note This small family contains only about fifteen species in our area. Related families have species that are parasites and predators on cockroach eggs, wood-boring beetles, as well as other wasps.

---

273 TRICHRYSIS TRIDENS
Cuckoo Wasp

Family Chrysididae
Order Hymenoptera
Length 7–11 mm.
Recognition marks Metallic blue-green, sometimes with a reddish cast; third abdominal segment of abdomen has sub-marginal grooves, hollowed out ventrally.
Habitat Parasitic on *Trypargilum politum*, a sand wasp.
Distribution United States east of the Rocky Mountains.
Note Cuckoo wasps are inquilines or cleptoparasites, that is, they kill the host larvae and their own larvae utilize the food that is stored in the nest of the host. These wasps, of which there are over 125 species in the United States, lie in the nests of solitary bees and wasps that build nests in the ground. These brightly colored wasps may be collected by an aerial net swept along the ground where they are searching for the nests of other Hymenoptera.

274 DASYMUTILLA OCCIDENTALIS
Eastern Velvet Ant

Family   Mutillidae
Order   Hymenoptera
Length   16–28 mm.
Recognition marks   Body blackish except for orange hairlike setae on abdomen.
Habitat   Adults on ground or on flowers. The female lays her eggs in the nests of bumble bees.
Distribution   Eastern United States south to Florida, west to Texas; related species and subspecies occur in the arid Southwest.
Note   Velvet ants, family Mutillidae, resemble true ants, family Formicidae, but they are almost always covered with long hairlike setae, usually of white, orange, or red, with black setae forming patterns. The females are wingless and are easily found running on the ground, but they sting and must be handled with care. Males are larger than the female and have wings. When they emerge from the pupae as adults they fly to the females for copulation. Although the species are widely distributed throughout North America, they are much more common and abundant in the arid Southwest.

---

275 DASYMUTILLA SACKENII
Western Velvet Ant

Family   Mutillidae
Order   Hymenoptera
Length   12–13 mm.
Recognition marks   Body is black, covered with pale yellowish hairlike setae; legs and underside of the body are black.
Habitat   The female lays her eggs in the nest of *Bembix occidentalis,* a sand wasp.
Distribution   Pacific Coast States and Nevada.
Note   Most velvet ants are active at night. The males sometimes come to lights. To collect the female, look at night near the ground nests of bees and wasps. Do not try to pick up the females because they can bend their bodies and sting. The stinger is nearly as long as the female's abdomen.

276 TRISCOLIA ARDENS
White Grub Wasp

Family Scoliidae
Order Hymenoptera
Length 25–30 mm.
Recognition marks Robust, hairy; black with red markings; hind coxae widely separated; apical portion of wings with numerous longitudinal wrinkles.
Habitat Adults generally found on flowers. The female flies over the ground in search of the white grubs (larvae of certain Scarabaeidae, order Coleoptera) which they parasitize. She digs into the soil and deposits an egg on the larva. The egg hatches and the wasp larvae feed on the beetle larva.
Distribution Southwestern United States and Mexico. Similar species are found throughout the United States and Canada.
Note The females of this and related species sting. Most of the following species of Hymenoptera have stingers. These are modified ovipositors with a connecting poison sac. The stinger can quickly pierce the skin, inject the poison, and immediately cause pain. This is a warning to mammals and predators to avoid these insects, and gives them a survival advantage. Many species are marked with bright orange as a warning that they sting.

---

277 POGONOMYRMEX BARBATUS
Harvester Ant

Family Formicidae
Order Hymenoptera
Length 6–7 mm.
Recognition marks Head and thorax are black; abdomen is red; pedicel is 2-segmented.
Habitat Harvester ants gather and store seeds and sometimes other insects. They build their nests in sandy areas.
Distribution Southwestern United States and Mexico, with related species throughout southern United States.
Note This species forms extensive colonies of several hundred individuals. They do not always confine their activities to the nest. They may extend their influence over a wider area by traveling along paths that radiate out from the nest as far as 30 meters (about 120 feet). These paths run into the surrounding vegetation from which the ants gather seeds or prey. The workers of these ants have a painful sting. There are many species of ants, some of which are illustrated here and on the following pages. They vary in length from 1–20 mm. in the United States. Some tropical species are larger. Usually they are dark colored, some are yellow or pale tan, or reddish brown. They can always be recognized by the pedicel or hump that separates the main portion of the abdomen (called the gaster) from the thorax. Their antennae are elbowed. The workers are wingless, but reproductives have wings and often swarm.

278 CREMASTOGASTER LINEOLATA
Lined Acrobatic Ant

Family Formicidae
Order Hymenoptera
Length 2.5–3.5 mm.
Recognition marks Light brown to black; body covered by yellowish pubescence, short and closely appressed; surface of thorax dorsally lined by striae interspersed with puncture; easily recognized by these lines and the heart-shaped abdomen.
Habitat Found in moderate to large colonies in exposed soil or under stones, logs, stumps, or in dead trees. The workers feed on aphid honeydew as well as dead insects. They also are predatory. The workers tend aphids, acquiring their honeydew and in return protecting them from aphid predators. This ant sometimes infests homes and may be found living in the woodwork of houses and outbuildings. Although they do not feed on the wood, their continuing enlargement of their nests can damage these structures.
Distribution Throughout southern Canada, and throughout United States east of the Rocky Mountains.
Note When disturbed, workers may attack human limbs, biting fiercely, and emitting repulsive odors.

---

279 SOLENOPSIS XYLONI
Southern Fire Ant

Family Formicidae
Order Hymenoptera
Length 1.6–5.8 mm.
Recognition marks Yellowish to reddish; gaster dark; body, especially the gaster, very hairy; surface finely sculptured; antennae 10-segmented with a small, 2-segmented club; mandibles straight with three distinct teeth.
Habitat Nests are in the ground, and colonies may be openly exposed or under the corner of stones and other objects. They rarely nest in wood, sometimes in woodwork or masonry of houses. Nests in soil consist of a loosely constructed irregular mound.
Distribution Southern United States from Florida to California.
Note The stings of ants are painful. This species has been reported to have stung an infant to death. Some individuals exhibit an allergic reaction to the stings and need medical treatment. Those that build mounds on lawns, in cultivated fields, and pastures are a particular nuisance. They are scavengers and may damage fruits, or enter homes and damage fabrics. The closely related ant, *Solenopsis geminata* is also a serious pest in the South.

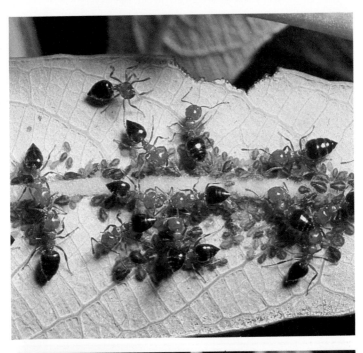

280 MYRMECOCYSTUS MELLIGER
Honey Ant

Family Formicidae
Order Hymenoptera
Length 6–12 mm.
Recognition marks Golden to brown, body covered with a fine pubescence; antennae 12-segmented, without a club, covered with fine pubescence; the storage caste have very large gasters.
Habitat This species is diurnal. The workers collect nectar and honeydew which is stored in their distended crops or honey stomachs until they reach their nests. There it is distributed by regurgitation to their larvae and sister ants. Some of the individuals serve as a storage caste, that is, they eat large quantities of honey which is kept undigested in the gaster. These individuals cling to the ceiling of the nest and hang downward, serving as living honey pots.
Distribution Southwestern United States and Mexico.
Note The honey storage ants have long been esteemed as an item of food by the Indians of Arizona and Mexico.

281 CAMPONOTUS PENSYLVANICUS
Carpenter Ant

Family Formicidae
Order Hymenoptera
Length 6–13 mm.
Recognition marks Light red to brown or black; gaster covered with ashy gray pubescence; eyes well developed; antennae 12-segmented, without a club.
Habitat This is a wood nesting species; the nest is dug out of the wood of dead trees, logs, stumps, and old wood of houses. The ants feed on dead insects, prey upon live insects, gather honeydew, and are attracted to the juice of fruits.
Distribution Throughout eastern North America, west to Texas.
Note The stinger is lacking in the workers of this species. However, they emit a strong odor of formic acid. The colonies may be very large. A typical colony may contain approximately 2,500 workers, a single queen, and some males. It takes from three to six years before they produce sexual individuals and swarm. Thus, they may invade a home and not be noticed for several years. They chew out an intricate system of galleries, usually in spots where the wood has somewhat decayed or where it has been damaged by other insects. The galleries may extend into the underlying soil. Although not as serious as termites, carpenter ants should be controlled by the use of chemical treatment of the wood.

282 FORMICA PALLIDE-FULVA
Mound Ant

Family Formicidae
Order Hymenoptera
Length 3.5–6.5 mm.
Recognition marks Mandibles have broad dentate apical border; gaster is yellowish or reddish brown; numerous hairs on the petiole.
Habitat This species is enslaved by *Formica pergandei*, another mound building ant. They form colonies, ranging in size from small to very large, in the soil, piling sticks and wood chips into piles. Their food is largely honeydew, but they also prey upon small arthropods.
Distribution Throughout eastern United States west to the Rocky Mountains.
Note This species is docile and easily enslaved by other species of ants. Formica ants represent one of the largest genera of this family. Many species are involved in slavery. This has long been of interest to biologists and there is a considerable amount of literature on the subject. Briefly, some ants raid the nest of other species in order to obtain pupae for food. Some of the pupae survive in storage chambers in the raiders' nest long enough to transform into workers. They emerge as workers and become a part of the colony although they are a different species. Because of their close similarity, they are accepted by their captors who serve as nest masters. This addition to the work force helps the colony as a whole and therefore raids are made not only for food, but for the purpose of obtaining additional slaves.

Ant nests are also the site of many invaders. Since their eyesight is not particularly good, shape and color are important for colony mate recognition only to a limited degree. Pheromones, odorous chemical substances more or less unique to the species, are important. Ant nest guests are often beetles, many of whom have evolved shapes similar to those of their hosts. Although they are not able to supply the proper odors, they can survive in the nest when other invaders would be torn to shreds and eaten, because they secrete substances that the ants like to lick. It is thought that perhaps some of these substances may have the effect of a drug since some colonies become "addicted" to the material supplied by their guests and spend more time tending them, rearing these beetles than they do their own young. The result is that the colony begins to deteriorate and finally dies out.

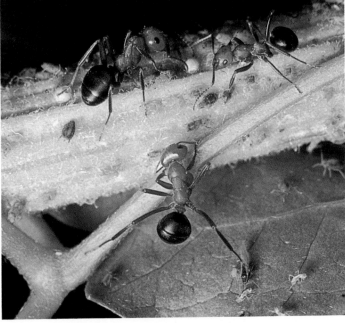

283 EUMENES FRATERNUS
Potter Wasp

Family Eumenidae
Order Hymenoptera
Length 13–17 mm.
Recognition marks Body is black with yellow markings on the thorax and abdomen; wings are smoky with violet iridescence.
Habitat Adults make a nest of clay in the form of a pot which is provisioned with the larvae of moths or beetles. The larvae are paralyzed by stinging but remain alive. The wasp attaches eggs on slender threads to the top or sides of the pot before the nest is stored with larvae. After the pot is filled, the cell is closed and the female flies away.
Distribution Southern Canada and eastern United States, west to Nebraska and south to Texas.
Note The behavior patterns of potter wasps differ from those of sphecid mud wasps. Potter wasps, as described above, do not lay their eggs on the prey, whereas sphecid mud wasps do attach their eggs directly on their larval food. Female potter wasps sting.

284 DOLICHOVESPULA ARENARIA
Aerial Hornet

Family Vespidae
Order Hymenoptera
Length 17–18 mm.
Recognition marks Brown with yellow markings on the head, thorax, and bands on the abdomen; wings folded longitudinally when not flying; hind femora not swollen; tarsal claws simple.
Habitat Nests are made of paper in trees, or in bushes near the ground.
Distribution Throughout United States and Canada as far north as the Arctic Circle.
Note Yellowjackets and hornets are aggressive. Their sting is painful and they must be collected with caution. Sometimes it is safe to approach the nest at night. The entire nest can be covered with a net, and chloroform or ether used to kill the inhabitants. However, this should not be done unless the wasps are a danger to homes or work areas. Wild hornets are an important part of our natural environment and they should not be needlessly killed.

POLISTES HUNTERI
Paper Wasp

Family Vespidae
Order Hymenoptera
Length 17–18 mm.
Recognition marks Reddish brown; antennae are dark, abdomen dark with the first abdominal segment above narrowly outlined with yellow; tarsi yellow (upper right).
Habitat The nests of paper wasps (lower right) are common on eaves of buildings, ceilings of porches, and other outdoor structures. The larvae and pupae live in the cells of the nest and are completely dependent upon the workers for food. A new colony is established each year by a young queen, the only surviver of the winter.
Distribution Eastern and southern United States, west to Arizona.
Note There are fifteen species of *Polistes* in the United States, most of which live in the arid Southwest. The nests of this species lack an outer paper covering. There is only one comb attached to a support by a rather thin pedicel. Polistine wasps have the greatest diversity of nest structure and social life of all of the Vespidae. The nests of *Polistes* species are small and simple, while those of other genera have more elaborate nests construction. Nests are made of wood pulp masticated by the wasps and glued together by their saliva. Number of combs, covers, and sites vary from species to species. Some are built underground by the excavation of soil, but still they are made of paper. Excavation may involve the removal of roots and shoots that interfere with the growth of the nest. The outer covering of the nest, which protects the combs from the effects of the weather, also insulates the colony from extremes of temperature; this is called the envelope. Inside are the cells, hexagonal shaped chambers in which live the larvae and pupae as they develop. Pillars support rows of cells within the envelope. Air spaces are necessary for proper ventilation in the nest and an attempt to maintain constant temperature. As the nest grows, older cells no longer in use are filled with fecal material. These cells are sealed off from the rest of the nest to prevent the possibility of the spread of disease. Nests thus can be simple, made up of ten to twenty cells, or massive nests with over 12,000 cells, with many variations in between—all constructed in approximately four months at the most.

286 PSEUDOMASARUS VESPOIDES
Mud Wasp

Family Masaridae
Order Hymenoptera
Length 8–18 mm.
Recognition marks Black, with yellow markings on the thorax and abdomen; wings transparent; antennae and most of the front of the head are yellow; antennae clubbed.
Habitat These wasps make a mud nest which is provisioned with pollen and nectar rather than insects. The nest is attached to twigs, or sometimes the sides of large rocks.
Distribution Western United States east to South Dakota, Colorado, and New Mexico.
Note This species is very common in the West, with related species in the East. They build nests of hard mud or sometimes sandy material or twigs, with one to thirteen cells placed vertically with nest tops in a straight line. They feed on pollen of species of *Penstemon, Salvia, Ranunculus,* and others.

287 PEPSIS FORMOSA
Tarantula Hawk

Family Pompilidae
Order Hymenoptera
Length 35–40 mm.
Recognition marks Satiny black with wings orange, smoky near margins; legs long; antennae usually held curled when at rest; wings held out at sides when not flying.
Habitat These are solitary wasps, probably the largest species of wasp in the United States. Most species burrow in the ground and form branching tunnels. The female hunts large spiders, stings them with her stinger, and returns to the nests with the paralyzed spider. She attaches her egg to the spider and when the egg hatches, the larvae will feed upon the spider. Pupation occurs in the ground and new adults will begin the hunt for spiders. Adults frequent flowers of trees, shrubs, and flowers such as milkweed.
Distribution Southwestern United States, north to Kansas and Nevada.
Note About twenty species of *Pepsis* occur in North America, many in the southwestern United States. The family includes over 250 species. Take care while collecting these species, and especially this species, because of their sting. This species probably has the most painful sting of any insect.

288 TACHYTES DISTINCTUS
Sand Loving Wasp

Family Sphecidae
Order Hymenoptera
Length 10–20 mm.
Recognition marks Abdomen is stalked at the base; middle tibiae have one apical spur; eyes are green; body is black with yellow hairlike setae on thorax; wings are transparent.
Habitat These solitary wasps provision their nests with grasshoppers and crickets. They nest in sandy areas. This species has been reported to start its tunnels in preexisting holes. The cicada killer holes or those of lizards are often used. The nests are excavated at night and a mound of excavated soil can be found at or around the nest entrance. The nests are usually multicellular, the cells either placed at the ends of branches that radiate from the main burrow or along the burrow. The main entrance is left open during the provisioning of the nest.
Distribution Throughout southern United States.

289 SPHEX ICHNEUMONEUS
Great Golden Digger Wasp

Family Sphecidae
Order Hymenoptera
Length ±25 mm.
Recognition marks Blue, part of abdomen and legs red or reddish with golden pile; wings smoky yellow.
Habitat The nest is made of mud and is provisioned with grasshoppers. Adults visit flowers of sumac, clematis, milkweed, and *Ceonothus* species.
Distribution Throughout United States and southern Canada.
Note These ground-nesting wasps are usually gregarious. Most colonies consist of fewer than fifty individuals. Sphex colonies may be maintained for many years and the record of twenty-five years has been recorded for this species. It nests in open areas with little vegetation. Other species nest in abandoned buildings in the floor.

290 AMMOPHILA AZETECA
Azetec Thread-waisted Wasp

Family Sphecidae
Order Hymenoptera
Length ±25 mm.
Recognition marks Gray to black; abdomen has patches of orange; wings are transparent; legs are long and black.
Habitat Thread-waisted wasps use insects and spiders to provision their nests. *Ammophila* species are generally solitary nesters, but a few are gregarious. Nests are dug prior to searching for prey. The nests are generally simple, short burrows ending in a single cell. When nest excavation is completed, the wasps usually make a temporary closure. Lepidopterous (butterflies and moths), and hymenopterous (wasps, ants, and bees) larvae are commonly used for nest provisions. This species has been reported to provision its nest with larvae of the alfalfa weevil, *Hypera postica*. They may bring smaller larvae to the nest in flight, or drag larger caterpillars across the ground. They also have been noted to maintain several nests at one time. The ability of these wasps to remember the location of several nests and their changing requirements is truly remarkable.
Distribution Throughout the United States.

291 AMMOPHILA WRIGHTI
Wright's Thread-waisted Wasp

Family Sphecidae
Order Hymenoptera
Length ±20 mm.
Recognition marks Abdominal petiole is 2-segmented; head and thorax are orange; abdomen is orange and black; wings transparent.
Habitat These wasps nest in the ground and provision their nests with caterpillars. They capture and paralyze the caterpillar and return with it to the nest. The paralyzed caterpillar provides food for the developing wasp. This species of *Amophila* captures its prey before it begins to excavate the nest. The larvae of caterpillars are the most commonly used provision. It is interesting to note that these species select hairless larvae over those with a large amount of setal hairs. Caterpillars are carried head foremost and upside down, held by the wasps' mandibles.
Distribution Widely distributed throughout southern Canada and the United States.
Note These species, as with other sphecids, have females that sting. One must use caution when removing them from the collecting net.

SCELIPHRON CAEMENTARIUM
Black and Yellow Mud Dauber

H

Family Sphecidae
Order Hymenoptera
Length 25–30 mm.
Recognition marks Slender petiole; hind wings have a large anal lobe; two apical spurs on the middle tibiae; body is black with yellow markings; pedicel twice the length of the abdomen; surface is nonmetallic.

Habitat This species is associated with human habitations and has thus been introduced into a number of new areas. Sceliphron females build their nests in a variety of sheltered situations. Each mud nest usually consists of several contiguous tubes or cells of mud. Each cell is mass provisioned with spiders. Cells are usually fully stocked in one day and sealed. If they are not fully stocked, they can be temporarily sealed at night. Adult wasps can be found at the edge of ponds or pools collecting mouthfuls of mud for nest construction. Nests are common under eaves of homes and other sheltered places.

Distribution Widely distributed throughout the United States.

Note This species can be collected in the spring and summer at the margins of pools and ponds or near their nests. They have a painful sting, so use caution. Use an aerial or sweep net. They make better specimens if the wings are spread; otherwise, the wings are folded lengthwise and the venation cannot be seen.

293 PODALONIA LEUCTUOSA
Caterpillar Wasp

Family Sphecidae
Order Hymenoptera
Length ±25 mm.
Recognition marks Abdomen is stalked at base; petiole is 1-segmented; hindwings have a large anal lobe; middle tibiae have two apical spurs.; head and thorax are black; abdomen is orange; wings are black.
Habitat These solitary wasps provision their nests with caterpillars. Species of *Podalonia* generally capture their prey before excavating their nest. Hairless, nocturnal feeding caterpillars of the moth family Noctuidae are preferred. Female wasps remove cutworm larvae from the soil during the daytime. The paralyzed caterpillar is carried in the wasp's mandibles. The wasp lays down the caterpillar and begins the excavation of the nest. One caterpillar is used per cell, and the egg is laid on the side of the caterpillar. In late summer or fall hundreds of females will gather in protected places to overwinter.
Distribution Throughout the United States and southern Canada. This species is less common than the *Ammophila* species.

---

294 SPHECIUS SPECIOSUS
Cicada Killer

Family Sphecidae
Order Hymenoptera
Length ±50 mm.
Recognition marks Black or rusty brown with bands of yellow on the thorax and abdominal segments 1-3; one or two apical spurs on the middle tibiae.
Habitat This species provisions its nest with dog-day cicadas, *Tibicen linnei*. It captures the cicada, usually in flight, who squeals loudly until quieted and paralyzed by the sting. The cicada killer carries the paralyzed cicada to an underground nest where the larvae of the wasp will feed on it when they emerge. This wasp is one of the largest of all sphecids and is a very strong flier.
Distribution Widely distributed throughout the United States.
Note The cicada killer appears in the middle or late summer. It digs a tunnel about six inches deep, makes a right angle turn, and tunnels for another six inches where it ends with one or more globular cells. Favorite sites include roadsides, under sidewalks, and along embankments. One or two cicadas are placed in a cell with one egg. The eggs hatch in 203 days, feed, and the larva pupates and hibernates in the cell until spring. This species sometimes causes damage to lawns because of their tunnels. The females are said to have one of the most severe sting of any insect.

295 BEMBIX AMERICANA
Sand Wasp

W

Family Sphecidae
Order Hymenoptera
Length 16–20 mm.
Recognition marks Stout-bodied wasps; labrum are long and triangular; black with yellow markings; wings are transparent; body is covered with fine pubescence.
Habitat Sand wasps nest in sandy areas where they construct a great many burrows. The food consists mainly of flies and true bugs. They are considered to be beneficial insects (upper right).
Distribution Widely distributed throughout North America.
Note *Bembix* species nest gregariously and maintain their colonies from year to year (lower right). They are not social in the usual sense, but may take part in mass "flights of intimidation" against intruders in the area. Because they provision their nests with flies, they are thought to have some effect on local fly populations, but probably not much. They readily become accustomed to human presence and are not truly aggressive or dangerous. The sexes meet in the air and copulation takes place on a plant or on the ground. Nests are built in sandy soils and consist of a mound of excavated earth, a sloping tunnel of several feet in depth, and a horizontal terminal branch or cell burrow. There is also a vertical spur for a resting area. Males pass the night in shallow burrows which they construct for themselves. Cell provisioning is progressive. Flies are seized and paralyzed either in flight or at rest and are transported to the nest carried by the middle legs. The fly is released at the entrance to the burrow, grasped with the hind legs, and dragged inside. At or near larval maturity the wasp closes the cell, and its occupant spins a cocoon. Overwintering takes place in the prepupal stage and the life cycle is completed in the spring.

296 EUCERCERIS CANALICULATA
Beetle Wasp

Family   Sphecidae
Order   Hymenoptera
Length   ±25 mm.
Recognition marks   Head is brown; thorax is dark brown and yellow; abdomen is yellow and brown; wings are brown.
Habitat   The nest is in hard-packed soil, gravel, or mud. They are provisioned with various kinds of insects.
Distribution   Southwestern United States with many related species throughout North America.
Note   *Eucerceris* species have been known to use the vertical shafts of old halictid bee burrows as a starting point for their nests. Weevils are commonly used by some species for food. The depth of the tunnels vary from 12 to 60 cm deep. The number of cells in a nest varies but eight appear to be a common number. The stock of weevils per cell ranges from four to ten.

---

297 COLLETES COMPACTUS
Plasterer Bee

Family   Colletidae
Order   Hymenoptera
Length   ±12 mm.
Recognition marks   Head is marked with yellow; body is black with white markings on the abdomen; body is covered with sparse pile; wings are transparent; antennae are black.
Habitat   These bees nest in the ground or in crevices in bricks and stones. They plaster the sides of the nest with a secretion that dries to a lustrous sheen. The pollen they eat mixes with the nectar inside their body. Pollen is regurgitated in the nest for the larval food.
Distribution   Throughout eastern United States, south to Georgia and west to Arizona.

298 ANDRENA VICINA
Mining Bee

Family   Andrenidae
Order   Hymenoptera
Length   11–13 mm.
Recognition marks   Brown; yellow markings on the clypeus only; wings are transparent.
Habitat   These bees build tunnels in the soil. They are usually found in flowers, particularly Umbelliferae, where they are able to suck nectar in spite of their short mouthparts. Both sexes overwinter as adults. Mating takes place in the spring. Some of these mining bees nest in large colonies, but they are not social. The nests, however, often damage lawns.
Distribution   Southern Canada and northern United States.
Note   Adults of some species are commonly found visiting flowers of apple, *Cretaegus* species, wild cherry, and others. They nest in large groups in the soil. Immatures can be found in earthen tunnels. The adults overwinter.

G

---

299 AGAPOSTEMON TEXANUS
Sweat Bee

Family   Halictidae
Order   Hymenoptera
Length   9–11 mm.
Recognition marks   Brilliant blue-green; scutum is shiny, doubly punctate, with sparse, coarse punctures superimposed upon a surface of finer and closer punctures; wings are transparent.
Habitat   Adults visit a wide variety of flowers. These bees nest in the ground in tunnels they dig.
Distribution   Southern Canada, United States, and Mexico.
Note   The majority of halictid bees nest in burrows in the ground, either on level ground or in banks along streams or embankments of roadways and railroads. Their main tunnel is vertical, with lateral tunnels branching off from it, each terminating in a single cell. An interesting feature in this family of bees is that this single group contains all the stages from the solitary to the social way of life.
The common name "sweat bee" stems from the habit of approximately 12 species seeking out animal and human sweat. If they are pinched as they lap up the salty fluid they will sting, but their stings are not very painful. The group is a very large one with about 460 species in North America.

W

300 NOMIA MELANDERI
Alkali Bee

Family Halictidae
Order Hymenoptera
Length 12–13 mm.
Recognition marks Black; pale brown hairlike setae cover the body with black bristles intermixed on the anterior part of the mesothorax; four light-green apical crossbands are present on abdominal segments 2-4.
Habitat These are important pollinators, especially of alfalfa. Reared in large numbers, the bees are released in areas near this crop, resulting in a greatly increased yield of alfalfa.
Distribution Western United States, with related species throughout North America.
Note Each female takes about thirty days to build a single nest of fifteen to twenty cells. The entrance to the shaft is marked by a mound of dirt. These bees are gregarious, so a large number of these mounds may be present in any given area. The bees hibernate in the prepupa stage and complete their life cycle the second year.

B

301 OSMIA COBALTINA
Mason Bee

Family Megachilidae
Order Hymenoptera
Length 7–18 mm.
Recognition marks Metallic blue; body is short and broad; abdomen has a pollen-collecting basket on the ventral side; the tongue and other mouthparts are elongated.
Habitat This bee nests in the ground or in natural cavities in wood.
Distribution Western United States; related species occur throughout North America.
Note The cells of the nests of these bees are supplied with pollen and nectar. An egg is laid in each cell. The larvae feed to maturity, but hibernate in the prepupal stage in a cocoon inside the cell. Mason bees lack the pollen baskets on their tibiae which are present in more advanced bees. They carry their pollen in a ''pollen brush'' on the underside of the abdomen.

W

302 MEGACHILE PASCOENSIS
Leafcutting Bee

Family Megachilidae
Order Hymenoptera
Length 7–9 mm.
Recognition marks Wings are transparent; head and thorax are black and densely pilose; abdomen has black pile; body is stout.
Habitat The leafcutter bees prepare a tunnel in the ground or in rotten wood. The female flies to a suitable flower and carefully cuts parts out of the petals, or sometimes the leaves. These round disks are brought back to the tunnel and used to construct what might be called a small cradle. A food pellet of pollen mixed with nectar is placed in the cradle as food for the young. The cell is then sealed over with additional pieces of leaves cut to fit the opening.
Distribution Widespread throughout United States. Over 650 species of this family occur in the United States and Canada.
Note It is easy to collect these and related bees as they visit flowers. However, their identification to species is dependent upon the use of many technical characteristics. Bees should be kept dry; otherwise the pile mats and the specimens are of a poor quality.

303 PTILOTHRIX BOMBIFORMIS
Digger Bee

Family Anthophoridae
Order Hymenoptera
Length 12–18 mm.
Recognition marks Black, without markings except for the hairlike setae which are pale; tarsi lack pulvilli; these bees resemble small bumble bees.
Habitat Adults burrow into the ground where they store a mixture of honey and pollen to be used as larval food. The pollen-collecting setae are located on the hind tibiae and the tarsal segments. Adults often are seen visiting the flowers of hibiscus.
Distribution Eastern United States from New Jersey, south to Florida, and west to Kansas and Texas.
Note There are over 900 species of bees in the family Anthophoridae in the United States and Canada. Obviously their identification is difficult and dependent upon technical literature.

304 EPEOLUS COMPACTUS
Cuckoo Bee

Family Anthophoridae
Order Hymenoptera
Length 12–20 mm.
Recognition marks Brown, with small patches of pale pubescence. These bees lack pollen-carrying baskets or brushes.
Habitat This group of bees is parasitic, usually on species of bees of the genus *Colletes*. *Epeolus* species are robust, short, pubescent, long-tongued bees marked with black and white, and with red patches on the legs. *Colletes* species are unrelated long-pubescent bees. *Epeolus* species also have been reported to kill the eggs and young larvae of their hosts.
Distribution Southwestern United States.

---

305 XYLOCOPA MICANS
Carpenter Bee

Family Anthophoridae
Order Hymenoptera
Length 14–27 mm.
Recognition marks Head and thorax are black; abdomen is black and shiny. These bees are often confused with bumble bees, but can be identified by their shiny abdomen and metallic color.
Habitat Males and females overwinter as adults in nests constructed in fence posts, wooden rails, tree stumps, and eaves of buildings. Adults visit flowers and take nectar, often by simply biting through the base of the flower instead of sipping it from the top.
Distribution Throughout the United States.
Note Carpenter bees are sometimes considered to be pests in porch posts, barn beams, and other wooden structures. They do not feed on the wood, however, and seldom excavate enough to be considered pests. Mostly people fear they may sting, although they are not aggressive and seldom do so. They can make tunnels up to 12 inches long in the wood which are partitioned into several cells separated by cemented wood chips. Pollen and nectar are placed in each cell together with one egg. The larvae hatch and feed. After development to the prepupal stage they hibernate through the winter, pupate in the spring and the adults emerge.

306 BOMBUS OCCIDENTALIS
Bumble Bee

Family Apidae
Order Hymenoptera
Length 17–27 mm.
Recognition marks Black and yellow; body is densely pilose; wings are transparent, but the veins are black. Some species are marked with red (upper right).
Habitat Bumble bees are important pollinators. They nest in the ground (lower right).
Distribution This species occurs along the Pacific Coast States, but bumbles similar to this species occur throughout North America.
Note Bumble bees are common throughout the temperate regions of the world and may even be found high in mountains and in the far north near the Arctic Circle. Only a few species live in the tropics, probably because of the competition with other bees. These insects are closely related to honey bees, but their life cycle resembles more that of the yellowjackets in that only the young queen overwinters. In the fall the female will mate with a male and this young queen will overwinter alone, the male dying shortly after mating. As spring approaches, the queen starts a new colony. She will use a hollow nest of some other bee, or find a similar cavity in the ground. Plant material is used to line the nest. Once completed, an egg cell is prepared and eggs are laid in the nest. A supply of pollen is placed nearby as food for the developing larvae. Next she constructs a waxen honey pot which she uses for food as she guards the nest and waits for the larvae to mature. The larvae feed on the honey and pollen mixture supplemented with special food supplied by the queen. Once they reach full size, which takes about ten days, they pupate. Soon adult females emerge but take over the duties of the workers. These females do not mate. After awhile males are produced and mate with the queen. Later in the season sexually active females are produced who will start new colonies in the following spring.

Bumble bees are very beneficial as pollinators. Unfortunately, chemical spray kills these insects along with the pests. Bumble bees sting.

APIS MELLIFERA
Honey Bee

Family Apidae
Order Hymenoptera
Length Queen 16–20 mm; Worker ±12 mm; Drone (male) 15–16 mm.
Recognition marks Body dark brown; abdomen reddish brown with apical segments black; lightly covered with short pile.
Habitat Honey bees are completely domesticated and live in hives provided by humans; however, they will leave these hives and form "wild" colonies in hollow trees, but there are no wild, native bees known.
Distribution Cosmopolitan.
Note Honey bees visit flowers to obtain nectar and pollen (upper right). The worker bees do this after spending the early part of their life with chores in the hive. Workers are sterile females and the most numerous of the individuals of the hive. In addition to gathering food they construct the waxy combs made from secretions of the wax glands. They tend the eggs and larvae as well as feed the queen and carry away the eggs produced by the queen. These workers are able to sting, but only once because the stinger is left in the victim's body, and the worker dies shortly thereafter. By the time the workers are ready to leave the hive and take up their new duties as foragers, their life is nearly expended. They can last at this final task for only a few days.

New colonies are formed when a swarm, led by a young queen accompanied by a group of workers, takes place. If the bee keeper anticipates this procedure, he is able to capture the young queen, place her in a new hive along with her following, and thus establish a new hive of bees. In a sense this group of individuals act as a single organism. The new hive is a form of reproduction. Bees are the only insects that are able to maintain themselves continuously with such a store of food and in such large numbers throughout several seasons. Other social insects tend to die out during the winter months and build up their colonies again in the following season. The workers have various bodily modifications for the tasks they must perform. For example, their legs are used for cleaning the antennae; hind legs have pollen baskets, and pollen scrapers, and so on. Pollen is removed from the pollen combs by a row of stiff hairs at the end of the tibia and then is pushed upward into the pollen baskets by means of the projection which is just below the tibial comb at the basal tarsal segment.

APIS MELLIFERA (Continued)
Honey Bee

Family Apidae
Order Hymenoptera

The queen (upper right) is the center of the hive. She provides all of the eggs, the majority of which develop into workers (lower right), some into males or drones, and a few occasionally become young queens. Queens are produced under three circumstances: when the reigning queen dies; when the colony is too large and must swarm; and when the queen is too old to produce the necessary quantity of eggs.

Pheromones, or ectohormones as they are sometimes called, play a very important role in the life of the honey bees. The queen produces the only sex attracting pheromone. Scent glands are found on workers only, and are used by scout bees when marking a food source. Alarm odors, produced when a bee stings, attracts other bees for a common defense. The African bee, which has apparently developed a strong alarm odor, is particularly aggressive. This varies considerably from strain to strain.

Honey bees are capable of passing on detailed information by means of their language. Karl von Frisch devoted much of his life studying this phenomenon. His experiments, now classics of science, clearly showed that worker bees communicate various bits of information by means of a dance, consisting of a series of circular movements in a particular direction, according to the position of the sun. The extent and direction of the dance then tells other workers the direction and distance to the honey flow, making it possible for them to go directly to the flowers and gather honey and pollen. The drones' sole function is to mate with the queen, and this is done only once. Drones cluster to one side of the hive out of the way of the workers, only flying on warm sunny afternoons. Otherwise, their life is one of complete subjugation. Once they have the opportunity to mate, the explosive shock which everts the male genitalia out of their abdomen kills the male almost immediately upon connection with the queen. Males that never have the opportunity to mate are stung, killed, and dumped out of the hive as winter approaches.

309 TIPULA ILLUSTRIS
Crane Fly

Family Tipulidae
Order Diptera
Length 15–22 mm.
Recognition marks Brown; wings have brownish markings; distinct V-shaped groove on prothorax; resemble long-legged mosquitoes.
Habitat The larvae of crane flies are aquatic. The adults are found around moist areas, often resting on shore vegetation. They frequently come to lights at night.
Distribution Pacific Northwest, east to Colorado.
Note These large insects are often mistaken for mosquitoes, but they do not bite or suck blood. They are widely distributed throughout the world. Over 1500 described species are found in the United States and Canada. Although not difficult to collect many species of this family, it is rather hard to identify them because of the great number of species involved. No comprehensive work has been written on this family. Specimens mounted on insect pins usually lose their legs which drop off very easily. It is best to store specimens in trays in order to keep the legs of each species together. The legs should be glued back onto the body when they become detached.

310 BITTACOMORPHA OCCIDENTALIS
Phantom Crane Fly

Family Ptychopteridae
Order Diptera
Length 10–15 mm.
Recognition marks Black with white markings on legs and abdomen. These flies are often confused with crane flies, but their coloration is usually a good way to distinguish them.
Habitat Adults usually seen on vegetation in deep, moist woods. The larvae live in wet soil or organic debris. They are equipped with an abdominal breathing tube, and are saprophagous.
Distribution Western United States; similar species occur throughout eastern United States.
Note These insects, members of the family Ptychopteridae, are called false crane flies, or phantom crane flies. Only about sixteen species occur in the United States.

AEDES TAENIORHYNCHUS
Salt Marsh Mosquito

Family Culicidae
Order Diptera
Length 3–4 mm.
Recognition marks Black; white bands on the proboscis; palpi are white at tips; abdomen is ringed with broad white bands.
Habitat The adults are abundant near salt marshes. The female sucks blood (upper right) and is an abundant pest mosquito, often carried by the wind considerable distances from the marshy areas into towns and cities where it is very troublesome.
Distribution Coastal regions of North America.
Note The larvae and pupae of all 2500 species of mosquitoes are aquatic (lower right). Most larvae feed on plant material such as algae, bacteria, fungi, and decaying vegetation. Some larvae are predaceous, particularly those that live in tree holes or in water that collects in leaf bases. The pupae, although active, do not feed. Both the larvae and the pupae are dependent upon free oxygen for respiration. The larvae have an abdominal breathing tube which pierces the water surface for a supply of air. The pupae have "ear trumpets" on the thorax for the same purpose. The habitats of mosquitoes vary from species to species. Some live in still ponds, others in woodland pools, and others in flowing streams. A few of our species live in pitcher plants while a great many tropical species are found in flower and leaf bracts containing water. Although many species of mosquitoes are pests because of their bloodsucking habits, by far the greatest problem is that they are vectors of many of the world's most serious diseases: malaria, yellow fever, dengue, and others. Mosquitoes are difficult to control without using chemicals that pollute the environment. DDT is still used in many parts of the world simply because it is the only way the population can be saved from death by malaria and yellow fever. Some fish eat mosquito larvae, making it possible to control at least some of the pest species by culturing these fish and releasing them in ponds, streams, and lakes to eat the larvae. Recent progress has been made in larval control through the use of nematod parasites.

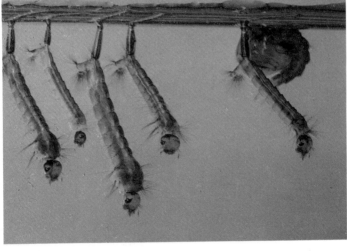

TOXORHYNCHITES RUTILUS
Elephant Mosquito

Family   Culicidae
Order   Diptera
Length   5–6 mm.
Recognition marks   Body is covered with shiny metallic blue scales; proboscis is long, curved, and inflexible, and not used for bloodsucking.
Habitat   Larvae live in tree holes, artificial containers, and the bracts of bromeliads. They are predaceous, using other mosquito larvae and other aquatic arthropods for food. The adults feed on plant juices and nectar. They never take blood meals (upper right, male).
Distribution   Southeastern United States, particularly South Carolina, Georgia, and Florida. The genus *Toxorhynchites* also occurs in tropical regions.
Note   Attempts have been made to use the larvae (lower right) of the genus *Toxorhynchites* for the biological control of other mosquitoes. They can be reared in large numbers in laboratories such as those of Insect Control and Research, Inc., in Baltimore, Maryland. The larvae are fed other mosquito larvae which are also raised in the laboratory. A laboratory can produce as many as a million mosquitoes a day. One way to distribute the mosquitoes is to gather their eggs, transport them to the field and "seed" the area to be controlled with these eggs. The larvae hatch and feed on other mosquito larvae. Unfortunately, it is necessary to continue this process from year to year because, of course, if the *Toxorhynchites* larvae are successful in controlling the other mosquitoes, they then run out of food themselves and their population decreases.

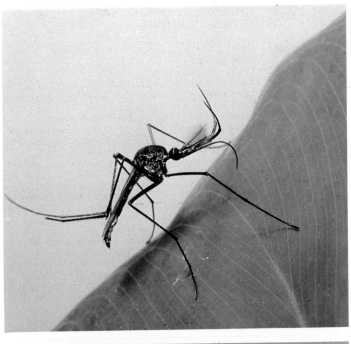

313 ANOPHELES QUADRIMACULATUS
Malaria Mosquito

Family Culicidae
Order Diptera
Length 4–5 mm.
Recognition marks Dark brown to nearly black; wings have black scales with patches of white scales forming four white spots.
Habitat Larvae prefer clean, still water with shady areas. The larvae feed in the sun and rest in the shade. Adults congregate in old buildings, particularly near cattle barns. They may enter homes and are found throughout the year.
Distribution Southern Canada south of the Great Lakes, and throughout eastern United States and Texas.
Note This mosquito was the principal vector of malaria in this country until the end of World War II when malaria was entirely eliminated in the United States. During the early 1800s, malaria was a cause of many deaths in the United States. Loss of life from both yellow fever (transmitted by another mosquito, *Aedes aegypti*) and malaria was very high during the building of the Erie Canal in New York State, and of course, in the early 1900s both diseases caused loss of life during the building of the Panama Canal. Malaria is transmitted only by species of mosquitoes of the genus *Anopheles*.

---

314 CHIRONOMUS ATTENUATUS
Midge

Family Chironomidae
Order Diptera
Length 5–5.5 mm.
Recognition marks Pale green to light brown; thorax and abdomen are marked with dark bands; wings are pale brown.
Habitat Larvae are aquatic and resemble mosquito larvae without air tubes; they are scavengers. The adults fly near ponds and streams and are attracted to lights at night in great numbers. They are often mistaken for mosquitoes.
Distribution This and related species are found throughout North America.
Note Some of the larvae of these midges contain a red pigment, similar to haemoglobin, used as a respiratory aid. These larvae usually indicate that the water is polluted and low in oxygen. As with mosquito larvae, these insects provide fish with food and are, therefore, an important part of the aquatic food chains. The family is large, and each area has many species which are difficult to identify without the aid of technical literature.

315 SIMULIUM AUREUM
Black Fly

Family Simuliidae
Order Diptera
Length 3–4 mm.
Recognition marks Black; thorax humped; antennae short; wings very broad at base, transparent; legs short.
Habitat The larvae (lower right) are aquatic and are usually found in rather swiftly flowing streams. The pupae are also aquatic. Each has gills and a hold-fast organ by which they attach themselves to the rocks.
Distribution Western United States with closely related species in eastern United States.
Note Black flies, family Simuliidae, are widespread in distribution, but not universal. They are mostly found in areas where there are swiftly flowing streams. The adult females of many species are blood suckers, and their bite is very irritating. In tropical regions they transmit diseases. In Africa, Central America, and parts of Mexico, the female black fly is a vector of onchocerciasis, a disease often called River Blindness, that is caused by a parasitic worm. When the black fly bites, the worm larvae are injected into the blood stream of the victim. These larvae migrate through the body, eventually reaching the eyes and causing partial or complete blindness. If the victim is fortunate enough to escape blindness, the worms cause other problems. They form nodes or bumps on the skin and weaken the body. Chemicals will hold the disease in check, but at present there is no known cure.

Black flies also are pests of domestic animals. Blood loss can so weaken some animals that they die from exposure. Swarms of black flies can irritate dairy cattle so that milk production is greatly decreased. Fishermen often have been seriously bitten by these flies.

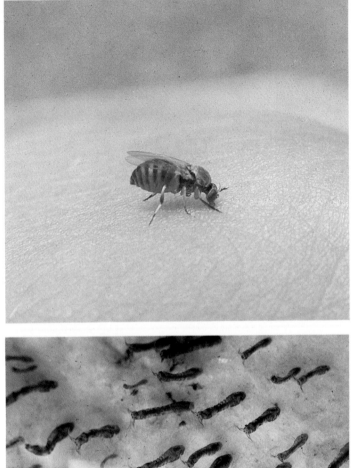

316 PLECIA NEARCTICA
Lovebug

Family Biblionidae
Order Diptera
Length 13–15 mm.
Recognition marks Black; thorax has brownish dorsal surface; antennae are short and 8-segmented; compound eyes are large, covering more than 50% of the head.
Habitat Adults fly in large swarms. The larvae breed in decaying vegetation.
Distribution Southeastern United States, west to Texas.
Note This species has become a pest in Florida in recent years where mowed grass decaying along interstate highways provides breeding areas for the larvae of this fly. Automobile exhaust attracts the flies to the highways, and they have become so numerous that cars encounter clouds of mating flies which smear the windshields and clog radiators. Flies mate in midair, the two sexes coupled together. This accounts for their common name: lovebugs.

317 HEDRIODISCUS TRIVITTATUS
Soldier Fly

Family Stratiomyidae
Order Diptera
Length 8–10 mm.
Recognition marks Head is green or yellow between the antennae and the oral margin; thorax is yellowish brown with prominent pale stripes on the mesonotum; wings lack markings; abdomen is flat and broad.
Habitat Larvae live in moist areas. Adults are attracted to flowers.
Distribution Southern United States, south into Central America.
Note The larvae of species of the soldier fly family, Stratiomyidae, live in a number of different situations including some that are aquatic, others in moss, decaying vegetation, cow dung, and under stones. The adults are usually found around flowers, especially the flowers of species of Umbelliferae such as Queen Ann's lace. They are often seen flying among the flowers along roadsides. Over 230 species of this family occur in the United States and Canada. They are relatively easy to catch in an aerial net.

318 PTECTICUS TRIVITTATUS
Yellow Soldier Fly

Family Stratiomyidae
Order Diptera
Length 6–7 mm.
Recognition marks Body is metallic blue, covered with dense golden yellow pubescence; eyes are black; abdomen is yellow, with dark bands; legs are yellow; wings are transparent; body lacks bristles.
Habitat Adults are found in wooded areas visiting flowers, particularly members of the Umbelliferae.
Distribution Eastern North America, west to Colorado and Texas.
Note The larvae of some species of Stratiomyidae are aquatic, and a few even live in salt water. These have a thick, leatherlike integument impregnated with calcium, distinctly a crustacean type exoskeleton rather than an insect type. Presumably, this offers a great amount of protection. Some species are able to live in hot springs because of this feature.

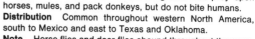

319 TABANUS PUNCTIFER
Horse Fly

Family Tabanidae
Order Diptera
Length ±10 mm.
Recognition marks Pale gray, mesonotum has fine grayish pile; abdomen is black; wings are black.
Habitat The adults are bloodsucking flies that prey upon horses, mules, and pack donkeys, but do not bite humans.
Distribution Common throughout western North America, south to Mexico and east to Texas and Oklahoma.
Note Horse flies and deer flies abound throughout the country, particularly in forested areas. They bite and suck blood, usually in shady areas where animals are likely to be resting after feeding. The larvae of most species are aquatic or semiaquatic and prey upon other insects. The adults emerge in the late spring and early summer. Although most Tabanids feed on wild animals, domestic livestock are often pestered by their bites, sometimes seriously weakening and even killing them.

320 TABANUS AMERICANUS
Greenhead

Family Tabanidae
Order Diptera
Length ±13 mm.
Recognition marks Thorax and abdomen are reddish brown; wings lack markings except along the front edge.
Habitat Larvae live in the mud by the roots of heavy vegetation near water. Adult females are pests of livestock.
Distribution Southern Canada, eastern United States, west to the Mississippi River and eastern Texas.
Note Tabanids not only cause a loss of blood, but cause animals to run wild so that they lose weight and may break their legs. They also attack domestic fowl. Even more serious, however, is their ability to transmit livestock diseases by mechanically passing pathogens from one animal to another and even to humans. Tularemia and anthrax are transmitted in this way. In Africa, a roundworm disease, *Loa loa,* is a human eye disease transmitted by tabanids.

321 CHRYSOPS FLAVIDUS
Deer Fly

Family Tabanidae
Order Diptera
Length 8–12 mm.
Recognition marks Brown to black with light tan markings; eyes are green to golden with zigzag stripes; antennae slender.
Habitat Adults occur in much the same areas as the horse flies, usually in marshy areas. The larvae are found in wet soil along the margins of lakes, streams, and ponds, particularly in very alkaline soil. Adult females are diurnal and the bite is painful.
Distribution Throughout eastern North America, south to Cuba, west to Mexico. Other species of *Chrysops* are found throughout North America.
Note The deer flies (genus *Chrysops* and related genera) are distinguished from the horse flies (genus *Tabanus* and related genera) by the patterns on the wings, which in general are distinctively marked. Horse flies have either clear wings, very small markings, or they are entirely dark.

322 RHAGIO MYSTACEA
Snipe Fly

Family Rhagionidae
Order Diptera
Length 7–16 mm.
Recognition marks Yellow; eyes are large and reddish brown; pronotum is yellow with four dark brown stripes; basal portion of each segment of the abdomen is dark brown; apical portion of each segment of the legs is dark.
Habitat Adults are common in woods, especially near moist places and may be found resting on foliage, in long grass, and on tree trunks.
Distribution Throughout eastern North America.
Note The abdomen of snipe flies tapers toward the apex; the wings may have small spots but no distinct markings. The larvae of these flies are predaceous, living in wood, under bark, in moss, and sometimes in water. The adults are predaceous on small insects. Most snipe flies do not bite, but members of the genus *Symphoromyia* are common biting flies of the western states, especially along the coast or high in the mountains.

323 RHAPHIOMIDAS TROCHILUS
Flower-loving Fly

Family Apioceridae
Order Diptera
Length 10–14 mm.
Recognition marks Dusty brown; eyes are dark green; abdomen is dark with light posterior bands on each segment; wings are brownish; proboscis is long and swordlike; thorax has fine dusty pile.
Habitat Adults are found on flowers in arid regions of North America. They are poorly known and very few of the larvae have been studied. One species, at least, has larvae that lie in sand.
Distribution Southwestern United States.
Note The adults of this family are similar to those of robber flies but have different wing venation and head structure characteristics.

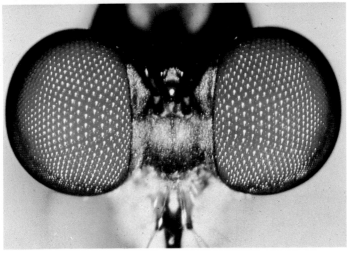

324 MYDAS CLAVATUS
Mydas Fly

Family Mydidae
Order Diptera
Length 20–30 mm.
Recognition marks Black with yellow or orange markings on the second segment of the abdomen; antennae are clubbed, apex is swollen; hind legs are large and black, with red and yellow markings.
Habitat Larvae live in wood or in soil. They are predaceous on beetles. Adults are also predaceous.
Distribution Eastern United States, south to Florida, west to Texas.
Note Species of mydas flies are generally large, black, and somewhat resemble wasps. Although little is known about their life cycle, some species have been reared from hollow decaying trees and rotten stumps. Adults have been known to emerge inside mobile homes, probably from the wall insulation. One species, *Mydas maculiventris*, is reported to be an important larval predator of plant-feeding scarab larvae in Florida. The flies get their common name because it is said that the antennae of these insects resemble the ass-ears of King Midas.

325 OPOMYDAS LIMBATUS
Juice Mydas Fly

Family Mydidae
Order Diptera
Length 20–25 mm.
Recognition marks Head and thorax are almost entirely dark reddish brown to black; antennal club is orange-red; abdomen is yellowish; male aedeagus is large, the apical portion bent down and forward.
Habitat Adults are predaceous on other insects. Larvae prey upon beetle larvae in rotting logs and stumps.
Distribution Arizona to California, south to Mexico.
Note Although there are only about forty species of the family Mydidae in North America, other species occur in Central and South America, including one of the largest flies in the world. A Brazilian species is over 2 inches in length. Collecting these flies is rather easy because they are reluctant to fly and often can simply be picked up and dropped in a killing jar.

326 EFFERIA AESTUANS
Robber Fly

Family Asilidae
Order Diptera
Length 20–30 mm.
Recognition marks Brown; grayish thorax; abdomen is darker with large pale yellow apical spots.
Habitat Adults frequent open spaces, resting on the ground or on dead weeds and twigs in fields, pastures, thickets, and along the edges of woods; abundant from June to August.
Distribution Eastern United States, west to Wyoming.
Note Robber flies are among the most active predators of the order Diptera. Their large eyes (upper right) bulge so that it appears that the top of the head is concave. Most species are very hairy, covered with a fairly dense pile of hairlike setae. Sometimes the face of the fly appears bearded. The adults (lower right) have a thick, stout proboscis, not elongated. They can capture an insect on the wing, alight, and suck it dry in a matter of seconds. Their abdomens are long, slender, and more or less pointed at the apex. The legs are covered with well developed bristles, some of which are used to hold onto captured prey. These flies are often abundant during part, at least, of the horse fly season. Sometimes they will take on a horse fly; after a great deal of buzzing and tumbling along the ground, the battle usually ends in a draw.

Robber fly larvae are found in the soil, in decaying wood, rotting vegetation, and similar locations. They too are predaceous. Unfortunately little has been done to encourage the development of these insects. Most of the larvae remain unknown to science. To our knowledge, no attempt has been made to use adults or larvae for biological control measures. Predaceous larvae have never been employed, for example, to feed on the many species of "root worms." Many of the over 850 species of robber flies in United States and Canada are large and rather showy. Like the horse flies, they present a challenge to the collector.

327 SYSTOECHUS OREAS
Bee Fly

Family Bombyliidae
Order Diptera
Length ±10 mm.
Recognition marks Black to pale with light gray pile covering the thorax and abdomen; body has rather long hairlike setae.
Habitat Adults often visit flowers. The larvae are parasitic on bees and egg cases of grasshoppers.
Distribution Pacific Northwest, south to California, east to Utah.
Note The bee flies, so named because they resemble bees, have stout, broad bodies, usually densely covered with thick hairlike setae. Their wings may be marked with brown or black, and are sometimes entirely dark. Some bee flies have very long probosci which are used to suck nectar from flowers. Often these insects are seen at rest on flowers with their wings outstretched. Most larvae of Bombyliidae feed upon the eggs of beetles, grasshoppers, moths, and bees.

About 750 species occur in North America, north of Mexico. Many species are widely distributed and each region has a complement of species. They seem to be more common in the arid regions of southwestern United States.

328 BOMBYLIUS MAJOR
Black-tailed Bee Fly

Family Bombyliidae
Order Diptera
Length 7–12 mm.
Recognition marks Proboscis is long and narrow; body has pale vestiture; front half of wings are dark brown, remainder is transparent; they resemble bees.
Habitat Adults visit flowers and probably are important pollinators for certain species. The larvae are parasitic on bee larvae. The adults fly from May to August.
Distribution Common throughout the United States.
Note Not all members of this large family of rather large flies resemble bees. In fact, about half of the species are covered with brightly colored scales instead of hairlike setae and they have short probosci. A few species resemble wasps more than bees.

329 CONDYLOSTYLUS CHRYSOPRASI
Long-legged Fly

Family Dolichopodidae
Order Diptera
Length ±5.5 mm.
Recognition marks Body is entirely coppery green with bluish reflections; eyes are well separated, somewhat projecting.
Habitat The larvae are predaceous, live in soil, under bark, or in water. Adults are very common along the shore of streams, in wet meadows, and moist areas of woodlands. They are predaceous, so far as is known. The adults of some species have been observed in a mating dance in swarms. The adults of one European species have been observed feeding on mosquito larvae they have captured and removed from the water.
Distribution North Carolina, south to Florida, west to Texas, Mexico, and Central America.
Note Members of this family have tapering abdomens, somewhat pointed in the female, and curved under in the male. The integument is smooth with metallic reflections of green, blue, or copper. The legs are noticeably long and slender as their common name suggests.

330 VOLUCELLA BOMBYLANS
Hover Fly

Family Syrphidae
Order Diptera
Length 10–11 mm.
Recognition marks Body is covered with hairlike setae; abdomen has distinct yellow and black markings; wings have distinct dark bands; they resemble bumble bees.
Habitat The larvae of this bumble bee mimic are scavengers in the nest of many social Hymenoptera. Adults are found hovering over flowers and feeding upon the nectar. They can be mistaken for bumble bees.
Distribution Widely distributed throughout eastern United States to Florida, west to Kansas and Texas.
Note Members of the family Syrphidae are usually called hover flies because they hover in one place in midair. Over 950 species occur in North America, north of Mexico. Many species are common and widely distributed. As can be seen from the illustration, this species and many others closely resemble bees. They do not, however, bite or sting.

331 ERISTALIS TENAX
Drone Fly

Family Syrphidae
Order Diptera
Length 12–14 mm.
Recognition marks Brownish to black; body is moderately covered with pile; scutellum is yellowish; eyes are not spotted, but have pile that forms a vertical stripe; a close mimic of the honey bee in color, size, and movements.
Habitat The larvae live in polluted water and in wet, decaying carcasses. They breathe by means of a tube which extends to the surface of the water or other liquid material. Adults are common in the summer months and, as with other Syrphids, they feed on nectar. They hover over and dart from flower to flower.
Distribution Cosmopolitan.
Note This species is introduced from Europe. There are reports of human infection by this insect. The adult flies may lay their eggs on soiled human bodies; for example, in vomit around the mouth of a child, or in mucus. The eggs are swallowed and the larvae grow in the intestinal tract where they may actually feed on living tissue.

332 METASYRPHUS AMERICANUS
Flower Fly

Family Syrphidae
Order Diptera
Length Approximately 10 mm.
Recognition marks Metallic, greenish; three abdominal crossbands are yellow, reaching the lateral margins, but those of the second and third abdominal segments are incomplete, not reaching the margins; front of head has a median black stripe; sides of the head are black.
Habitat Larvae are predaceous on aphids. The adults frequent flowers.
Distribution West Coastal region, south to Mexico, east to Florida.
Note The descriptions and classification of Syrphidae are based on variations in the arrangements of the wing veins. One very easy way to recognize members of this family is to find the "false vein" that runs lengthwise across the wing. This vein does not originate at the wing base, but rather seems to originate in the middle of a wing cell, run across other veins, and end near the margin of the wing, but in the middle of another cell.

333 CHRYSOTOXUM INTEGRE
Yellowjacket Fly

Family Syrphidae
Order Diptera
Length ±10 mm.
Recognition marks Metallic, hard integument; body is pitted; abdomen has only four visible segments; they resemble cuckoo wasps, family Chrysididae, order Hymenoptera.
Habitat The larvae stages are unknown. Adults are uncommon, but have been seen flying low through brush at lower elevations.
Distribution Rocky Mountain region.
Note During World War II the Sperry Rand Corporation spent vast sums of money for research on the flying mechanisms of the Syrphid flies. Their studies contributed greatly not only to our knowledge of insect flight, but to the development of gyroscopes used to stablize the flight of airplanes and similar applications. It is now well known that the aerodynamics of insect flight, because of the small size, is quite different from that of large animals and of airplanes.

334 THECOPHORA OCCIDENSIS
Thick-headed Fly

Family Conopidae
Order Diptera
Length ±5 mm.
Recognition marks Black; head is narrower than most species of this family; antennae are long with an enlarged terminal segment.
Habitat Adults are found feeding on pollen and nectar of flowers. The larval stage is spent as an endoparasite of bees and wasps. They feed on fluids and tissues of the host. The pupal stage takes place inside the host. When the adult flies emerge and mate, the female deposits her egg on the abdominal region of the next bee or wasp host, probably when it visits the flowers frequented by the flies.
Distribution Throughout most of North America.
Note Most species in this family have heads that are wider than the thorax and antennae that are rather long, slender, and clubbed. Their mouthparts are long and slender, as is the abdomen. These flies resemble somewhat thread-waisted wasps and other wasps, and they are usually the same color. Females have long ovipositors. Although only about seventy species occur in the United States and Canada they are often collected from material in sweep nets swept over flowers, especially those in meadows, along roadsides, and along railroad tracks.

335 PHYSOCEPHALA BURGESSI
Wasp Fly

Family Conopidae
Order Diptera
Length ±5 mm.
Recognition marks Black; facial grooves are yellow; sides of the head are reddish yellow; front of coxae is black; hind femora are irregularly thickened at the base.
Habitat The larvae are internal parasites of the bumble bee, *Bombus sonorus*. Adults visit flowers for pollen and nectar.
Distribution West Coastal Region, east to Alberta, and south to Texas.
Note These flies hover over flowers. Most of them seem to visit only flowers of the mint family. It is reported that some species are associated with ants and others may parasitize Orthoptera. Little is known about most of the species of this family.

336 POECILOGRAPHA DECORA
Marsh Fly

Family Sciomyzidae
Order Diptera
Length 6–7 mm.
Recognition marks Yellow with brown patches on the wings; body has few bristles; antennae are aristate, the arista has bristles; proboscis is rather large; the bristles of the head and thorax arise from conspicuous brown spots.
Habitat The larvae are parasites of freshwater snails. The adults are common flying about the banks of ponds and streams.
Distribution Northeastern North America, west to Colorado.
Note All species of this family, so far as is known, are parasites or predators of freshwater snails. Nearly 150 species occur in our area. The family is more abundant in tropical regions. Their habit of feeding on snails has led to attempts to control the snails that are vectors of the dreaded disease of the blood, Schistosomiasis. This parasitic flatworm has become a major disease organism in many parts of the world, including Puerto Rico, other areas of tropical America, and Africa.

337 EPHYDRA CINEREA
Shore Fly

Family Ephydridae
Order Diptera
Length 2.5–4 mm.
Recognition marks Opaque gray with shining, silky, green frons; tibiae and tarsi are yellowish.
Habitat Adults (upper right) lay their eggs in extremely salty water. The larvae of this species breed only in Great Salt Lake, Utah. They become so abundant that masses of dead adults form (lower right) in wind rows along the shore at certain times of the year.
Distribution Great Salt Lake, Utah. There are about 350 species of this family in North America, north of Mexico, with many species recorded from each region.
Note The larvae of the species of this family are all aquatic or semiaquatic. The adults are generally found along the shore near where the larvae live. They are generally considered to be beneficial because they reproduce in great numbers and are excellent fish food. A few species are reported to be leaf miners and sometimes become abundant enough to damage such crops as watercress, rice, and even barley and other grains. Other species of these flies breed in crude petroleum. The Salt Lake brine fly shown here has been studied in some detail. It is estimated that at times there are over twenty-five adults per square inch, extending over an area of about 18 feet wide.

338 DROSOPHILA MELANOGASTER
Fruit Fly

Family Drosophilidae
Order Diptera
Length 2.5–4.5 mm.
Recognition marks Usually with red eyes (although various strains have brown eyes, and some lack eyes entirely); body is brown; wings are held crossed over the abdomen.
Habitat This species is common around decaying fruit. The larvae live in the flesh of the fruit. However, laboratory specimens are reared on yeast, agar, and various nutrients combined into a cake of standard quality.
Distribution Cosmopolitan.
Note The family Drosophilidae contains several hundred species with varied habitats. Most of the species are found around fruit and sap flows. They also live in decaying fungi, decaying succulent plants such as cactus, and even some on carrion. Some species are of economic importance because of their abundance around food processing plants and food markets. They are sometimes involved in the transmission of fungus diseases of plants.

This species has been widely used in laboratories and classrooms for the study of the principles of genetics. Kits may be obtained commercially and they are easily reared.

339 LIRIOMYZA SATIVA
Leafminer Fly

Family Agromyzidae
Order Diptera
Length 2–2.5 mm.
Recognition marks Grayish black; front of the head is dark below, more yellowish above.
Habitat The yellowish larvae make winding tunnels (mines) between the margin and midrib of the leaves of holly, as shown in the photo. They form a puparium inside the leaf and hibernate there throughout the winter. The adults emerge in the spring.
Distribution Introduced from Europe, now widely distributed throughout North America.
Note The mines of leafminer flies are much easier to identify than the flies themselves. The mine pattern is often characteristic of the species. Some leafminers are very host specific, and others are more general feeders. Some of the common leafminers are the chrysanthemum leafminer, *Phytomyza syngenesiae* and the aster leafminer, *Calycomyza humeralis*. Leafminers sometimes are serious pests of ornamental plants.

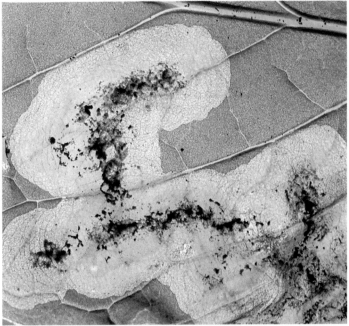

340 SCATOPHAGA STERCORARIA
Dung Fly

Family Anthomyiidae
Order Diptera
Length ±9 mm.
Recognition marks Body is grayish brown, clothed with yellow to reddish hairlike setae; thorax has long, heavy, black spines. Males are bright yellow due to the longer, heavier covering of pile.
Habitat Adults fly from April to October around fresh cow manure. The larvae live in the manure.
Distribution Throughout North America, Europe, and Asia.
Note This large family of flies is represented by over 500 species in North America, north of Mexico. They resemble house flies, family Muscidae. Wing venation and antennal characters are used for the identification of species, but this is very difficult without a good binocular microscope. The larvae of most species live in dung or in decaying plant material. Some species have aquatic larvae, others may be parasitic on other insects, and some bore into plants. Among the more common species are some pests: the onion maggot, *Hylemya antiqua*, the cabbage maggot, *H. brassicae*, and the turnip maggot, *H. floralis*. All three species are at times serious pests and require control measures.

341 MUSCA DOMESTICA
House Fly

Family Muscidae
Order Diptera
Length 7–8 mm.
Recognition marks Thorax is black with stripes of gray pile; head and abdomen have brown markings; sponging mouthparts.
Habitat House flies breed in decaying food materials. Their larvae, called maggots, are white and legless. The female deposits approximately 150 eggs at one time, laying them in the larval food material which includes manure, human and animal. It takes about two weeks under optimum conditions for the larvae to mature, pupate, and for the adults to emerge. In cool weather, the cycle is longer, but nevertheless rapid. This perhaps accounts for their very great abundance.
Distribution Cosmopolitan wherever food material is available.
Note House flies invade our homes, but not only are they a nuisance, crawling on our bodies and our food, they are also mechanical transmitters of many diseases, particularly typhoid fever. Although most of the control measures involve chemicals, it is rather easy to control them by screening homes, barns, manure, and decaying vegetation. If manure is used on fields for fertilizer, it should be plowed under to prevent fly breeding.

342 LUCILIA ILLUSTRIS
Blow Fly

Family Calliphoridae
Order Diptera
Length 6–9 mm.
Recognition marks Bright metallic green, varying to dark blue; palpi are yellow; body has heavy, black setae.
Habitat Larvae, or maggots (lower right), live in garbage, carrion, and excrement. The adults are attracted to fresh meat and will lay their eggs on it, if it is not protected. They also oviposit in sores or wounds of animals and man.
Distribution This is a common species in western United States, but related species occur throughout North America.
Note The family Calliphoridae is a very large one. The flies are all very similar in appearance, many of them metallic in color. The group includes the common blue bottle and green bottle flies. As is true of many flies, their life cycle is very rapid, hence they multiply rapidly under favorable conditions. They are also involved as disease carriers. Domestic fowl contract a highly fatal disease, limberneck, which is caused by the bacterium *Clostridium botulinum*. Poultry may eat blow fly larvae that breed in carcasses containing botulism bacteria. Wildfowl are also similarly affected. It is not unlikely that human botulism under certain circumstances might be contracted in the same manner. Many species of blow flies and other flies that breed in carrion may cause cutaneous myiasis. Flies are attracted to wounds that have not been properly treated, providing a suitable site for the invasion of maggots. Usually the fly larvae feed on the necrotic tissue, but under extreme conditions heavily infested healthy tissue may be eaten as well, causing great pain.

343 SARCOPHAGA HAEMORRHOIDALIS
Flesh Fly

Family Sarcophagidae
Order Diptera
Length 10–14 mm.
Recognition marks Black with gray markings; aristate antennae plumose at basal half.
Habitat The larvae are scavengers. They may breed in human excrement as well as in the human digestive tract.
Distribution Cosmopolitan.
Note A large family of flies, this and other flesh flies are widely distributed. The larvae live in a wide variety of habitats. Some feed on animal carrion, but others are scavengers in bee, ant, and termite nests. Many larvae feed on decaying vegetation, but never on living plant tissue. Some live under the skin of reptiles and amphibians. One interesting species lives as predators in pitcher plants. A few are parasites of insects. Adults feed on nectar, honeydew, and other plant liquids. They do not bite. Aerial and sweep nets are adequate for fly collecting. Because of the many spines and setae, most flies should be pinned. The insertion of the pin must be done carefully to prevent the destruction of setae necessary to be seen in order to make an accurate specific identification.

344 EUMACRONYCHIA SCITULA
Banded Flesh Fly

Family Sarcophagidae
Order Diptera
Length 4–9 mm.
Recognition marks Body is grayish; thorax has dark longitudinal stripes; abdomen has white and black crossbands; tip of abdomen is orange.
Habitat This species lays its eggs in the nests of wasps. They presumably follow the wasp back to her nest as she provisions it with prey. Once she has left the nest the fly enters, destroys the wasps' eggs and lays her own in their place. The fly larvae then feed on the food provided by the wasps for her own young.
Distribution California; other species of the genus *Eumacronychia* occur throughout the arid Southwest.
Note Adult Sarcophagidae are very strong fliers who lap up nectar from flowers in order to refuel themselves. Some interesting biology classroom experiments can be conducted with these flies. Hungry adults are glued to the end of an applicator stick. Solutions of sugar and water are prepared, varying in sugar concentration. The fly is then held close to, but not touching, the sugar solutions, starting with the lowest concentration and working up toward the highest concentration. As soon as the "threshold" concentration is reached, the fly's mouthparts will dart out in an attempt to feed, thus showing the sensitivity the fly has for sugar.

345 PARADEJEANIA RUTILIODES
Moth Parasite

Family Tachinidae
Order Diptera
Length ±14 mm.
Recognition marks Body is orange-yellow; thorax is darker above; abdomen has long, dense, black spines.
Habitat Adults are found in the early autumn on blossoms of wild buckwheat. The larvae parasitize various lepidopterous larvae.
Distribution Southwestern United States, north to Oregon.
Note The family Tachinidae is composed of a great many parasitic flies. They are second only to the parasitic wasps as nature's way of controlling insect populations. The various species vary in length from 5–15 mm. Many of them resemble house flies. Others, some examples of which are shown here and in the next four illustrations, are very colorful. This family is defined by the following technical features: the antennae are aristate and usually bare of bristles; heavy bristles are present on the body; and the postscutellum is well developed. The identification of the species is very difficult. It is necessary to use very technical descriptions in order to make accurate identifications of these flies.

---

346 TRICHOPODA INDIVISA
Hairy-legged Fly

Family Tachinidae
Order Diptera
Length 9–11 mm.
Recognition marks Reddish brown; eyes are brown; abdomen has patches of yellow; wings are brown; hind tibia has wide, leaflike expansions fringed with long, stout setae.
Habitat Females of *Trichopoda* species fasten unincubated eggs externally on the adults of various bugs. Adult flies visit flowers and feed on pollen and nectar. The larval host records include rearings from cicadas.
Distribution Southwestern United States and Mexico.
Note The family Tachinidae is the second largest family of flies in North America, north of Mexico, with over 1200 described species. They occur in all regions. Many species have never been associated with an insect host; therefore, their biology is unknown. Whenever these flies appear from the cocoons or pupae of other insects, both the flies and the hosts should be preserved and accurate identifications made for the records.

347 XANTHOEPALPUS BICOLOR
Yellow and Black Tachinid

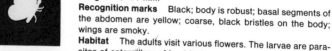

Family Tacinidae
Order Diptera
Length 9–11 mm.
Recognition marks Black; body is robust; basal segments of the abdomen are yellow; coarse, black bristles on the body; wings are smoky.
Habitat The adults visit various flowers. The larvae are parasites of caterpillars of Lepidoptera.
Distribution Southwestern United States, north to British Columbia.
Note The adult female of these flies deposits her eggs directly on the host insect, or sometimes, on the plant that the host will visit and feed upon. The tachinid eggs are eaten along with the plant material. The egg hatches in the digestive tract of the host. In both cases, the larvae of the fly are internal parasites on the insect larvae or nymph. It feeds on the host, usually killing it after it has matured, and in the case of holometabolous insects, after it has made its pupal cell or cocoon. Thus, rather than a moth or beetle, and so on, a fly will emerge.

348 JURINELLA LUTZI
Brown Tachinid

Family Tachinidae
Order Diptera
Length 9–11 mm.
Recognition marks Robust body; brown; abdomen is black; body has coarse, long, black bristles; wings are brown; eyes are red; arista of antenna is prominent and black.
Habitat Larvae parasitize the larvae of moths, particularly various species of armyworms.
Distribution Southwestern United States and Mexico.
Note Adults of the Tachinidae do not bite or sting. Search for them in flowers, particularly in meadows, along fence rows, or in open fields.

349 PHASIOMYIA SPLENDIDA
Orange-spotted Tachinid

Family Tachinidae
Order Diptera
Length 8–9 mm.
Recognition marks Black; eyes are red; legs are black; wings are smoky; tip of abdomen has a large orange spot.
Habitat The life history of these flies is unknown. Their relatives usually parasitize Hemiptera, the true bugs, but some have been bred from ground beetles, family Carabidae.
Distribution Northeastern North America, west to British Columbia and Washington.
Note Many species of Tachinidae have been used as natural controls of various insect pests such as the gypsy moth, the brown-tail moth, both pests of forest trees, and the European corn borer.

B

350 CUTEREBRA CUNICULI
Rabbit Bot Fly

Family Cuterebidae
Order Diptera
Length 20–25 mm.
Recognition marks Black, stout flies, covered with short pile on the body which is light gray on the thorax; antennal arista is plumose.
Habitat This large fly is parasitic on rabbits. The larvae invade the skin or natural body openings after hatching from eggs laid on the rabbit's body. After a short period of migration through the tissues of the rabbit, it settles down just below the surface of the skin where it matures. It makes a small hole in the skin through which it breathes. This lesion oozes serum and may become secondarily infected with bacteria. Finally the mature larva drops out of the body and burrows into the ground where it pupates. The adult flies emerge in about two weeks.
Distribution Throughout southern United States.
Note The human bot fly, or torsalo, *Dermatobia hominis,* is related to this species. Although its natural hosts are cattle, sheep, dogs, cats, and rabbits, humans frequently become infested with this parasite. It is a painful pest and must be surgically removed from its position beneath the skin. It does not occur in the United States, but is abundant in cattle-raising regions of Central America.

L

GLOSSARY

abdomen the posterior section of the three main body divisions of the insect.

aedeagus the male intromittent organ, refers to the penis plus accessory structures, used to introduce sperm into the female.

alluvium clay, silt, sand, gravel, or similar detrital material deposited by running water.

ametabolous without metamorphosis, insects that lack metamorphosis at all points in their life cycle, i.e., apterygote orders.

androconia the modified wing scales producing a sexually attractive scent in certain male butterflies.

annulated with ringlike segments or divisions.

antenna (pl. antennae) in insects, a pair of appendages, located on the head above the mouthparts, used as sensory organs.

apical at the end, tip, or opposite to the base, i.e., apical segment of antennae is the segment most distant from the head.

aposematic conspicuous coloration, warning coloration.

apterous wingless.

apterygote insects that belong to the subclass Apterygota. Insects in this subclass are wingless (apterous) and include the orders: Protura, Diplura, Collembola, and Thysanura.

aquatic living in the water.

arista a large bristle located on the apical segment of certain antennae; found on the antennae of some diptera (true flies).

aspirator a device used to collect small insects by suction, especially useful for small insects such as fruit flies, springtails, and leafhoppers.

basal   at the base, opposite to apical; refers to the point of attachment.

beak   proboscis, refers to the protruding mouthparts of insects with piercing-sucking mouthparts, i.e., aphids, true bugs, and cicadas.

Berlese funnel   an insect-collecting device, the Berlese funnel includes a large funnel containing a piece of screen or hardware cloth, with a killing jar or container of alcohol below it; the material, such as leaf litter, is placed in the funnel and usually a light is placed above the funnel to force the insects into the container.

binomial nomenclature   the use of two Latin names, the genus and species, for each plant and animal.

bisexual   dioecious; having male and female reproductive organs in different individuals.

brackish water   this is a mixture of salt water and fresh, usually found in the mouth of streams and rivers emptying into the sea.

camouflage   to conceal or disguise.

cantharidin   material secreted by certain species of meloid beetles (Coleoptera: Meloidae) and others which, when in contact with the skin, can cause blisters.

capitate   with an apical knoblike enlargement, antennae that are capitate have the apical segments enlarged.

carnivorous   feeding on the flesh of other animals.

caste   a form or type of individual in social insects: reproductives, workers, and soldiers all represent castes; ants, many bees, and termites are social insects with castes.

caterpillar   the larval stage of butterflies and moths, known as an eruciform larva, with distinct head capsule, chewing mouthparts, thoracic legs, abdominal prolegs, and cylindrical in shape.

caudal   posterior end of the abdomen.

caudal filament   a threadlike process at the posterior end of the abdomen, present in many insects including mayflies, stoneflies, and silverfish.

cell   (in entomology) refers to a space in the wing membrane that may be closed (surrounded by veins) or open (not surrounded by veins); the word cell usually refers in biology to a mass of protoplasm surrounded by a cell membrane with or without a nucleus.

cephalothorax   a body region consisting of the head and thorax joined together.

cercus (pl. cerci)   one of a pair of appendages at the posterior end of the abdomen, usually long, filamentous, and extending beyond the wings and abdomen.

chelicera (pl. chelicerae)   anterior clawlike or pincerlike paired appendages of Arachnida.

chitin   a complex nitrogenous carbohydrate forming the main skeletal substance of the arthropods.

class   a taxonomic category, a subdivision of a phylum containing a group of related orders, i.e., class Insecta.

clavate   refers to gradually enlarged tip; clavate antennae have gradually enlarged 4–6 apical segments which resemble little baseball bats.

clubbed apical or distal segments enlarged as in clubbed antennae.

cleptoparasite a parasite that feeds on food stored for the host larvae.

clypeus a sclerite on the face of insects just above the labium and below the fronds, serves as the attachment point for the labium.

cocoon a silken case in which the pupa is formed.

communal insect colonies in which members of the same generation cooperate in nest building but not in the care of the young.

complete metamorphosis life cycle with an egg stage, larvae, pupa, and adult, sometimes called homometabolous; complete metamorphosis is found in the majority of insect species.

composites a family of plants, Compositae, including sunflower, goldenrod, and aster.

compound eye the major insect eye located on the head and made up of many individual facets; the facets represent separate lenses and may be hexagonal or somewhat circular in shape; in many insects the paired compound eyes take up considerable area on the head.

copulation sexual reproduction, males and females of dioecious organisms mating.

corbicula in the bee the pollen basket located on the hind tibia; this structure is bordered on each side by a fringe or long curved hairs for collecting pollen.

corium the elongated, usually thickened, basal portion of the front wing in members of the order Hemiptera (true bugs).

cornicle one of a pair of dorsal tubular structures extending from the dorsal area of the abdomen on aphids.

coxa (pl. coxae) the basal segment of the insect leg.

crawler the active first instar nymph of a scale insect.

crochets small hooked spines located at the tips of the prolegs on butterfly and moth larvae (Lepidoptera).

cutworms the larval stage of certain species of lepidopterans, namely, members of the moth family Noctuidae.

deciduous parts that may fall off or shed; in entomology refers to wings, such as those of termites, that are shed after nuptial flights.

deflexed bent downward.

depressed flattened dorsoventrally.

dermatosis refers to inflammation of the skin; in entomology dermatosis is caused by the presence of lice, fleas, bed bug bites, etc.

dioecius having male and female sex organs in separate individuals.

discal cell a more or less enlarged cell in the basal or central part of the wing.

diurnal active during the daytime, opposite of nocturnal.

dorsum the back or top side.

drone the male bee.

ecdysone the molting hormone of metamorphosis.

ectoparasite   a parasite that lives on and feeds on skin of the host; lice (Anoplura) and keds (Diptera) are obligate ectoparasites of man and animals.

elbowed antennae   antennae in which the first segment is elongated and the remaining segments branch off of the first segment in a right angle.

elytron   (pl. elytra)   the thickened, leathery, or hard front wing of most Coleoptera and some Dermaptera.

ensocial   insect colonies displaying a caste system with reproductive and nonreproductive individuals and division of labor and overlapping generations.

entomology   the study of insects and related organisms such as spiders, ticks, and mites.

exoskeleton   a skeleton or supporting structure on the outside of the body.

eye (see compound eye and ocellus)

family   a taxonomic category below the level of order; families contain related genera; in zoology family names end in *idae*.

fauna (pl. faunae)   the animal species of a given region.

feign   to pretend; feign death refers to insects, especially some beetles that pretend to be dead to avoid capture.

femur (pl. femora)   the third leg segment located between the trochanter and the tibia.

filament   slender threadlike structure; filamentous usually refers to slender abdominal tails.

filiform   hairlike or threadlike; filiform antennae are long and slender.

flora (pl. florae)   the plant species of a given region.

fontanelle   a small depressed spot on the front of the head between the eyes, found in some species of termites, Isoptera.

furcula   in springtails (Collembola) a forked springing apparatus.

gall   an abnormal growth (tumor) of plant tissue, caused by the stimulus of an insect, fungus, or bacteria.

gaster   the rounded part of the abdomen posterior to the node-like segment in ants; abdomen.

genitalia   the sexual organs and associated structures; the external sexual organs.

genus (pl. genera)   a taxonomic category that includes a group of related species. This is the first name of a species; it is Latinized, capitalized, and when printed it should be italicized.

gill   respiratory organs found in some aquatic insects used for gas exchange.

girdle   refers to the insects, especially some cerambycid beetles, that feed on bark and gnaw grooves about stems and twigs.

gregarious   living in groups.

halter   the hindwings of the Diptera; small knoblike structure located on the metathorax and used for balance.

head   the anterior body section; the region which bears the compound eyes, ocelli, antennae, and mouthparts.

hematophagous   feeding on blood.

hemimetabolous   have incomplete metamorphosis, egg stage, nymph, and adult; no true pupal stage.

herbivorous   feeding on plants.

holometabolous   complete metamorphosis: egg, larvae, pupa, and adult stages.

honeydew   a liquid discharge from the anus of certain Homoptera, i.e., aphids, treehoppers, etc.

host   the animal or plant harboring or infected with a disease.

hypopharynx   a median mouthpart structure anterior to the labium. The ducts from the salivary glands open from this structure.

incomplete metamorphosis   life cycle with egg stage, nymph or immature, and adult, also called hemimetabolous.

integument   the outer covering or skeleton of insects and other invertebrates; in insects and other arthropods the integument is primarily composed of chitin.

invertebrates   animals without an internal skeleton of cartilage or bone.

labial palp   one of a pair of small feelerlike or antennalike structures arising from the labium.

labium   one of the insect mouthparts, the so-called lower lip.

labrum   one of the insect mouthparts, the so-called upper lip.

lamellate   composed of or furnished with layers.

lanceolate   spear-shaped, tapering at each end.

larva (pl. larvae)   the immature stage between the egg and the pupa in holometabolous insects; the immature stages vary in morphology and structures and many have common names, i.e., grub, caterpillar, maggot, and wireworm.

leaf miner   an insect that lives and feeds upon the leaf cells in between the upper and lower surfaces of the leaf.

looper   a caterpillar that moves by looping its body, also called inchworm or measuring worm. These lepidopterous larvae move by anchoring the front of the body and moving the rear portion up to the anchored front.

luminescent   producing light. Some insects such as some beetles (Lampyridae) produce light to attract a mate.

maggot   the legless larva without a well-defined head capsule found in many flies.

mandible   one of the anterior pair of mouthpart structures, commonly called jaws.

mesothorax   the middle or second segment of the thorax.

metathorax   the third or posterior segment of the thorax.

maxilla (pl. maxillae)   one of the paired mouthpart structures immediately posterior to the mandibles.

maxillary palp   a small feelerlike or antennalike structure arising from the maxilla; sensory in function.

metamorphosis   a change in form during development.

millimeter   0.001 meter, or 0.03937 inch.

mimic   insects that imitate others in color and form; in mimicry the insect that is mimiced is the model.

mimicry   the ability of an animal to imitate or mimic another species of animal or plant.

monoecious   possessing both male and female sex organs, hermaphroditic.

muslin   coarse cotton fabric used for some types of insect nets, especially beating nets.

myiasis   the invasion of living animal tissue (including humans) of dipterous larvae (maggots).

naiad   an aquatic nymph.

nasutue   a soldier in the termite caste system whose head projects forward into a point able to spray fluid on enemies.

nocturnal   active at night.

nymph   an immature wingless stage following hatching that later develops wing pads, or undeveloped wings, with undeveloped or immature reproductive organs. The nymph applies to ametabolous and hemimetabolous insects only, that is, insects without the pupal stage.

ocellus   (pl. ocelli)   a simple eye of an insect.

omnivorous   feeding on both plant and animal materials; refers to animals that feed on a wide range of food.

ootheca   the covering or case of many eggs; cockroach egg cases are ootheca.

order   a taxonomic category below the level of class containing similar or related families.

osmeterium   a fleshy, tubular, eversible, Y-shaped gland located at the anterior end of some caterpillars (Lepidoptera).

oviposit   laying eggs.

ovipositor   the egg-laying apparatus of the female, the external genitalia.

palp (pl. palpi)   a segmented extension, antennalike, located on the maxilla and the labium.

parasite   an animal that lives in or on the body of another animal. The parasite may be on the host for its entire life cycle as an obligate parasite or for only a part of the life cycle, a temporary parasite.

parasitic   living as a parasite.

parasitoid   an organism alternately parasitic and free-living.

pathogen   a specific causative agent such as a bacteria, virus, fungus, or protozoan that is capable of causing disease in animals and plants.

parthenogenesis   development of an egg without fertilization, common in some Hymenoptera.

pedipalps   the second pair of appendages in the arachnids, usually used for sensory purposes and in courtship.

petiole   a stalk or stem, the narrow stalk in the Hymenoptera that attached the thorax to the abdomen.

pheromones   ectohormone, a substance given off by an animal that causes a specific reaction by individuals of the same species; includes trail substances, sex attractants, and alarm substances.

phylogenetic   refers to the arrangement or placement of animals or plants in some type of evolutionary tree or evolutionary classification arrangement.

phylum   a major taxonomic category of the animal kingdom containing classes and orders.

phytophagous   feeding on plants.

pile   covered with fine hairlike setae.

plumose   featherlike; plumose antennae are featherlike antennae like those in many moths.

population   a group of individuals of the same species living together in a limited and defined space.

predaceous   feeding on other animals.

predator   an animal that attacks and feeds on other animals (its prey), usually animals smaller or less powerful than itself.

prepupa   a quiescent stage between the larval period and the pupal period; also the last nymphal instar of thrips.

proboscis   the extended beaklike mouthparts.

pronotum   a dorsal sclerite of the prothorax.

prothorax   the anterior section of the three thoracic segments.

pterygote   winged, an insect in the subclass Pterygota.

pubescent   downy, covered with short fine hairlike setae.

punctate   with punctures, microscopic pitlike depressions.

pupa   (pl. pupae)   the stage between the larva and adult in insects with complete or holometabolous metamorphosis; a nonfeeding, usually inactive stage.

puparium   (pl. puparia)   a case formed by the hardening of the last larval skin in which the pupa is formed in some diptera.

quasisocial   insect colonies with members of the same generation using the same nest and cooperating in brood care.

raptorial   fitted for grasping prey as in raptorial front legs of mantids.

recurved   curved upward or backward.

reproductives   the members of an insect caste system, male and female, capable of reproducing; their numbers usually limited, males sometimes termed kings; females usually are termed queens; found in both Isoptera (termites) and some Hymenoptera.

reticulate   like a net, netlike.

saprophagous   feeding on dead or decaying plant or animal materials, such as carrion, dung, dead plant parts.

scavenger   an animal that feeds on dead plants or animals; also one that feeds on decaying materials or animal wastes.

scales   found on the wings of butterflies, moths, and skippers; scales are actually outgrowths of the body wall; modified setae.

scutellum   a triangular shaped sclerite located behind the pronotum in Homoptera, Hemiptera, and Coleoptera.

sedentary   remaining in one place, attached, not migratory.

semisocial   insect colonies with members of the same generation cooperating in brood care and with some reproductive division of labor, i.e., egg layers and workers.

seta   (pl. setae)   a bristle, located on the external surface of some part of the body.

siphon   a breathing tube located on some aquatic insects including mosquito larvae, and some bugs.

soldiers   members of an insect caste. Soldiers protect the colony or nest from invaders; found in ants and termites, nonreproductives, adapted for fighting.

species   a group of individuals or populations that are similar in structure and physiology and are capable of interbreeding and producing fertile offspring.

sphecids (pl. sphecidae)   a family of hymenopterous insects which includes the solitary wasp.

spiracle   the external openings of the tracheal system, a breathing pore.

spittle   the waterlike material that is secreted by the nymphs of the spittlebugs or froghoppers (Homoptera: Cercopidae); the material is used for protection and is secreted from anal glands.

stridulate   to make a noise by rubbing two surfaces together.

subsocial   insect colonies in which the adults care for nymphs or larvae for a period of time, but not in the colony.

suture   impressed line where two body sections meet or where two elytra meet when closed in the case of the Coleoptera.

symbiosis   two species living together in close association with mutual or reciprocal benefits.

tarsus   (pl. tarsi)   the leg segment immediately beyond the tibia, consisting of one or more "segments" or subdivisions.

terrestrial   living on the land.

thorax   the body region between the head and abdomen which bears the legs and wings.

trachea   (pl. tracheae)   a tube of the respiratory system of arthropods.

transparent   to see through; clear.

triungulin   the active first larval instar of some beetles and stylopids.

tumblers   the aquatic pupa stage of mosquitoes.

vector   an animal capable of transmitting a pathogen to another animal or plant; usually part of the life cycle of the pathogen takes place within the vector, the remainder of the cycle in the host.

vertebrates   animals with some type of internal skeleton of cartilage and/or bone.

wigglers   the aquatic larval stage of mosquitoes.

INDEX OF ENTRIES